Treason on the Airwaves

Three Allied Broadcasters on Axis Radio during World War II

Judith Keene

Foreword by István Deák

University of Nebraska Press
Lincoln and London

Manufactured in the United States of America
♾
First Nebraska paperback printing: 2010

Library of Congress Cataloging-in-Publication Data
Keene, Judith.
Treason on the airwaves: three Allied broadcasters on Axis radio during World War II / Judith Keene; foreword by István Deák.
p. cm.
Originally published: Westport, Conn.: Praeger, 2009.
Includes bibliographical references and index.
ISBN 978-0-8032-3292-1 (paper: alk. paper)
1. World War, 1939–1945—Propaganda. 2. World War, 1939–1945—Radio broadcasting and the war. 3. World War, 1939–1945—Collaborationists—Biography.
4. Radio in propaganda—History—20th century. 5. Amery, John, 1912–1945.
6. Cousens, Charles, 1903–1964. 7. Tokyo Rose, 1916–2006. 8. Nazi propaganda—Great Britain. 9. Propaganda, Japanese—Australia—History. 10. Propaganda, Japanese—United States—History. I. Title.
D810.P6K44 2010
940.54'8870922—dc22   2010006813

Contents

A photo essay follows page 78

Foreword

Here is a fascinating triptych, lucidly and authoritatively etched, of World War II broadcasters who engaged in activity that was deemed treason. The three accused—an Englishman, an Australian, and an American—were all brought to trial following the end of hostilities; the nature of the sentences that were handed down to each of them varied enormously according to the extent of post-war public resentments and the personality of the accused.

The most familiar among the three is perhaps Iva Toguri—a young American of Japanese origin who was popularly known as "Tokyo Rose"—though the profiles of the other two are equally compelling. The Englishman John Amery, a virulent anti-Communist and anti-Semite who spoke openly of Winston Churchill as a "Jew-lover," became enchanted early on with fascist doctrines and unwisely linked his star to the triumph of Nazism in German wartime broadcasts. The Australian Charles Cousens, a popular radio personality at home, became equally prominent abroad among prisoners recruited by the Japanese to broadcast war news. Iva Toguri, who was stranded in Japan at the outbreak of the war, accepted the radio broadcast post that was offered to her out of necessity rather than initiative or conviction.

As the author examines their stories, all three accounts provoke thoughtful questions as to the nature of justice and retribution. What constitutes the special contribution of Professor Keene is her emphasis less on the political climate surrounding the trials—amply covered in many scholarly tracts—than on the social and racial overtones manifest in the course of the three-fold prosecutions. Her thesis, that the dominant motive for the traitor John Amery as well as for the judges of the alleged traitor Tokyo Rose was racism, will certainly lead to a spirited debate among the readers of this book.

The author is scrupulous in examining the small, personal details that were often ignored in official accounts and which allow for a balanced view in forming any judgments with regard to the three protagonists. Because the destinies of all three were tied to their facility with the microphone, the powerful propaganda role of that early-twentieth-century instrument looms large in Professor's Keene's pages.

This exhaustive study, remarkable both for clarity and vigor; adds substantially to our knowledge of post-war retribution, especially as its targets were not Germans or denizens of countries allied to or occupied by the Nazis but citizens of nations proud of their unblemished record in opposing the enemies of freedom and democracy during World War II. The haste with which some "traitors of the airwaves" were tried and sentenced after the war shows that even the great victorious democracies felt it necessary to engage in purges similar to all other countries that had emerged from the war.

István Deák
Columbia University in New York City

Preface

In the late summer of 2005, when I was researching this book, there burst on the scene in my hometown of Sydney, a spate of violent racial incidents. The groups involved fought over access to the much-vaunted Australian icon, "the beach." On a couple of strips of sand in the southern suburbs what the press and the rioters called "the Lebs" battled it out with, similarly described, "Aussie surfers." While in other parts of the city people struggled home with bags of Christmas shopping, the police in the contested areas set up roadblocks and closed the streets. At a time of the year when the heat is at its most enervating and schools, university and businesses wind down to a month's annual holiday, these disturbing events took place. Predictably, in a country that makes much of the supposed laid-back nature of its citizens, the politicians said little that was useful. Ineffective leaders, perhaps, are the collateral damage in a society that claims as its national ethos "she'll be all right." On a prosaic note, I wondered where these young "Aussies" had acquired the flags they so wantonly draped around their shoulders or flew on the flagpoles that sprouted on their cars. In my recollection, the closest I had ever been to an Australian flag was in primary school. But even then the raising and lowering of the national standard only ever took place on special days and was a task restricted to a few gold-star pupils.

It was unnerving seen even from the safety of the multicultural inner-city. The smiling woman who sells my bread is modestly dressed from her scarf-covered head to her invisible toes. The butcher is halal and the corner shop, a model of Chinese capitalism, is run under the gimlet-eyes of two brothers from Shanghai. But, more and more, the example of the people from World War Two, with whom I had been engrossed, seemed apposite. In all their variegated contexts, racism had been the catalyzing factor. John Amery and his anti-Semitic confreres understood so little about human existence that they imagined Jews were the source of the world's problems. Iva Toguri and her generation of Japanese Americans were excluded from full acceptance in their own place of birth, on the West Coast of the United States. Equally, they were never at home in Japan, the land of their forefathers. Many Australians and Americans of Charles Cousens' generation accepted with equanimity that the price of ending the Pacific war was that the atom bomb would reduce to ash civilians in Hiroshima and Nagasaki. Increasingly, in all of this, I wondered what disloyalty means in a racist society. The young Australians posturing on the beach, their tee shirts emblazoned with racist insults, or the fervent Japanese in 1940 cheering the flag of the rising sun and, equally, the pro-Nazi anti-Semites in Occupied Europe, all responded to their own sense of social crisis by retreating into exaggerated and self-aggrandizing nationalism.

Writing this book has made me aware of the strain in the relationship between the individual, the citizen and the nation. And wartime adds volatility to the whole concoction. In coming to close terms with John Amery, Charles Cousens and Iva Toguri, I have discovered, as well, that the big patterns of history are made up of a great many micro-histories, individual stories, writ small and even smaller. My purpose, however, is not advocacy for these individuals. Rather the objective is to illuminate these three related stories by setting the protagonists within the choices that separately were available to them in World War Two in Europe and in the Pacific and, in turn, examine the ways in which their particular governments held them accountable for these choices after the war. In the end, all that an historian can hope for is to elucidate a large issue in the past, treason in this case, by reconstructing how it was worked out in the lives lived by the individuals caught up in it.

Acknowledgments

The research for this book has been supported by a number of people and institutions. I am glad to acknowledge generous backing between 2001 and 2004 from the Australian Research Council. The University of Sydney through Sesquicentenary grants, Research and Development funding and seeding money from The Research Institute for Humanities and Social Sciences has also enabled the research. In what are embattled times for humanities, I consider myself lucky to be part of the Faculty of Arts at The University of Sydney. The Dean, Stephen Garton, is a distinguished scholar and an efficient administrator, a fortunate combination that is repeated in the History department, chaired by Robert Aldrich. Over the last three years, colleagues in History and in European Studies in Sydney and elsewhere have put up with my endless talk about treason, the state and what, in the twentieth century, it means to be tagged as disloyal. That I remain friends with most of these people is a tribute to their tolerance. At the New South Wales Asylum Seekers Centre, I have seen firsthand how precious are the rights of citizenship and how dire the consequences when governments withhold them from individuals needing asylum.

Librarians and archivists, to paraphrase Eric Hobsbawm, are to the historian what the opium producer is to the addict. The Inter-Library Loan Section at Fisher Library, including Rod Dyson and Bruce Isaacs, provide exemplary service. A great many archivists have helped with the research for this book. They include those at the National Archives of Australia, in Canberra and Sydney, the Australian War Memorial, the British Library, the Public Record Office at Kew, the House of Lords Records Office in London and, in particular, Edward O. Barnes, at the National Archives and Records Administration in Washington. At NARA in San Bruno I especially thank William Greene who oversees the voluminous papers relating to Iva Toguri's prosecution. Toshika McCallum, at the Hirasaki National Resource Center within the Japanese-American National Museum in Los Angeles guided me through the extensive files and newspaper series that the center holds on Iva Toguri and Japanese-American community in the 1940s. The museum's permanent exhibition on the lives of Japanese-Americans interned in the United

States during World War Two is moving and memorable. Linda Wheeler and Carol Leadenham, at the Hoover Institution on War Revolution and Peace at Stanford University, unearthed material and, as always, gave good advice. The overseer of manuscripts at the Cambridge University Library, Godfrey Waller, was helpful, as was the staff at the Churchill Archives Centre, Cambridge where the Amery Family papers are deposited. John Entwisle at the Reuters Archive steered me to new Amery material and Clare Brown at the Lambeth Palace Library found important files and arranged copies. Colin Harris at the New Bodleian Library was generous in answering long-distance questions.

Finally, I thank those who have aided the project or read the chapters and papers that have come out of it. They are Richard Bosworth, Phillip Bradley, Catherine Branson, Alison Broinowski, David Cannadine, D. M. Carment, Wayne M. Collins, Tim Cousens, Robert Cousens, Patrizia Dogliani, David Dutton, John W. Dower, Bridget Griffin-Foley, Amirah and Ken Inglis, Yves Lancelot, Laurence Maher, Roger Markwick, David Marr, Ross McKibbin, Dirk Moses, John and Vera Parkes, Marian Quartly, Liz Rechniewski, David Ricquish, Elizabeth Roberts, Kerry Robinson, Marta Ruiz Jiménez, Philip Taylor, William Rubinstein, Michael Sexton, Robert Stitt, Edith Vincent, Richard Walsh, Grahame White, Shane White and Shannon Woodcock. In my household I am grateful for the friendship and loving support of Trudi Valleau; Jonathon Likely; and Emma, Sam and Jock Keene. In relation to the last, I cannot better Leo Amery's words of gratitude for a life with a beloved spouse in which each year has been even better than the one before. This book is dedicated to the memory of my goddaughter Anne Jackson who brought optimism and joy to those around her.

Abbreviations

AIF	Australian Imperial Force
BBC	British Broadcasting Corporation
BEF	British Expeditionary Force
BPHOL	Beaverbrook Papers, House of Lords, London
CAC	Churchill Archives Centre, Cambridge
CIB	Japanese Cabinet Information Bureau
DPP	Director of Public Prosecutions
JACL	Japanese American Citizens' League
JANM	Japanese American National Museum, Los Angeles
LAP	Leo Amery Papers
LVF	Légion des volontaires français contre le bolchevisme
MAE AG	Spanish Foreign Ministry Archives, Madrid
NHK	Japan Broadcasting Corporation
PC	Press Cuttings
POW	Prisoner of war
NAA	National Archives of Australia
NARA SB	National Archives and Records Administration, San Bruno
NSWRO	New South Wales Record Office, Sydney
PPF	Parti Populaire Français
PRO	Public Record Office, Kew
RA JAF	Reuters Archive, John Amery File
SCAP	Supreme Allied Command
SOE	Special Operations Executive
TP CUL	Templewood Papers, Cambridge University Library
TSD	Typescript Diary
UCLA	University of California, Los Angeles

Introduction

Traitors in wartime have a long history. Since the establishment of the nation state there have been individuals, from conviction—in anticipation of material reward or out of fear—who have acted in ways that promoted the success of the other side. Invariably, too, governments have carried out retribution against their own countrymen who were seen to be supporting the enemies of the nation.[1] During World War Two, both Allied and Axis governments used enemy nationals to broadcast propaganda. And, at the end of the conflict, the Allied victors charged with treason a number of their own citizens who had been involved in enemy radio.

This book traces the experiences of three such individuals. They were broadcasters over Axis shortwave and after the war were tried as traitors. John Amery, an English civilian and the son of a senior figure in the British government, made pro-Nazi broadcasts and speeches across Occupied Europe. The Australian, Charles Cousens, a leading figure in commercial radio before the war and a volunteer soldier in the Malaya campaign, became a broadcaster over Radio Tokyo while a prisoner of the Japanese. Iva Toguri, a young American freshly graduated from UCLA was stranded in Japan visiting relatives when war broke out and became a disc jockey on a Japanese program that was beamed to Allied soldiers in the Pacific.

The three stories highlight separate, national experiences that link the wartime theatres of Europe and the Pacific. As radio broadcasters they were part of the expanding networks of shortwave radio at a time when almost all belligerent nations were committed to shortwave broadcasting in the belief that propaganda disseminated over the airwaves went hand-in-hand with military victory. Postwar all three were charged with treason by their home governments. Their trials in Britain, Australia and the United States, respectively, provide a reminder that immediately after the war there was widespread anger towards collaborators and loud calls from the public for retributive justice against suspected traitors. As recognizable figures on Axis shortwave and as the protagonists in much-publicized trials, the three postwar cases attracted a good deal of attention. Later, as the preoccupations of peace took over and public interest in war issues flagged, the memory of their era faded.

John Amery was the playboy son of Leo Amery, who in turn was a high Tory intellectual and a member of Churchill's government. From 1940 to 1945, despite the father's involvement in the British war effort, the elder son traveled in Occupied Europe, part of a motley cavalcade of pro-German propagandists. His speeches, regularly beamed back to England, castigated the "Jews, Toffs and Plutocrats" around the "Jew-lover" Churchill and the inept efforts of the "stuttering King George VI." John's wartime activities caused his family pain and embarrassment. Though the son's beliefs were refracted through a virulent anti-Semitism, they were sourced from the same wellspring that fed the ideas of the father. These were an obsession with the British Empire and a visceral hatred of communism.

The detail and the substance of John's ideology were elaborated during his time in Nationalist Spain during the Spanish civil war. There, he was part of the crowd of foreign camp followers—admirers, ideologues and opportunists—that circled around Franco's headquarters. Members of the extreme Right in Europe, whether they traveled to Burgos or not, laid great store by Franco's "Crusade." For them, the conflict in Spain was much more than a civil war.[2] Instead, they viewed what was taking place on the Iberian peninsula between 1936 and 1939 as a preparatory bout in the keenly anticipated final round of the show-down in which an ebullient European Right would trounce democrats, republicans and their "Bolshevik masters." At Franco's court, rubbing shoulders with European fascists and proto-Nazis, Amery absorbed many of these ideas. And exactly like these proto-fascists and pro-Nazi franquistas, when the larger civil war was declared, Amery took the political experience and his contacts from the pro-Franco movement into Occupied Europe where he trumpeted, on and off the air, the virtues of the coming New Order under Nazi auspice.

Captured at the end of the war fleeing north with the rag-tag of Mussolini's supporters, Amery was brought back to London, tried as a traitor and for a range of reasons, pled guilty. In a desperate effort to raise a pardon, the Amery family marshaled a dossier of testimonials and psychiatric reports to prove that John had been "morally insane" since a very young age. Subsequently, this material has been used to explain Amery's traitorous leanings. Certainly, it is legitimate to ask why the cosseted son of the English establishment would become a Nazi sympathizer; however, the explanations that rely uncritically on the Amery family sources are unsatisfactory. The indulged first sons of doting parents often grow into headstrong and unmanageable young men. Among the members of the Amery class this was not uncommon as was the practice of family members using their influence to protect their sons from the consequences of their unruly escapades. Indeed, as we shall see, one need only to look at John Amery's younger brother, Julian, to see that a similarly protected and privileged upbringing could produce a patriot who led an exemplary public life.

The subject of the second narrative, the Australian Charles Cousens, became a broadcaster on Radio Tokyo. Before the war, his voice was one of the most recognized on the Australian airwaves. Having enlisted when war broke out, Cousens was in Singapore when the British Expeditionary Force surrendered to the Japanese and with some fifty thousand Allied prisoners was herded into Changi prison camp. The Japan Broadcasting Corporation, at the time, was actively expanding their shortwave networks and, having identified Cousens as a prisoner with radio experience, sent him to Tokyo. Like a great many British and Australian soldiers, Cousens had been shocked and disoriented by the collapse of the Malaya Command and distressed by the condition to which the defeated force was reduced. Initially he assumed that he could intercede in some way in Tokyo with the victors and, like many others caught up in what later would be categorized by the home government as collaboration, he had no way of foreseeing what lay in store for prisoners like himself or what would be the consequences of his social actions in captivity.[3]

In Tokyo, Cousens became a leader of a contingent of Allied prisoners of war drafted on to the Japanese airwaves to produce engaging English-language programs for transmission into the Pacific. Hitherto, very little has been known about these British, American and Australian broadcasters, though they played a crucial role in the Japanese shortwave network. Cousens and the group, including the young Japanese American woman, Iva Toguri, produced a series of programs over Radio Tokyo that drew dedicated American and Australian listeners, probably the only Axis propaganda broadcasts anywhere to achieve such audiences. American and Australian soldiers in the Pacific tuned in for the latest dance music and POW families at home were drawn to their sets by Nippon shortwave networks that spiced their emissions with lists of names and occasional messages from prisoners in Japanese camps.

When Japan surrendered, Cousens was arrested in Tokyo and sent back under guard for trial in Australia. Like a great many of those similarly charged elsewhere, Cousens maintained that his aim always had been to send useful information to Allied headquarters. His arraignment in the Sydney magistrate's court took place in an atmosphere of high emotion, coinciding with the return of soldiers and ex-POWs and the local press headlining reports from Tokyo of Japanese war crimes. Among the several hundred Allied soldiers and civilian prisoners whose voices had been heard over Radio Tokyo, only two Australians were charged; Cousens the single ex-serviceman. After a rowdy pretrial hearing, the magistrate found that Cousens had a case to answer on the charge of treason. Later, as a consequence of the complexity of state and federal legal jurisdictions, the charge lapsed, but Cousens suffered egregious penalty at the hands of the Australian Army.

Iva Toguri—an American whose narrative comprises the third part of this study—was probably the most famous of the three wartime broadcasters, though much of the material put out about her was based on rumor and misinformation. Among many returned servicemen in the Pacific and their families, "Tokyo Rose," as they called her, had become a household name: the symbol for all that was thought to be evil in the Japanese character. Her experiences during the war and her treatment afterwards, however, can only be understood when set within the context of her background as a Nisei, a first-generation American born within the Japanese American community of the United States. Along with several thousand young Nisei, she was stranded in Tokyo when war broke out, and like several hundred of them, considered herself lucky to find work in the English language section of the Japanese broadcasting service. Unlike a great many of fellow countrymen in Japan, however, Toguri resisted all Japanese efforts to make her take up Japanese nationality.

Toguri was charged with treason after the war despite her wartime marriage to a Portuguese citizen and without regard to the assistance she had provided to Allied prisoners of war at Radio Tokyo—one of whom was Charles Cousens. The trial in San Francisco took place in an atmosphere of palpable racism towards all Japanese, whether they were in Japan or on the American mainland. The retribution that her conviction comprised was loaded with animosity and fear sourced from the preceding era of wartime.

Overall, in analyzing these three linked examples, my own perspective on treason and traitors is that the term covers a "complex set of behavioral options," that are only possible to understand when set within the historical context in which they took place.[4] A good deal of the writing that hitherto has dealt with traitors has focused on the personal peculiarities of the individuals, particularly their character flaws and sexual proclivities. As well as in the explanations of John Amery's "aberration," the tendency can be seen most clearly, perhaps, in the great many studies that have been made of the Cambridge traitors, the group of young men around Burgess and MacLean who betrayed Britain between the wars and later.

In my study I carefully reconstruct the individual lives of Amery, Cousens and Toguri, before and during the war, but equally, I attempt to recreate the milieu in which their respective governments made the decision to categorize their behavior as treason. Even if it were in doubt, the diversity in outcomes—Amery executed, Cousens no-billed and Toguri receiving a heavy prison sentence—would signal the importance of historical context and contemporary contingency. The legal definitions of treason in Great Britain, in Australia and in the United States were precise. In practice, however, behavior that fell under that legal rubric evoked a whole range of responses and at each stage in the process of identification, prosecution and verdict, the conjunction of individual behavior, wartime context and historical contingency came into play.

The Laws of Treason and the Prosecution of Traitors

Treason is the oldest and most heinous of crimes. In Britain, the United States and Australia, the concept of treason evolved from the specification of the original English crime with subsequent changes made to each country's legal system according to historical events in each place. The English Treason Act of 1351 spelled out the categories of conduct that were seen to challenge the authority of the monarch and constitute the capital offense. The death penalty was the punishment for attempted regicide, for disrupting the royal succession, for corrupting the national currency and for challenging the authority of the monarch's agents. As well, the law proscribed the capital crimes of waging war on the monarch, adhering to the monarch's enemies, and giving them aid and comfort within the realm or elsewhere. In the course of five centuries, English treason prosecutions buttressed monarchical power, originally versus the aristocracy and then the gentry and, as the English state was democratized, they reached further down into the social structure. Over this long history, the application of the English Treason Act resulted in thousands of executions. Even after the death penalty was abolished in the United Kingdom in 1977, treason has remained a capital offense.[5]

When facing the exigencies of wartime, the British government promulgated several new laws to streamline the prosecution of traitors. Traditionally, there had always been opposition in Britain to the implementation of legislation that limited the rights of "free born Englishmen" [and women]. Wartime laws and regulations in 1940 were brought in against strong parliamentary opposition, and at the end of the conflict were quickly rescinded.[6] British chariness toward implementing restrictive legislation, however, was not carried over into a reluctance to detain individual Britons who were suspected as traitors. The Treachery Act in May 1940 expanded the crime to include all acts of espionage by citizens or foreigners operating within any British jurisdiction. Faced with the great many Britons identified and later charged as traitors, a new treason act was implemented in June 1945 that maintained the substance of the earlier definition of the capital crime, but simplified the requisite evidential proof to bring it into line with the charge of murder. Instead of the previous legal requirement for two direct witnesses to the traitorous act, proof of the crime required only a single witness.

In the course of World War Two, Allied intelligence units cooperated to draw up a Watch List of Renegades. These were Allied citizens whose behavior had been reported via various intelligence and underground networks as indicating that the named individuals harbored pro-Axis sentiments and had collaborated in some way or another with the enemy. Once renegades were identified, wartime governments expended considerable resources to keep tabs on them in order to collect evidence for their potential postwar prosecutions.[7] Some were resident in Occupied countries; however, most had been held in captivity abroad, as prisoners of war or in civilian detention camps. As soon as possible after the armistice, officers of Allied Military Intelligence moved to arrest those whose names were on the Watch Lists. In Britain, senior Scotland Yard detectives, who had been seconded to MI5, collected affidavits and evidence against suspected traitors in preparation for the laying of charges in English courts.

Suspected collaborators could be tried under the British Treason Act, for which a conviction carried an automatic capital sentence. Alternatively, they could be prosecuted for breaching British Defense Regulation 2A by assisting the enemy, which carried a maximum punishment of penal servitude for life. According to the Director of Public Prosecutions, Theobald Mathew, his department operated on the principle that renegades who were "thought not to be deserving of death" were indicted for violation of Defense Regulation 2A.[8] By April 1946, at least one hundred and twenty-five Britons had been charged with having aided the enemy abroad. The defendants consisted of sixty-eight civilians and fifty-seven service-men, almost all of whom were prisoners of war or civilian internees; most of the actions that brought the charge had taken place in camps in Occupied Europe.[9] It is not always possible to establish the precise outcome of each charge; how-ever, the arraignments took place between the end of 1945 and early 1947. In February of that year, Mathews indicated that, using Defense Regulation 2A, his department had achieved verdicts against twenty-one British citizens who had made Axis broadcasts. Overall from a welter of prosecutions, and including at least nine capital convictions, there were three executions for treason. As well as Amery's in the week before Christmas 1945, the others were the civilian broad-caster William Joyce, better known as "Lord Haw Haw," who was put to death in Wandsworth Prison on January 3, 1946; and the British serviceman, Theodore Schürch, executed in Pentonville Prison on January 4, 1946.[10]

What is notable about these postwar British trials is the wide range of sentences that were handed down, even for what were very similar crimes. One observer has suggested that where there were executions it was because the British government "wished to demonstrate the maximum retribution against anybody who seriously challenged it."[11] However, this was not so. Certainly, the British citizens con-victed under the Treachery Act as German wartime spies and executed between mid-July 1941 and March 1944 may have constituted a challenge to the British state.[12] But the other "ordinary" prosecutions under the treason act did not. Nei-ther William Joyce nor John Amery posed a threat to Britain. Joyce was never a British citizen and though he had obtained a British passport illegally, that in itself was a straightforward criminal offense. His ranting on the Berlin airwaves in the end amounted to no more than that. Amery, an unreliable fantasist who certainly brought the good name of his family into disrepute, offered no substantial chal-lenge to the British government. Indeed, one could observe that in constituting a continuous and considerable drain on the German purse, Amery aided the Al-lied war effort. In further proof of the lack of official consistency, charges were dropped against Edward Bowlby, just after Joyce's execution, even though Bowlby was without question a British national who had traveled on a valid English pass-port to Berlin from where he made a series of tawdry anti-Semitic broadcasts that were directed at wartime Britain.[13]

Some forty British individuals, of whom at least nine were servicemen, made pro-Nazi broadcasts from Berlin. Thomas Cooper and the soldier Walter Purdy received capital sentences that were subsequently commuted. In the end the two, separately, spent less than a decade behind bars. Norman Baillie-Stewart, fac-ing his second trial as a traitor and despite his having abjured British citizenship in 1938, received five years of hard labor.[14] P. G. Wodehouse, extricated from internment in Occupied Europe in return for making broadcasts from Berlin, was never charged.[15] Also, the English courts were kind to the half-dozen fe-male broadcasters in Berlin among whom the longest sentence meted out was for eighteen months handed down at the Old Bailey to Susan Hilton. The best indicator of the severity of sentence was the trial's proximity to the end of the war. The further away from the armistice that it took place, the less likelihood there was of a heavy sentence. This phenomenon of chronology, with Iva Toguri a notable exception, held sway, as well, in Australia and the United States.

In Australia, treason within the country and its territories was designated as a capital offense under the Commonwealth of Australia Crimes Act, 1914.[16] Individuals enlisted in the military services could also be charged under the Defense Regulations Act. The latter might bring a heavy custodial sentence, but never capital punishment. The legal complication that tangled the government's attempts to press treason charges against two Australians, who had been broadcasters on Japanese shortwave radio, was that their traitorous actions had taken place outside Australian territory. Therefore, the indictments had to be brought within the jurisdiction of English common law in which, as we have seen, it was a crime to aid the king's enemies whether at home or abroad. Prior to the Australian law reforms of the 1960s, English common law prevailed in the ex-colonies, that is, in what after Australian Federation became the states of Australia. Therefore, when the Australian government wished to prosecute Charles Cousens, and later the civilian broadcaster John Holland, the Attorney General was forced to navigate a set of complex legal pathways. When the rivalry between state and federal instrumentalities constituted an insurmountable obstacle, the Commonwealth of Australia was forced to turn to the British courts for assistance.[17]

The United States Constitution (Article III, Section 3) defines treason as the act of levying war against the nation or adhering to the nation's enemy by providing aid and comfort, whether within the country or outside. It also includes the requirement of proof from direct testimony of two witnesses to the overt act. Unlike the British, and undoubtedly influenced by American revolutionary tradition, treason laws in the United States for the most part have been only "sparsely used."[18] And again, unlike British practice, "not one man" has ever been executed for committing treason against the United States.[19]

After World War Two, a dozen American servicemen were brought before military tribunals with a single soldier executed when found guilty of desertion. At the same time, eleven American civilians were arrested as suspected traitors. Of those in Occupied Europe, nine had been employed as broadcasters on German shortwave networks based in Berlin; five of them were convicted of treason.[20] The American justice system gave no special consideration to convicted females. For example, Mildred Gillars, who had broadcast under the call sign of "Axis Sally," received a sentence of twelve years, part of which she served in the Alderson Federal Women's Reformatory where Iva Toguri later also became an inmate.

From the Pacific Theatre of War, three Americans were charged with having aided the enemy. John Provoo (a staff sergeant when taken prisoner in the Philippines) used his position to harm an American officer. Later, Provoo joined the POW broadcasting unit in Tokyo. Tomoya Kawakita, a civilian with dual Japanese American nationality who had been working in Japan when war broke out, became an interpreter in a Japanese mine and munitions factory where he harshly treated Allied prisoners. Both Provoo and Kawakita were convicted of treason but managed subsequently to have their sentences ameliorated. Provoo, indicted twice, successfully appealed to have his verdict quashed on the grounds that he had been denied a speedy trial. Kawakita's death penalty verdict in 1948 was commuted to life imprisonment in 1953 by President Eisenhower, and in November of 1963, in one of the President's last directives, J. F. Kennedy pardoned Kawakita.[21]

Iva Toguri is the exception to the patterns of postwar treason trials. She faced court at the end of 1949, one of the last from World War Two, and received a ten-year custodial sentence and a hefty fine. Her insistence on retaining her American citizenship during her years in wartime Japan—instead of choosing the loophole of "voluntary expatriation" as did thousands of her countrymen in Japan—counted against her. By contrast the strategy adopted by American Nisei enabled them to "shed" their United States citizenship and transfer their allegiance with impunity to America's wartime enemy. After the Japanese defeat, these ex-Americans simply reapplied to the U.S. Embassy in Tokyo to have their American passports restored.[22] Toguri's stoicism in the face of the extreme tenor of racism and misogyny that characterized her trial in California seemed also to inflame antagonism towards her. The trial and subsequent unsuccessful appeals took place at the conjunction of two corrosive social currents. The deep distrust that many Anglo-Americans at the time expressed towards all things Japanese, including Americans of Japanese descent, provoked the response from leaders in the Japanese-American community whereby, determined to demonstrate their patriotism at all costs, they shrank from the publicity of the trial of "Tokyo Rose." None spoke out against the racism and the injustice that was Toguri's lot. Both community responses, the Anglo and the Japanese American, fed into a cold war paranoia that was manifest in the desire to exclude all individuals and groups who appeared not to fit the invented mold of the imagined American mainstream.

PART I

Broadcasting to Britain from Wartime Berlin

CHAPTER 1

Execution of the British Traitor: John Amery

In Wandsworth Prison on December 19, 1945, just before 9 A.M. and after the regular inmates had been moved to the exercise yards on the far side of the building, the governor and the chaplain escorted a slight young man from his cell to the execution chamber. Waiting for him was Albert Pierrepoint, already dressed in the hangman's khaki garb and black hood. The previous day, he had made the preparations; surreptitiously observing the prisoner to estimate height and weight to ensure the correct length of the noose and a counterweight of sand to enable a fatal drop that was quick and clean. The condemned man was led to stand on the trapdoor immediately below the noose while the hood was placed over his head and the rope around the neck. This done, the executioner stepped back and threw a lever. Instantaneously, the prisoner's body dropped, its weight severing the spinal column with a single jerk.[1]

Almost immediately, the doleful tolling of a bell announced the prisoner's demise. Shortly afterwards, an official emerged through a small door in the main prison entrance and affixed two notices to the gate. The first recorded the time of the execution; the other, a surgeon's certificate, indicated that the prisoner, indeed, was dead. Hardly were these somber proceedings complete when a car, waiting since early morning in the nearby street, sped off. At the wheel was a young man in military uniform with a dark-headed woman weeping at his side.[2]

John Amery was the prisoner executed that day. Thirty-three years of age and the son of a prominent London family, he had been convicted three weeks before of High Treason. Specifically, he had pleaded guilty at the Old Bailey to eight charges of having offered aid and comfort to the king's enemies in wartime. The offenses encompassed three sorts of treasonous acts: broadcasting over enemy radio; giving talks and lectures on behalf of Germany; and encouraging British prisoners of war to join the military forces of Germany. The couple in the car was Amery's younger brother, Julian, a soldier recently returned from war service in the Middle East, and John's common-law French wife, Michelle Thomas.[3]

Execution is always a dispiriting affair. John Amery's took place in the immediate aftermath of the Second World War when the public mood strongly favored retribution against those who had supported the defeated Axis. English papers were filled with reports of the great many trials of traitors that were taking place. In Amery's case, the tabloids fulminated against him as a "rat," a "madman in a black shirt," and a "failed West End playboy with a lust for the limelight." The dailies were in agreement that a violent end was an appropriate finale to his squalid and worthless life.[4] The quality press emphasized Amery's lack of remorse and his unshaken belief in Nazi ideology. Though there was sympathy for the parents because they had given devoted service to nation and empire, there was little for the son. A single correspondent to the *Manchester Guardian* asked whether the effect of Amery's activities was equal to the gravity of his punishment.[5] A poignant letter by his mother to the same paper pleaded to spare the lives of the others facing the charge of treason after her "own dear son has paid the penalty for his sincere if mistaken beliefs."[6] These, however, were small voices whistling against a very strong wind.

Between 1940 and 1945, John Amery had hitched his star to the Nazi victory. Of that there was no doubt. Before and after his arrest, he made no secret of his pro-Nazi stance and his supporting activities. When the Second World War broke out, Amery had been living in Europe and in a very short space of time offered his services to the pro-German forces in Vichy France. Subsequently, he hooked up with a motley cavalcade of pro-German propagandists traveling in Occupied Europe. In Paris, Prague, Berlin, Budapest, Bratislava and Belgrade and on German-controlled radio in Milan, Amery gave talks in English, French and Italian to hail the power and glory of the "New Europe" that was emerging under Axis auspice. The content of the speeches was highly repetitive. In them, Amery contrasted the vitality and strength of the fascist states with the sclerosis of Britain: "plutocratic," "Jew-ridden" and rapidly passing into the evil maws of an international Semitic cabal. Constantly he harped on the theme that the "Jew-lover," Churchill, had led the British people into a pernicious alliance with Bolsheviks and Americans. The latter, in their turn, constituted the Janus-face of international Jewry that had no other aim than to steal away the precious jewels of the British Empire.[7] Although in wartime these were treasonous words—and in Britain, treason was a capital offense—Amery's execution (and the speed with which it was carried out) was highly unusual.

The mode of John Amery's prosecution (and of his defense) was closely linked with that of William Joyce. Before the war, Joyce had been a member of the British Union of Fascists and at the end of August 1939, he and his wife had moved to Berlin where he became a core figure in Goebbels' overseas propaganda unit and made several broadcasts a week that were beamed back to England. Dubbed "Lord Haw Haw" and using the distinctive call sign of "Germany Calling," Joyce achieved notoriety in wartime Britain. Brought back to England for trial after the war, he drew hostile onlookers and unsympathetic press coverage whenever he appeared. He was first arraigned at the Bow Street Magistrate's Court on September 17, 1945 and proceeded through a series of hearings until his final, unsuccessful appeal to the Privy Council on December 18, 1945. This was the day before Amery was executed.

Amery's broadcasts were beamed to England from November 1942 to January 1943.[8] In them, a standard refrain was his harangue that the "Jews, Toffs and Plutocrats" in the British government were out of touch with ordinary English working people. As he repeated many times: "Apart from the midwife who brought them into the world and the undertaker who puts them in their coffin, English leaders never, by the remotest chance, come into contact with English working people. All English plutocrats had a nurse when they were born, all went to the same private school, Eton or Harrow, and then to the Universities of Oxford and Cambridge and from whence into the political parties, the big clubs or the big banks." In Amery's view, without exception "they feel more at home with the Plutocracy in Washington, than with the ordinary English workingman and woman."[9] There was truth in the description of the gulf that separated the prewar English elite and the working classes. But the hypocrisy of the message was striking when it came from one whose own life had been that of privilege and comfort. What is not in doubt is the humiliation that these talks caused the Amery parents, as they were forced to endure what his father referred to as the "miserable ordeal" of listening to John's immoderate oratory over the airwaves. Even more distressing than the direct insults to Churchill was the son's habit of deriding George VI as a "stammering idiot" and the living proof of the degeneration of the English leaders.[10]

In the collective biography of the Amery family, John's wartime activities constituted a painful chapter. Leo Amery had been a conservative member of Parliament since 1911 and a figure of considerable gravitas in conservative and imperial circles. His denunciation of Chamberlain's ineffective war policy is famous. On May 7, 1940, in the House of Commons, he had thundered the powerful words that Cromwell had used to rout the Long Parliament: "In the Name of God Go!" It was the final straw that brought down Chamberlain's administration. Churchill, succeeding Chamberlain as prime minister, took Leo Amery into the new government as Secretary of State for India, a post that he retained for the rest of the war. Leo's wife, Florence, was a devoted mother and an active MP's wife in her husband's Birmingham electorate. At least until her son's execution, Mrs Amery led a busy public life as patron and promoter of a thicket of organizations that were dedicated to Empire Unity and British Imperial Preference. Julian, John's younger brother, left Balliol College, Oxford, when war broke out in order to enlist, becoming a highly decorated member of the British Army's Special Operations Executive. In this unit, and to great effect, he used his expertise in the languages of the Middle East and the Balkans to organize behind the lines the pro-British factions of the resistance in Albania and Yugoslavia.[11]

Commentators at the time and indeed subsequently have puzzled over why it was that a son of Leo and Florence Amery would be attracted to the European, anti-Semitic, extreme Right. They have speculated, too, about how was it possible

that the first son of these devoted parents could have, so humiliatingly, deni-
grated their politics and public works. Indeed, any parent might wonder what it
was about the Amery household that could produce such a contrast between the
life experiences of the siblings: the public successes of the younger, Julian; and the
failures of the older, John. The answers that have been offered to these questions,
with a few exceptions, are far from satisfactory. Most fail to place John within
the setting of his family, and in turn, the members of the Amery family within
the specific historical and political context in which their private and public lives
were played out. Not only is a contextual approach enlightening for the individual case of John Amery, but it is also a useful way in which to understand traitors
and treason in general. Before setting the context and the details of John Amery's
biography, therefore, it is worthwhile laying out some of the explanations and
documentary evidence that have been offered to account for the phenomenon
of John Amery, quintessential son of the English establishment and pro-Nazi
traitor.

One of the first explanations of John Amery's behavior came from Inspector
Leo Burt of Scotland Yard. His memoir contains much material about the British
spies and traitors whom he captured and prosecuted in a long career in British
security.[12] Before the Second World War, Burt was "England's premier sleuth"
and afterwards rose to the rank of Commander in Chief of Special Branch, the
unit within Scotland Yard that oversaw national security. During the war, British
Intelligence cooperated with the Allied war effort to produce a Watch List of
Renegades. As far as it could be managed, while the conflict was in progress,
Military Intelligence kept traces on these individuals who were pro-Axis Allied
citizens and resident in occupied territories. Long before 1945, preparations were
under way for the trials that would take place as soon as peace was declared.[13]
Leo Burt had been seconded from the Murder Squad at Scotland Yard to the Intelligence Corps in MI5, where he played a prominent part in preparing these future
prosecutions. When John Amery and William Joyce were captured in Europe,
Burt and another M15 officer were immediately dispatched from London to in-
terrogate them, and to collect proper affidavits and evidence that would stand up
under English law. In both the Joyce and Amery cases, and in many others like
them, Burt accompanied the arrested individual back to England. He went as well
to Spain in 1945 with the head of Public Prosecutions and another MI5 officer to
investigate Julian Amery's efforts to head off his brother's treason prosecution.

In Burt's estimation, John Amery was a "queer card." Indeed, among all of
the traitors Burt had known, Amery was the "strangest of them all." At their first
interview, in the Italian prison camp at Terni, the young man was "completely
cocksure." Burt was taken aback when his prisoner declined to wear the civilian
suit that the detective had carefully brought from the Amery family in England,
preferring instead to arrive home wearing what Burt called Amery's "war paint"
of "full fascist uniform." It consisted of jack-boots, greenish-gray breeches and
black shirt. A shortage of planes forced the two to make a roundabout trip and
they spent a good deal of time together. A kindly man, by his own account, Burt

attempted to make the journey appear as if they were "two friends traveling in company." Burt found Amery to be "loquacious," a characteristic that the English detective had noted among all English prisoners. Ever a patriot, perhaps, Burt understood that these Englishmen were "thankful after a time in a foreign prison to pour out their hearts to an English compatriot." Indeed, when he had been arrested, Amery had asked for a typewriter, and had written a long and detailed statement setting out his activities in Occupied Europe and the reasons for his beliefs. As the two men made their way back to London, Amery's excited talk was almost entirely about the dangers of communism and his firm belief that he would not be prosecuted in England because his father would be able to have the charges against him dropped.

Burt had won a fearsome reputation as a tough handler of hard-bitten criminals, but in the end he came to feel sorry for both John and his de facto Michelle Thomas, she also incarcerated at the Terni camp. The couple drew the detective into the schemes they were hatching to regain the possessions they claimed the Italian partisans had purloined when the two were arrested. While bemused that anyone would worry about such things when they faced such serious charges, Burt went off on a wild goose chase to the Como partisan organization in an unsuccessful attempt to retrieve their possessions: the fur coat that Thomas had been wearing, as well as two silver fox pelts, the pigskin luggage and the Lancia Aprilia tourer in which they had been driving when the members of the Italian resistance had caught up with them on the autostrada heading to Switzerland.

During Burt's interrogation, Amery showed himself to be what the English detective described as "internationally minded" rather than English. Burt surmised that this was the result of Amery having had a French nanny who spoke only in French and filled the boy's head with dubious Gallic ideas. Even more importantly, though, for Burt, the thirty-three-year-old Amery was typical of the generation that was the "product of the long-weekend of the 1930s." By this, Burt meant that members of the cohort after the 1920s were different from the generation that had preceded them. In the decade immediately after the Great War, the national mood among the young had been one of "mafficking"; the "sinful, ginful twenties" had encouraged "Bright Young Things" to behave as though the hardships of war were over forever. By the 1930s, however, the mood had changed. This was an era in which "Youth" was spelt with a capital "Y" and the dizziness of 1920s gave way to more serious politics. Young people coming of age in the later decade had been hit by the Depression and international events such as the Spanish civil war. Burt pointed out that at home many of them rallied to calls such as those from the Prince of Wales who announced that to relieve the plight of the Welsh coalminers: "Something Must be Done."[14] As Burt saw it, the 1930s generation of young people had no experience of war or of the need to trim their sails to meet their pragmatic responsibilities. Certainly though, as he explained, it was no "cozy age" in which to be an adolescent because the era encouraged young English men and women to "think extravagantly about politics and act extravagantly in private life." And in this sense, Burt considered that John Amery was a symbol of his generation and in another era may have been quite a different fellow.

The English journalist Rebecca West, commissioned by the *New Yorker* to write a series of articles on the trial of William Joyce, offered an explanation from the vantage of a contemporary. She sat through a great many of the proceedings against traitors held in the London courts immediately after the war. Her collected essays, *The Meaning of Treason,* was published in 1949 and later expanded to include the postwar prosecutions of British scientists caught up in pro-Soviet espionage and the Cold War rivalry to develop an atom bomb.[15] Because the essays cover a long chronological sweep and she writes with verve, West has been very influential in the broad understanding of British traitors and treason. Her take, however, is highly idiosyncratic and her analysis solipsistic and overwrought. For example, William Joyce, who receives most of West's attention among the Second World War traitors, was a character whose flaws were attributed to his Irishness. At first sight of him in the dock, she was overwhelmed by his "real Donnybrook air" and that "he was a not-very-fortunate example of the small, nippy, jig-dancing kind of Irish peasant." What struck her too was his unprepossessing physical presence. His hair was "mouse-colored and sparse, particularly above the ears, and his pinched misshapen nose joined to his face at an odd angle"; he had a "long neck, shoulders narrow and sloping, his arms were short and thick, and his body looked flimsy and coarse." In her estimation he was a "queer little bog-trotter with a brogue." There is not much discussion by West of the legal ins and outs of the trial, but rather she offers an engrossing reconstruction of the traitors' biographies and the putative effect of their psyches. To take the example of Joyce again, West suggests that after the members of the senior Joyce family had been harassed in Ireland for their pro-Britishness, William was chagrined to find that in England he was looked down upon as an "Irish nobody." As a consequence, he was ineluctably drawn to Nazism, finally achieving the ultimate in broadcasting hate-driven tirades sent back to Britain. A great deal of what West writes about Joyce, his brother, and his wife and about Joyce's thoughts as he surveys his fellow-traitors in Berlin, makes entertaining reading, but ultimately is fanciful and highly embroidered fiction.

West's portrait of John Amery is quite different. She evinces great sympathy for his parents who, unlike Joyce's, were her class equals. John Amery was, she says, "like an automobile that will not hold the road." As a child, he was the sort that in company quickly turns from a "pet to a pest." West, however, dismissed as "useless" any attempt to conceive of John as a "mercenary trafficker or a dogmatic fascist." Rather, he was an "excellent broadcaster" with an overriding "hatred of Russia and communism." As it happens, we now know that West shared a fear of the Soviet Union, an obsession which won her the confidence of J. Edgar Hoover, the head of the American FBI.[16] Whether for these reasons or not, West passed over John Amery's anti-Semitism and the specifics of his ideological posturing. When she saw Amery in the dock, "a sick little monkey and yellow with fear," she thought only that his broadcasts would have made his listeners in England "feel sympathy for his family" and cause them to believe that the "Germans were terrible cads."

Hartley Shawcross was the prosecutor in the Amery and Joyce trials. The British attorney general's crisply written autobiography, *Life Sentence*, powerfully evokes the spirit of the times; more remarkably so because Lord Shawcross was in his nineties when the memoir was published.[17] Before the war, he had enjoyed a highly successful career at the Bar and as a Labor MP. When the party swept into government in July 1945, Shawcross was immediately appointed attorney general. His first major task was to deal with war criminals in Europe and traitors at home. Shawcross sat on the bench of international jurors at Nuremberg in the trials of the Nazi leaders and moved directly from there to the prosecution of high-profile British traitors.

In *Life Sentence,* Shawcross writes in detail about William Joyce and the difficulties involved in successfully prosecuting the crime of treason. The mode of John Amery's prosecution and of his defense was closely linked with that of Joyce. In both the Joyce and the Amery cases, Shawcross' adversary in court was the London silk, Gerald Slade KC, who also appeared for a great many "ordinary" traitors at the end of the war.[18] In Joyce's trial, Slade argued that because his client was not English he had no case to answer. Joyce was an American, born in New York to Irish parents, who became a German citizen before the United States entered the war. Joyce had held a British passport, but it had been acquired under false pretences. Slade claimed that an alien might hold allegiance to a country while resident in it, but could not be expected to do so when residing outside that country.[19] If Joyce could not be required to show allegiance to Britain, it followed that he could not be charged with disloyalty to the British monarch. By contrast, Shawcross for the prosecution argued that, whether by illegal means or not, the possession of a British passport extended the protection of the British crown to the holder who, in turn for enjoying such protection, had a reciprocal obligation of allegiance to the British king. In the Old Bailey and later on appeal before the Privy Council, Slade's defense was rejected. From the bench, Sir Fredrick Tucker opined that Joyce had left Britain "wrapped in the Union Jack," having made his home in England and when he stepped outside the country he was "armed with the protection that is normally conferred on a British subject."[20]

Although the prosecution carried the day in court, Shawcross later observed in *Life Sentence* that the outcome had been unsatisfactory. While most British people had hated Joyce during the war, many felt that because he was an American national, his conviction had been unfair. The sense of injustice was heightened when Joyce was put to death on January 3, 1946, immediately after the appeal decision was handed down, and before the Law Lords had given the reasons for their decision.[21]

Shawcross was much less forthcoming about John Amery's trial, observing only that he did not wish to cause "further distress" to Amery's "relatives" for whom he had the "highest respect." He noted, however, that Amery was "morally insane." As we shall see, this was the claim put forward by the experts hired by John's parents when they sought to have the death penalty lifted. Shawcross concluded that it was a great pity that the British government did not listen to Home Office specialists, who at the time were in agreement with the Amery family, as this would have facilitated a reprieve.

As the Attorney General and chief prosecutor, Shawcross would have been aware of the flurry of reports and counter reports about Amery's state of sanity in mid-December 1945, the fraught time in which the government had to make the decision whether to reprieve him or allow the execution to go ahead. For whatever reason, Shawcross was incorrect in concluding that the Home Office specialists opposed the death sentence. It was a much more complex matter. The prison medical officers who were in charge of John after he was brought back from Italy for trial most decidedly disagreed with the phalanx of Amery family experts who wished to prove that John was insane. As well, the Home Office legal experts pointed out that feeble-mindedness and a lack of understanding of the consequences of an action, which would have been justification for a reprieve, were not the maladies from which John Amery suffered.

The medical reports from the prison staff uniformly state that John Amery was composed, fully aware of his own actions and quite sane. Dr Grierson, the Senior Medical Officer at Brixton Prison, where John was held on his return to Britain, and Dr John Methuen at Wandsworth, where he subsequently was transferred, kept the prisoner under close observation. They maintained a detailed record of Amery's health and his state of mind from the time of his arrival from Italy until the morning of his execution.[22] In their daily dealings with him the medical staff apparently found Amery an unappealing character. The reports describe him as an "insignificant-looking and weedy individual"; "indolent and slovenly"; and "untidy and not over-clean in his personal attention."[23] Amery had disclosed that he had contracted syphilis at age seventeen, but that it had been successfully treated. According to the medical officers in 1945, there was "no sign of physical disease" and no positive indication on the Wasserman Test.[24] Amery's prison doctors also noted, with some distaste, that he was profligate, chain-smoking immediately the ration of fifteen cigarettes issued per day; he was also less interested in his own hygiene "than an English person," and possessed "Continental habits" whereby he preferred coffee over tea and had requested cognac on the night before the execution. But, unequivocally, the reports note that in Amery's mental state there was "no sign of insanity or mental deficiency."[25]

After more than half a century, there are several studies that attempt to explain John Amery's behavior. Two of them are concerned with his anti-Semitism and are discussed in the third chapter, which deals with Amery's activities during World War Two. The historian and ex-military intelligence officer, Adrian Weale, has studied Amery as part of a two-hander on traitors, bracketing him with Roger Casement, executed for treason during the First World War.[26] Weale, building on Rebecca West's claim that John Amery was the dysfunctional son of a pitiable family, argues that Amery received harsh treatment because his parents were part of the British elite. While this may be so, it is equally the case that from his elevated position as a member of Parliament and senior Tory figure, Leo Amery protected his son and the family from publicity, and even punishment, in many of John's more egregious scrapes. Much more problematic, however, is the evidence on which Weale uncritically relies and the decontextualized manner in which it is applied. Almost in its entirety, Weale's biography reproduces the material that the Amery family collected in the three short weeks between the handing down of the verdict and the execution. These documents have a specific historical provenance: They were created, with great urgency, between the end of November and the middle of December 1945, for the singular purpose of swaying the British Home Office to set aside John's capital sentence. This material cannot be used as though it provides a straightforward window into John Amery's motivation or his actions. Exactly as the Amery family intended, Weale accepts that John Amery was "morally insane," had been in this unenviable state from a very young age, and as a consequence should never have been hung. Sean Murphy, in his recent collection on British traitors in World War Two, accepts Weale's approach.[27] Much more substantial is David Faber's *Speaking For England. Leo, Julian and John Amery-The Tragedy of a Political Family*[28] that sets the three Amerys within the context of their familial relationship and the father's public life. Faber also uses the reprieve material for John in an unmediated fashion, but intertwines it with dense analysis of British political history.

The circumstances in which the material was collected influenced the content of these documents that have been central in the reconstruction of John Amery's biography. When he was brought back to London for trial, the Amery family solicitors, J. E. Lickford and Sons, briefed the king's counsel, G. O. Slade who had acquired a reputation in defending many of the Britons accused as traitors in Occupied Europe. He also was the legal counsel for William Joyce. In that case, Slade's carefully crafted defense rested on the fact that Joyce was not a British citizen and therefore could not be punished for having forsworn allegiance to the British king. In the lead-up to Amery's trial, the preparations for which came close on the heels of Joyce's arraignment, Slade advocated a similar defense. It was based on John's claim that while he was in Spain with Franco during the Spanish civil war, he had become a Spanish citizen. This defense collapsed, however, on the eve of John's trial. Joyce had been unsuccessful using this line of argument. Moreover, as we shall see, the prosecution had documented proof that the evidence of John's nationality, collected by his brother Julian in Madrid, was a fabrication. Faced with the collapse of the initial legal strategy, the family and Slade changed tack, recommending that John plead guilty outright in the hope that this would facilitate an act of clemency. Leo noted in his diary that when John, in jail, was informed of this new defense, he was agreeable, but had responded humorously that "if it were true that he was insane, he was certainly the last person to know about it."[29]

A guilty verdict for treason carried an automatic death sentence. When it was handed down on November 28, 1945, the Amerys and their friends went into high gear to obtain a reprieve. The plan was to have the sentence set aside on the principle that applied in the McNaghten Rules. Common in murder trials, and a capital offense, these stated that a person who could be proven to be insane could not be held responsible for his actions and therefore could not be put to death.

Leo, Florence and Julian collected fourteen sworn statements to show that at every stage throughout his life, John had been insane.[30] Some of the affidavits were solicited from individuals who had an involvement with the family. Others were prompted after friends had offered their condolences. The sheaf of documents was then given to Lord Horder, a Tory MP and, previously, the king's physician. A family friend, Dr Edward Glover of Wimpole Street, a specialist in mental disorders, also involved himself in the case. These two medicos made a diagnosis of John's condition, though without examining him in person. In addition, four psychiatrists of note were brought in to review the reports and provide further confirmation of John's diagnosis by the original two, though like them, the later experts had no opportunity to interview John face to face.[31] The Amery family medical experts were unanimous that in John Amery they were confronted with a patient who suffered a clear case of "long-standing psychopathic disorder," allied with "moral insanity and moral imbecility." He suffered "diseased mental processes," a disorder of the "total personality structure" and was "devoid of the moral sense by which normal people control their actions and their utterances." Moreover, the evidence showed that he had been suffering from a very early age the inability to distinguish between right and wrong and was, without question, "morally insane."[32] Armed with this report, family members and friends lobbied the Cabinet for clemency, particularly James Chuter Ede, the Home Secretary.[33]

The documents that were provided by the family to the Home Secretary catalogue in immense detail incidents that purported to prove John's "abnormality and moral insanity." Yet many of the events described do not suggest derangement. A great many of the statements about John's childhood and youthful behavior will sound familiar to parents in a child-centered present. As often happens, children with well-off and doting parents find school difficult. At home they have been led to believe that their opinions matter a great deal, only to discover at school that this is not the case. John Amery was such a child. As a small boy, an adolescent and a young man, he was greatly indulged at home and was accustomed to having his own way. It seems that servants and staff entrusted with the unenviable task of reining him in found a young charge who was arrogant and hard to manage. And long before the war, he had caused heartache to his parents. But even if all of these things are true, they do not constitute psychopathic behavior. Indeed, the younger brother, Julian, confronted a very similar situation while growing up, but in the end was able to create an identity for himself as an intellectual and an exceptional individual. Like his brother, Julian depended on his father's position and in turn Leo was assiduous in promoting his younger son's military, journalistic and political career. As well, in relation to John, it is worth emphasizing that most of the evidence on which the family psychiatrists relied was commissioned from tutors and schoolmasters who knew the gravity of the outcome at stake. Also, their statements suggest that these educators accepted as quite normal a level of bullying which today would be considered unacceptable in the handling of a schoolboy. In their comments on John Amery's school days, his masters advocated a form of institutionalized violence on which were predicated upper-class notions of schoolboy "honor, patriotism and true pride," as John's headmaster at Harrow expressed it. That between the wars "violence formed the background of much public school life, especially in the first years" made the application no easier to take for the individuals, like John Amery, who were on its receiving end.[34]

The earliest evidence in the family dossier comes from the statement of Caroline Mead who had joined the Amery household as a nursery maid when Julian was born. At Julian's birth, Jack, as the family always called him, was seven years of age, and a second nursery helper, Nanny Mead, was hired for the baby. A young French girl, Jeanine La Gallen or "Pipette" as the family called her, had been Jack's nursemaid previously and continued on as his governess. Nanny Mead wrote to Florence Amery when she heard about John's arrest. In a labored hand and with uncertain spelling, Mead recalled the nursery behavior from those early years. Later, she provided the same information in a sworn statement to the family psychiatrists.[35] Nanny Mead recalled that Jack was a "queer little boy." He could be "so loving and natural, but had no self control." Between the ages of three and four he had had episodes of bedwetting and often was given to tantrums. The nanny observed that the arrival of his baby brother "had a bad effect" on the older boy. Just after Jack had seen Julian for the first time and he and the nannies were taking tea, Jack without warning "took his egg and bread and butter out of the nursery and stormed and raved." Apparently, while Jack was upset like this, the nannies found him "uncontrollable" and could do nothing with him. Afterwards he would be "exhausted" and have to be put to bed. Nanny Mead recalled that on one occasion when his brother was in the pram, Jack had tried to tip him out; and at another time had struck a match that he tried to throw into the pram. When Julian was about six months old, his brother had put metal polish in the bottle in which the baby's mixture was prepared. When reprimanded, Jack had told Nanny Mead that he "wanted to poison his brother." As the nanny noted, in her experience children by four years of age should have self-control, and even at seven Jack's was "poor." As a consequence, she had always thought that "as a child [Jack] was not quite normal" and indeed "feared that he was not right." Half a century later, some of the behavior that concerned Nanny Mead would probably be seen as the manifestation of a severe dose of sibling jealousy, a not-uncommon phenomenon in families where there is more than one offspring and parents peruse child rearing manuals.

The headmistress of Jack's kindergarten, laboring under the eponym of Irene Ironside, also recalled the six-year-old as a handful.[36] From what she remembered, the Amery boy bullied other children and took discipline very badly. He was "unused to not having his own way," and she found him an "eccentric child" who "clung determinedly to his own ideas" and "had a tendency to shut himself in and live inside himself." He preferred to color in his letters, what he called "putting in fantasy," rather than forming them correctly and when chastised he wrote "silly words in chalk under the desk." At one stage he had astonished his teachers and playmates by coming to school wearing a "long necklace of colored wooden beads," which he could not be persuaded to take off and eventually had been sent home.

Jack boarded at West Downs Preparatory School in Winchester from May 1921 to July 1925, that is from the age of nine to twelve. It was the same story all over again.[37] The headmaster, Mr K. L. S. Tindall, recalled that Jack had been a "boy of very unusual character." Though he "clearly felt affection for his parents and other people," it never prevented him from getting into scrapes. Jack seemed often not to be "touched by the ordinary school boy's code of loyalty to one's fellows or the necessity for physical courage." And his naughtiness did not come from "a love of adventure or the desire to shine in the eyes of his fellows." There was, the headmaster recalled, an incident which epitomized young Amery as "a young boy who was unusual to the point of abnormality." Another boy, nursing a grievance arising from something that Jack had done, asked the headmaster if he might fight Jack. Permission was given as long as proper boxing conditions were followed and the headmaster was present. When all the boys had gathered as spectators and the putative pugilists were brought into the ring, Jack refused to join the fray. Despite much noisy urging, he simply lay on the ground and would not get up. The headmaster was shocked at such behavior from a boy who he believed could not have "failed to realize the contempt that such an action would arouse in the minds of school staff and his fellow students."

At Harrow, Mr J. A. Boissier, the housemaster in the headmaster's house where Jack was placed, recorded that he had been "the most difficult boy [that he had] ever tried to manage."[38] In his view, because Jack hated games and sports, the avenues were closed off to him in which normal boys seek "notoriety and limelight." As a consequence, Jack tried to distinguish himself by holding "ultra" views on many subjects and expressing them openly on every occasion. This meant that Jack "continually fell foul of masters and boys."

Sir Cyril Norwood, Harrow's headmaster, wrote separately to the Home Secretary and gave evidence to the Amery's psychiatrists. To James Chuter Ede, at the Home Office, Norwood pointed out that he was a supporter of capital punishment and "one who loathes treason as much as any other." He also admitted to feeling "the deepest sympathy for the Amery parents," though this was not why he had written. Nor did a "liking" for their son move him. Rather, he regarded this young man as "contemptible and repulsive."[39] At Harrow, on his arrival, young Amery had "instantly been in trouble" and even after several terms it had been "impossible to make anything of him." Among all the boys Norwood had known, and it was a "number running into the thousands," young Amery had been the "most abnormal and presented the most difficult problem." What astonished Sir Cyril was that although Jack's father had been the head boy of the school and had gone on to a highly distinguished career at Oxford, these facts "moved the son not at all." Even more so, while Leo was a Governor of the school and a

Minister of the State, the boy had been caught "committing petty theft." Worse, John had run away and, when brought back, claimed that he "wished to become a garage-hand in France" because in such an occupation "he would be his own master." Despite Sir Cyril's pointing out firmly that such a vocation would "let down his parents" and preclude the splendid future which might be his, Jack had persisted with this outlandish notion.[40] What struck the Harrow headmaster most forcefully was Jack's lack of interest in sport, so central to the school's ethos. Not only was he "idle on the playing fields," he was also "afraid of being hurt at games and therefore played badly." In the end, Jack ran away after an "exhibition of insubordination and slackness on the field for which there was no excuse" and for which he would receive the beating from the captain of cricket which he had "rightly earned." According to Sir Cyril, the combination of an inability to distinguish right and wrong and Jack's physical fear of beatings had made him an "abnormal boy." With some stretch, he concluded that, given these shortcomings of character, it was not so surprising that young Amery had gone on to become a traitor in World War Two.

After John Amery quit Harrow in 1927, the parents employed a number of private tutors. Those that could be contacted at the end of 1945 added more detail to the mounting evidence of young Amery's moral depravity. One of them, Leander Jameson, was in charge of Jack for most of 1927, the year in which the boy turned fifteen.[41] It was also in the second half of that year that his parents were away from home on their travels through the Dominions. Jameson noted that his pupil had shown signs of a "marked moral imbecility" from the very beginning. Here was a boy who "preferred anarchy to order," and was "much given" to adolescent "moods and introspection." His heroes were some "obscure Chinese warlords" and the French *Croix de Feu*, but despite these role models as action-oriented figures, Jack slept with his windows shut tight and hated the outdoors. At this time, the boy also had a Red Setter, which shared his bed so that his room "smelt like a kennel." He had no friends, but was, in the tutor's view, "abnormally interested in the opposite sex," even those girls who were "not of a desirable sort." On their second day together while Jameson and Jack were riding on a London bus, Jack lit a cigarette, ignoring the tutor's remonstrance that it was "against his father's wishes." When Jack continued to smoke, Jameson took the offending object from the boy's mouth and threw it out of the window, whereupon Jack threatened to report the tutor for assault. He left the bus and approached a nearby policeman, but on reaching him simply asked the time. In most situations, Amery was friendly and cheerful, but could become "sullen and difficult" when forced to undertake outside exercise. After an altercation over this matter, Jameson had caned Jack and noted that, at least in the tutor's estimation, corporal punishment had produced a "marked improvement in demeanor." Jack was enrolled in a riding school in what proved to be a forlorn hope that this activity would draw him into an enjoyment of the outdoors. He behaved badly, however, in front of the other riders, many of whom were younger than he and Jameson was left with the decided impression that Jack had no "self-confidence in his ability to ride" and "covered this ineptitude with outbursts of bad temper." Presumably, an earlier excursion with the local hunt when his horse bolted and left Jack "beside himself" did little to improve his confidence. Much more to his liking was the automobile. That year Amery was given a car, a Morgan, and over the summer he drove himself and Jameson around Scotland. The tutor noted that the fifteen-year-old had "very bad road manners," and drove irresponsibly and aggressively.

The Amery *pères* decided, in 1928, that what their son needed was a survival trip that would involve camping outdoors in Iceland. A new tutor, Kingsley Walton, was hired. In his statement in December 1945, Walton recalled that at first he found the sixteen-year-old Jack to be "charming" and an "enthusiastic camper," but was later perturbed by his pupil's tendency to "fail to connect his action with accepted boyhood standards."[42] For example, while they were in London, before departure, the tutor had had to extract Jack from the lounge of a West End hotel where he had wanted to order them both alcoholic drinks. The lad also tended to behave impulsively. He smashed some long-playing records, of which he was very fond, by sitting on them, apparently on purpose. Any threat by the tutor to leave, however, had pulled Jack up short because it seemed that he was anxious to earn a good report on the trip with which to please his parents.

Another tutor, G. C. Nock, who oversaw Jack's education for three months in the summer of 1929, related in December 1945 examples of Jack's cryptofascist attitudes. In reality, these descriptions resonate much more with adolescent bravado than with fascism. In Nock's view, Jack saw "society as sheep" and himself as a "lone wolf"; also he liked to boast of sexual conquests, both male and female.[43] Nock begrudgingly recorded that his pupil's "one good point lay in his personal charm," but that Jack nevertheless displayed a "pathological absence of affection." Nock's conclusion that Jack's "character was one complete flaw" hardly suggests that Leo had spent well in hiring a teacher who would keep at the forefront the development needs of his pupil. Indeed, as we shall see, it was while under Nock's tutelage that Jack contracted a venereal disease.

As the medical group that the Amery family marshaled in 1945 was composed predominantly of psychiatrists, it is not surprising that they were much interested in John's sexuality. And, like the reports discussed above, this information came tagged with a particular provenance. Under the heading "Sexual Abnormalities" the expert report notes, presumably drawing on material from Pipette via Mrs Amery, that Jack had masturbated at the age of five.[44] At about six years of age he had made "obscene drawings" which were of figures with breasts. To these he sometimes added a penis. The drawings would then be shown to his French governess. Edward Glover has written in the margin beside this information the startling comment that "this behavior in children is an early sign that the individual is abnormally bisexual and prone to develop homosexual perversions."

Una Wing, Jack's first wife, was the source of most of the information about Amery's sexual proclivities. Her comments, only a selection of which found their way into the final report produced in December 1945, are extremely interesting.

The details of her marriage to John Amery are discussed more fully in the next chapter. Here, it is sufficient to indicate the conditions under which her statement was produced. Una and John had married in Athens in a minor blaze of publicity in March 1933. She was from a modest background and may at some stage even have been a prostitute. The parents were very unhappy about the relationship, but as there was little that they could do, they hoped that, as eventually did happen, the attraction would fizzle out. When the marriage took place, Leo and Florence accepted the inevitable and Leo provided his new daughter-in-law with the quite considerable allowance of eight pounds a month. John and Una were together from 1933 at least until 1938, a good deal of that time being spent in France. When in London the couple appeared at luncheons and family functions at the Amery's home in Eaton Square. Separated by the war, the two drifted apart. John took up with new partners and, with him outside the country, there are no more references in Leo Amery's diaries to Una's ever having been invited again to Eaton Square.

When John was arrested, there was a news report in the *Sunday Pictorial*, which was accompanied by two photographs. The first was of Amery's French common-law wife, Michelle Thomas, and the other was of Una. According to the paper, Una had provided the photograph of herself. It was claimed that she had contacted the paper and asked that her photo be published so that Amery's second wife would know that she had joined up with a bigamist. The *Sunday Pictorial* presented Una as a patriotic woman who had been wronged by a traitorous bounder. According to the first wife, she had not seen John Amery since before the war. And unlike him—the "hang dog cur doing the dirty work of Goebbels," as the paper put it—she had been virtuously engaged from 1940 in the British war effort, first in a hospital and later making munitions in an airplane factory.[45]

Julian Amery interviewed Wing when he was marshaling the psychiatric dossier on John. She provided evidence that her ex-husband was, as the psychiatrists baldly put it, a "sexual pervert." He had been attracted to males and females and, it was suggested as an indication of presumed masochistic tendencies, would "obtain an erection when he was afraid." The psychiatrists quote Una in detail as proof that John presented as "a typical case of *psychopathia sexualis*."[46] In further interviews, Una pointed out that Jack was obsessed with a fear of having no money; and was a "braggadocio" with "high-flown and quite unrealizable plans for financial coups."[47] It seems, too, that he had practiced masochism and been "beaten up by mistresses and prostitutes" and there was some question of his having had perverse "'tying up' practices." According to Una, John had a "tremendous fear of being thought respectable or of settling down"; it was as though he seemed "to want people to think badly of him." She observed, in a comment that was not included in the final report, that her ex-partner had "almost a mental scar resulting from the beatings he had at school and which colored his whole recollection of school life."[48]

It may well be that John Amery was afflicted with various kinds of sexual problems. It is also the case that, as for many married couples, wartime provided the cover under which one or other could evade their marital responsibilities. Una's information, though, like that in the other statements collected in December 1945, must be considered in light of her own self-perception as a wronged wife who had been cold-shouldered by her erstwhile in-laws. Whatever the effect of this may have been, certainly the Amerys did not include her in the family gatherings in John's final days. Hers was not among the names registered as visitors with permission to see the condemned man. When she attempted to visit John at Wandsworth the day before the execution, she was turned away. By then, of course, Michelle Thomas was in London, seeing John every day, accompanied by his mother and other close family associates. And it was to Michelle Thomas that John wrote his final love letters.

Even if all the incidents described above reveal John Amery as an unpleasant, disobedient child; a difficult, arrogant young man; and even one with uncommon sexual leanings; none necessarily is a portent of his future politics and their fatal outcome. There probably is no doubt that the events, to which the psychiatrists refer, took place in one form or another, but many of them are typical of a rebellious and volatile adolescence. Moreover, the documents in which Amery's personality is described were created in a very specific and urgent context—namely to prevent the carrying out of the sentence of death.

The Home Office, the recipient of these documents, considered the legal position very carefully. The role of James Chuter Ede, the Home Secretary, was critical to the final outcome.[49] Ede was relatively new to the office, having taken up the post after Labor's victory in July 1945. A clear-cut majority had provided Labor with a mandate to implement wide social and economic reform. From the last quarter of the nineteenth century there had been a movement to abolish capital punishment in Britain and the new Home Secretary, purportedly, was an abolitionist. Later, he supported the end of capital punishment for murder. Treason, however, is a different kettle of fish, and even after 1977, when capital punishment in Britain was formally abolished, treason and mutiny remain crimes that incur the death penalty. Various family supporters—among them John Amery's godfather, Sir John Simon, and his maternal uncle, Hamar Greenwood—made approaches to the cabinet asking for clemency. Lord Horder went so far as to telephone Chuter Ede at home on a private line.[50] When the two met (Ede very reluctantly), Horder explained that Leo Amery had pressed him to make the contact, and Horder had acceded to a father's desperate wish. Ede pointed out firmly that legal precedent that allowed a prisoner to be medically examined applied only before a trial had taken place, never after the sentencing. And in all cases, the government always relied for advice on its own experts "paid from the public purse," not ever on those provided by the accused.[51]

Anxious not to appear unwilling to countenance a reprieve, the Home Secretary finally commissioned two senior Prison Service medical officers to assess Amery's mental state.[52] They were W. N. East, formerly the Medical Commissioner for His Majesty's Prisons, and J. S. Hopwood, then the serving Medical Supervisor at Broadmoor Criminal Lunatic Asylum. Their brief was to establish whether Amery's state of mind brought him under the particular sections of the Criminal Lunatics Act 1884 which preclude the mentally insane and the feeble-minded from criminal prosecution.[53] The Home Office doctors interviewed the prison staff who had overseen Amery, and took evidence from Amery's parents, his brother Julian, and John's estranged first wife, Una Wing. As well, Sir Cyril Norwood, the Headmaster of Harrow, provided the information he had already contributed to the family's psychiatrists. In addition, the doctors carried out two extended interviews with John Amery himself.

The final report, submitted on December 14, contained two separate sets of evidence that pointed to contradictory conclusions.[54] From the family's evidence, the Home Office medicos concluded that "although Amery had been brought up in a healthy home and sent to good schools, he had consistently exhibited criminal tendencies." From a young age he had been "grossly mentally abnormal." To those who had known him well it seemed that John suffered what medically was the "extremely rare condition" that he was, in effect, "morally defective": he was one of the unfortunate people who are "incapable of profiting from their own past mistakes." The report found Amery much less responsible than an ordinary offender, and in light of all of this, they considered that they could recommend that his capital punishment could be commuted on medical grounds. At the same time, though, East and Hopwood also noted that the prison medical officers, who conscientiously had dealt with Amery, considered him to be of "average intelligence or above," and to have never given them any reason to consider that he was "insane or unaware of his own actions." East and Hopwood also found no evidence of organic disease of the central nervous system or active disease of the lungs. The results of an electrocephalogram indicated no sign of a malfunction in the brain. All of this, of course, was in line with the previous prison medical reports.

The Home Secretary's office commissioned opinions from their own legal experts. The unambiguous advice from all quarters was that John Amery was not insane within the meaning of the McNaghten Rules and, if this defense had been adduced at the trial, it would have failed. On the question of the difference in law between moral turpitude versus mental insanity, Chuter Ede's legal advisers pointed out that criminals often were "morally abnormal," but at the same time were well aware of the legal consequences of their actions. In the eyes of the law, "idiocy, imbecility and feeblemindedness" were of a different order from "moral deficiency or moral defectiveness." With any of the first three conditions, the perpetrator of a crime would not be able to understand the consequences of the action and therefore was not culpable.[55] By contrast, the moral defective and those who are morally deficient are able to understand that their actions are wrong and that they will lead to a penalty, but they persist with the action in any case. The medical evidence relating to John Amery suggested that he may well have been morally deficient, but he was still cognizant of his actions. In one of the legal opinions, which had canvassed all possible outcomes of the Amery case, it was noted as well that the British people accepted capital punishment for treason because in their eyes it remained the most heinous crime. If there was any special handling of the Amery case, such as a last-minute reprieve, it must be based strictly on legal grounds so as to make it clear that the family was not being treated in a way that was different from other people.

It was probably not surprising that on December 17, 1945, the Home Secretary announced that he was "unable to find any sufficient ground to justify him in advising His Majesty to interfere with the due course of the law."[56] In the assessment of the Prison Service's own experts, John Amery was sane and fully aware of his own actions.[57] Therefore he had made his guilty plea in full knowledge of the significance and the consequences of it, and since he had admitted to treason, the British government had no other response than to carry through the death penalty.

The last document that was added to the family's portfolio (and has remained important) post execution, was Leo's statement, submitted with the psychiatric assessments to the Home Office. After John's death, and with slight alterations, it was privately printed for friends as a posthumous tribute.[58] Leo explained that he felt in part responsible for his son's death because it was his own place in the British government that had led the Germans to give prominence to John and his ideas. And, as the father stated, when faced with no legal defense John had taken the "courageous and manly decision" to plead guilty. Since he had foregone the opportunity in the courtroom to speak, Leo wished to provide a "coherent explanation of his son's behavior." This was that John sincerely believed he was acting in Britain's best interests and only ever wished to save the British Empire and Europe from the Soviet Union which he believed would win the war and unleash the forces of communism. In the later pamphlet, Leo added that "events in Eastern Europe, Persia and China" had indicated that in holding this position John was not entirely wrong.

Probably it is not surprising that in writing a son's obituary, the father would pass over the unpalatable truths of the outspoken anti-Semitism and the manifest admiration for fascist Italy and Nazism. By highlighting John's devotion to the British Empire and his anti-communism, Leo had restored his son to the ideological pale inhabited by the Amery family. Chuter Ede's reply to Lord Horder is pertinent, when the latter argued that the sincerity of John's beliefs were grounds for a pardon. The Home Secretary pointed out that treason is about actions, not about motivation or intention, and that a "great many people who have been properly found guilty of treason have believed that they were taking the right course."[59] However carefully considered Ede's comments may have been and how closely tied to the strictures of the law, the examples of Amery, Charles Cousens and Iva Toguri show that historical context and timing are critical factors in the outcomes of those charged with treason.

CHAPTER 2

Life in the Amery Family

Born in London on March 14, 1912, John Amery grew up on the "Imperial side of the River Thames".[1] His family was part of what David Cannadine has termed, the "post-patrician elite": the very upper layers of the English bourgeoisie whose influence had been entrenched a century before and whose members dominated government, civil administration and diplomacy in the interwar decades.[2] Their success depended not on aristocratic origins or inherited family wealth but on education, energy and the shared values that had been forged in the common experience of schooling at the great English public schools and a stint at Oxford or Cambridge.[3] Individuals with these desirable attributes found easy entrée into the networks of the Conservative Party and from there, through sponsored mobility, into Parliament and the higher reaches of British government.

The Amery Family

The career of John Amery's father, Leo, epitomized the trajectory of this meritocracy. Amery senior had been an outstanding student and in 1887, on scholarship, entered Harrow where he shone in academic studies and on the playing fields and became head prefect. Winning an exhibition to Balliol College, Oxford, he continued to cover himself with distinctions and prizes, earning firsts in Classics and Literature and a university blue as a champion cross-country runner.[4] Subsequently he was elected to All Souls, Oxford as a fellow in history. By this time the incisiveness of his thoughts, the clarity of his writing and the energy of his expression had attracted attention within the English newspaper world and the circles of the Tory Party. It was the start of a long career in which he made a name among British conservatives as a serious political commentator with a special expertise on imperial questions.

For Leo Amery, matters of Empire were at the heart of the political enterprise. The Amery family forbears enjoyed "strong Imperial connections."[5] Leo's father,

Charles Frederick, of Devon share-farming stock, had followed a peripatetic life through the British Empire. He had prospected for gold in Australia, planted tea in Assam, spent a long stretch of his career in the colonial forestry service in India, and died in 1901 in British Guyana.[6] According to recent research, Leo's mother, Elizabeth Johanna, was from a Hungarian family of assimilated Jews.[7] They had been converted to Anglicanism and migrated to England where she met her husband and followed him on his colonial ventures. Leo, the eldest son, was born in 1873 near the Afghan border and retained a lifelong interest in the politics and art of that region. In 1877 Leo's mother returned, alone, to England, near penniless and with several children. In 1886 she divorced Leo's father on the grounds of desertion, and henceforth he played little part in the family's life. By contrast, Elizabeth Amery, the mother, was highly ambitious for her children and struggled to send the sons to be educated at Harrow.[8] W. D. Rubinstein, who has traced the family's Jewish origins, claims that Leo Amery went to great lengths to conceal the "extraordinary secret" of his Jewish background and that to do so was "one of the central obsessions of his life".[9] In Rubinstein's view, Leo's stalwart and lifelong support for the state of Israel—from his involvement in drafting the Balfour Doctrine to the lasting friendships with key Zionists such as Chaim Weizman and Vladimir Jabotinsky, the founder of the modern Likud Party—was a function of the "philo-Jewishness" that was anchored in Amery's maternal upbringing. Probably, Leo's facility with foreign languages also came from his mother's polyglot background. Thus, although he was committed to putting the British Empire first, he was no mono-cultural Little Englander. Leo had spent time in Germany, the Balkans, Turkey and the Middle East and was fluent, or reasonably proficient, in French, German, Italian, Russian, Turkish, Hungarian, Bulgarian, Modern Greek and Serbo-Croatian.[10]

Leo Amery became among the most public, articulate and committed advocates of a system of Imperial Preference in trade between Britain and the Empire. His seven volume history of the Boer War, based in large part on his own experiences as the *Times* war correspondent on the ground, was completed in 1909. While in South Africa he had become a disciple of the colonial administrator and theorist of British imperialism, Alfred Milner, and later was part of the so-called Milner Kindergarten, the group that founded the journal *Round Table* to propound the great man's ideas. Broadly, these were that white colonial expansion would foster the wealth of the metropole to the point where, in Amery's words, "the fountain of colonial excess would overflow into coffers of the motherland." As he put it bluntly in 1932, it was "our duty to help the trade of our fellow-citizens of the Empire in preference to helping the trade of foreigners."[11]

From 1924 to 1929, he was the secretary of state for the colonies and the Dominions, in Baldwin's government, and from 1940 to 1945, secretary of state for India in Churchill's cabinet.[12] In Amery's view, an economically self-sufficient British Empire would provide a market for colonial and Dominion exports, protect Britain from foreign competition, and quarantine the British voter from what he called "the advances of Socialism." Between the wars, a number of civil and political associations were created in an attempt to wean the Conservative Party away from what at an earlier date had been a rusted-on commitment to free trade. From a safe base in Sparkbrook, a conservative seat within Joseph Chamberlain's bailiwick in Birmingham, Amery stumped party gatherings and wrote reams of articles spreading the good word on imperial protection.[13] He was, as well, the moving spirit behind the Empire Marketing Board, which, from 1926 to 1933, promoted the sale of Empire products through marketing, publicity and research.[14]

Amery's robust love of Empire was not simply intellectual. It accorded with his own boundless energy and great zest for strenuous activity taken in the outdoors. A "pocket Hercules," as the press often called him, he was a small man, no more than five feet four inches and extremely fit, priding himself on his athletic prowess in boxing, cross-country running, tennis playing, and, above all, mountain climbing. All his life he remained an exponent of a regimen of physical exercise with which to tone up the body at the start of each day.[15] Mount Amery in the Canadian Rockies was named for a climb he made in 1929, and another steep peak, which he scaled later, was called Mount Julian after his younger son. Mountaineering remained a lifelong passion, providing recreation and consolation when Amery was out of office or, during the Second World War, while dealing with the private and public stress caused by John's behavior.

Florence Amery shared her husband's imperial enthusiasms. She, too, came from colonial stock. On her father's side were Welsh emigrants to the United States, and her mother's family, having sided with the British in the American War of Independence, had been rewarded for their loyalty with generous land grants in Canada. Subsequently, the Greenwood family returned to Britain and flourished.[16] The three sisters and their brother Hamar, later Viscount Greenwood of Holbourne, retained a lifelong attachment to the Empire and its colonial peoples and a belief in the importance of strong imperial-colonial links. Throughout Leo and Florence's life together, their house was a gathering place for visitors from the colonies and the colonial elite in Britain. Mrs Amery was "at home" to visitors on Tuesday afternoons; the numbers swelling when there were important events on the Empire calendar. When the Imperial Conference was held in London in July 1934, for example, among the two hundred guests gathered in her drawing room was "everyone in England who mattered in colonial affairs."[17]

In London in the 1930s, Florence Amery chaired the Women's Committee of the Fellowship of the British Empire. Colonial food was her specialty. An old hand at "eating the Empire," Mrs Amery was regularly photographed on The Strand at Australia House at Christmastime stirring the dried fruits into the large Christmas cake which was prepared and presented with suitable fanfare each year to the little princesses, Elizabeth and Margaret.[18] In December 1928, at the Olympia Cookery Exhibition, she unveiled a seven-foot high King's Empire Christmas pudding, prepared in one-hundred separate cake tins and made entirely from Empire ingredients.[19] The Empire Marketing Board had regularly sponsored Empire Shopping Weeks and talks on the BBC about the need for "Buying British."

Empire Marketing Board posters proclaimed the importance of "Keeping Trade in the Family" and of remembering an empire "Filled with Your Cousins."[20] In 1927, Mrs Amery explained the principles of Imperial Preference to British housekeepers: "the more we spend on another Briton, the more that the other Briton will have to spend on you and the richer will grow what I have called the British family."[21] A movement for "Empire Meals on Empire Day" was launched in early 1932, with Mrs Amery at its head. At gatherings and press conferences she urged British women on Empire Day to use at their tables only "food products from Empire lands."[22] At other times, too, they should favor colonial and British products over those imported from the United States and the rest of Europe. In Mrs Amery's words, "the English housewife" must realize that "she has the power in her own hands to make or break the success of imperial food." English mothers should understand that the Empire was a "sort of suburban cooperative store" which could feed the English family healthily and cheaply.[23] In mid-May she emphasized that at home she "emphatically observed the rule of an all-British larder" adding "Cook, too, is just as particular."[24]

In the second half of 1927, Amery, accompanied by his wife, set off on an extended trip through the Empire. A cinematographer accompanied them to make a movie about the Dominions and the first such visit by a member of the British cabinet. The couple were greeted everywhere by welcoming crowds, none more enthusiastic than in Florence Amery's old hometown of Whitby near Toronto. Wherever he went, Leo took the opportunity to point out the virtues of imperial preference in Britain and the Empire.[25]

By the standards of many in their social circle, the Amerys were not rich. An enduring theme in Leo's diaries is his worry about the annual shortfall in the family's finances and his constant grumbles at what he saw as the high surtax levied on his income.[26] When compared with the great bulk of the English middle class, however, the Amerys led a life of wealth and comfort.[27] In the early years, the family lived in rented accommodation, but some of it, as when Leo was the First Lord of the Admiralty, was palatial. By 1924, they were settled in the large house at 112 Eaton Square, which remained the center of family life until the death in 2001 of the younger son, Julian, by then Lord Amery of Lustleigh.

Between the wars, the Amerys enjoyed the accoutrements of the lifestyle of the high bourgeoisie. At Eaton Square there was a cook, a butler, and a "houseful of maids."[28] Each of the boys had a nanny. Caroline Mead, hired when Julian was born, left when her charge reached four years of age. "Pipette," Jeanine Le Gallen, a dark-haired and lively Breton who had been with the family since John was small, had arrived in England in 1915 as a refugee. She became the boys' governess and a fixture in the household. Speaking little English and only ever French with the children, she gave them fluency in the language from a very young age. With French Royalist politics, her paper of choice Charles Maurras' *L'Action Française*, Pipette ran the nursery according to her own Gallic ideas of child rearing.[29] The Amerys traveled frequently to France. Mrs Amery, always well turned out, bought her clothes there on regular shopping trips. In Paris, the Hotel Bristol was a home away from home. According to Julian, the family did not possess a country house because his father preferred to spend the money on extended holidays away from England.[30] Every year the Amerys took long vacations abroad. In the winter they skied in the Alps and in summer took walking tours in the south of France or went on climbing expeditions in the mountains. And there were regular "after cures" at the Italian lakes.[31]

Leo and Florence (or "Bryddie," as she was affectionately called by close friends) were a devoted couple who had married in 1910. After almost three decades, Leo tenderly noted in his diary that "every year for us [is] better than the last."[32] When John was born, his father was 39 years of age and when Leo was 46, a second son, Julian, arrived. Leo and Florence's attitudes to parenting, and the tenor of the relationship which they sought to create with their sons, reflected the new child-rearing concepts of the interwar bourgeoisie. Perhaps as well, they were influenced by their own un-English upbringings. Leo and Florence relished the intimacy of close family life, doting on the two small boys and, whenever possible, spending time with them.[33] They delighted in the signs of precocity in their offspring: the proficiency in French, the charmingly childish observations about the world, and their naughty pranks even when they were directed at distinguished guests.[34] In a less child-centered household, some of the children's behavior would have earned a stiff reprimand.

Leo, worrying that his sons would be overawed by the gulf between their small selves and the public figure of their father, insisted that the children call him "Coco," even though the practice sometimes struck visitors as very odd.[35] The boys were included in many adult activities. They were regularly brought downstairs to greet important guests, and from an early age were included in gatherings, dinners and soirées, where they were encouraged to ask questions and put their own points of view.[36] One of Julian's earliest memories was as a four-years-old when the family lived at Whitehall during his father's tenure at the Admiralty. His mother's sitting room was located beside his father's study and Julian was allowed to "play bears" between the two. His playmates included Mr Baldwin, Sir Austen Chamberlain and T. E. Lawrence. Similarly, the little boy regularly sent signals from the nursery window to the First Sea Lord seated at his desk in his office at the Admiralty next door.[37]

Even when they were away from them, the children were at the forefront of their parents' thoughts. During the six months in 1927 that Mrs Amery was traveling with her husband through the Dominions, a favorite topic in interviews was her belief in the importance of a mother's involving herself in the rearing of children. In almost every report from the antipodes, she spoke proudly about her own two boys and their wonderful achievements.[38] At their homecoming, Julian remembered his parents bringing "a trunk of gifts" for himself and his brother collected during the trip or presented as gifts by the people who had entertained the English visitors.[39] Like a great many modern parents, Leo and Florence worried constantly about the health of their boys and endlessly planned their futures. And whenever the opportunity availed itself, over the long span of Leo and Florence's public lives, they fostered their two sons' careers.[40]

Nicholas Henderson, later to become a senior British diplomat, has left a delightful memoir of the Amerys *en famille* as he came to know them when he and Julian were boarders at Summerfields prep school in the 1930s.[41] He found them fascinating and quite unlike any of the other families in his experience. There was a "faint aura of foreignness" about Julian. He spoke French perfectly, which greatly annoyed the French master, and seemed always to impart the impression that "his holidays were spent in *wagons-lits*" and that "his spiritual home was in the Balkans." Henderson recalled that Julian was "uninhibitedly devoted to his parents in a demonstrative and scarcely English way." When all the parents came down to the school for half-term, the other boys were astonished that Julian was quite "unabashed to be seen kissing his mother and father in public and being kissed by them in return." At school, Julian was called "Pompo," short for "pompous" because his manner was "so different" from everyone else's. In Henderson's view, Julian as a schoolboy was "by nature defiant." He founded the "Anti-Authority League whose main purpose was to challenge the right of the masters to tell [the boys] how to organize [their] spare time." Also, unlike the other boys at that time, Julian was "unfashionably in favor of strong men." He used to speak about "Winston" in the same casual way that other schoolboys mentioned Donald and Gubby, the famous cricketers, Bradman and Allen. Equally unusually, Julian loathed organized games and "valiantly refused to conform to the standards of bravery expected on the rugger field." The only game he willingly played was golf, for which he insisted on carrying an oversized bag of clubs and wearing slightly ridiculous plus fours. When teased, Julian would reply haughtily that Lloyd George and Briand also favored the game. In Henderson's recollection, Julian had little contact with the masters whom he never regarded with awe. Indeed, he behaved in general as though "school was a place of limited and transient importance, a mere frontier stop on the way to adult political life."

Henderson spent a half-term holiday with the family in London and found it quite unlike the other "tongue-tied outings" with which at that age he was familiar. First up, Mrs Amery met the boys at the train herself, taxi and porter in tow, with a "sense of joyful expectation as though this was the moment she had long been waiting for, the return of the beloved son from exile." Her behavior seemed to suggest, as well, that a great many "other people in London had been yearning for this moment, too." Later, at home over lunch, the parents and Julian made it clear that they "wanted to get down to the political agenda as soon as possible." Henderson was nonplussed by the intense discussion at the table about current politics. Julian spoke a great deal, giving the impression that "he was completely *au fait* with everything despite having been forced to spend a tiresome interval away from London."

Julian's own assessment of his school days fits this picture. In his words, he "endured Summerfields and Eton rather than enjoyed them."[42] When he began prep school, he was made miserable by the cold baths; horrible food; smelly, door-less lavatories and the relentless conformity imposed by the bullying older boys. He soon found, too, that many of the masters were unaccommodating of pupils who made original observations. This was especially so in French where the master was not kindly disposed to having his syntax and pronunciation corrected in the classroom. In the beginning, when ragged by older boys, Julian lashed out, in an early incident splitting the lip of the "jeering" senior who called him a "cry baby" and later with a scout knife gashing the forehead of another. In marked contrast to the response that similar behavior had evoked in his older brother's prep school, the headmaster at Summerfields was understanding, explaining the virtue of "turning away wrath with a soft answer" and of "showing some regard to public opinion as well as the letter of the law." Subsequently, Julian was sent to Eton in the hope that it would be less rigidly disciplinarian than was his father's old school of Harrow. Knowing how miserable John had been there, his mother was fearful that the same fate would befall her second son.

In his memoir of Eton, Julian recalls that he hated sport of the sort pursued at school. He was also unhappy with the beatings meted out by fagmasters and prefects and, as a consequence, was involved in a good many scrapes. Fortunately, in the end, none was catastrophic as he managed to "mitigate" the unpleasantness of fagging by staying clear of the boarding house as much as possible during the day. Later he acquired a fagmaster with whom he came to an arrangement whereby Julian ghostwrote the senior boy's essays in return for being left alone. Eventually, he and several other boys always took breakfast at a local café and even rented lodging in the village which they used as a private sitting room away from school. By these strategies, Julian managed to carve out an identity for himself as an unusual and intellectual boy and avoid being overwhelmed by school rules and regulations.

The habits and the rhythms of the Amery family were bourgeois. Leo set great store by the virtue of work, particularly the intellectual kind, and was keen to instill the same values in his children. Over the span of his life, Leo produced a string of books and articles. In 1938 when Julian was keen to publish some pieces about his travels in wartime Spain, his father was delighted to invest several days' labor working over them, making suggestions and rewriting parts of the final text. He was, similarly, indefatigable in his public responsibilities as a member of Parliament.[43] In the interwar years, as well as a heavy involvement with the school board at Harrow, he was a conscientious Fellow at All Souls, traveling regularly up to Oxford for college dinners and gatherings. Often, he was heard on the BBC giving interviews and talks about the British Empire. He spoke in public, as well, for a great range of other causes. In the same way, Mrs Amery followed a punishing schedule of public duties. Indeed Leo often teased her that she needed a "surgical operation for a hypertrophied conscience."[44]

Fathers and Sons: Leo, John and Julian

Despite the obvious and genuine affection between Leo Amery and his sons there were strains in the relationship. It is almost commonplace that young men who are the offspring of distinguished fathers can find it difficult to make their own way in the world. When Randolph Churchill, for example, reached his majority, an editorial in the *Times* put it succinctly: a famous father was "no light handicap because the son's failures are accentuated by comparisons; and his successes explained away by heredity."[45] Equally, these fathers may not accept that it is not easy for their sons to repeat the paternal achievements. Again, the tension between Winston Churchill and Randolph is close to home. Randolph navigated his entire life in the powerful wake of his father. In the brutal assessment of an American newspaper columnist, Winston's son "generates no heat of his own and reflects only the little light that shines from his illustrious parentage."[46] Similarly, across generational divide, only the younger Amery son successfully followed in his father's public footsteps, thereby fulfilling the parental expectations. Julian went on to Balliol, though without scholarship, led the university Conservative Party, enlisted early when war began, and gave distinguished service in the Middle East and the Balkans. And, when he entered the House of Commons in 1950, he was the youngest Tory MP ever to have done so.

Julian's career, however, was not clear sailing. Many of his successes, especially those achieved as a young man, relied on his father's backing. Like any other proud parent, Leo was always ready to intervene on his son's behalf. In late 1939, Julian was press attaché to the British Embassy in Belgrade and Leo, who enjoyed a long friendship with the British Ambassador, had played a part in his son's obtaining the post. Once Julian was ensconced, his father continued to help. Julian was trying to expand the pro-British content in the Yugoslav press and his father wrote articles that could be used and solicited contributions among political acquaintances. And when Julian disagreed with policies on the spot, he went over the heads of his immediate superiors to appeal to his father in London. Not surprisingly, this caused ill will. In late 1940, Julian intrigued with the opposition groups in Belgrade and Istanbul who wished to overthrow Prince Paul and King Boris because they were suspected of being pro-German. Even though these suspicions were proven correct, Julian's activities contravened official British policy, at this time still supporting the monarchists. Quite understandably, the Ambassador construed Julian's actions as insubordination and had him removed. Despite Leo's own long career in British public administration and what, one suspects, would have been his own stern rejection of a subordinate who had flouted well-defined lines of authority, Leo backed his son entirely, moving heaven and earth to have Julian reinstated in an equal position elsewhere.[47]

Another incident in the summer of 1942 demonstrated Leo's determination to put his son forward. Julian was home on leave from Cairo, and like many soldiers in a similar situation, talked to his family about what he had seen of the war and what he thought were the problems in the way it was being run. At this time, there were doubts among the home population about the likelihood that the British Expeditionary Force could achieve success in Egypt. Julian's observations were apposite, though they were no more than those of a young captain and one who was stationed in Cairo itself. He reported that at all levels there was poor morale among the British troops and that the only antidote to this undesirable state of affairs would be a visit from Winston Churchill, himself. Leo, impressed with his son's ideas, pestered Churchill to give Julian a hearing. After several notes and phone calls, a visit to Number 10 was squeezed into the Prime Minister's busy schedule so that for twenty minutes, the twenty-one-year-old addressed the Prime Minister and the Chief of the Imperial General Staff, Sir Alan Brooke, about the shortcomings of the British Army command. A highly unusual incident, it infuriated Brooke, who noted in his diary that Julian was a "most objectionable young pup" in a sinecure in the city of Cairo and had been allowed to impugn the reputations of experienced senior officers in the field.[48]

John's relationship with his father unraveled over several years, in a series of stages. In April 1920, he entered West Downs Preparatory School in Winchester where, in his father's words, "he did not do too badly." John was "on the whole happy there" and "the boys thought him amusing."[49] As we know, though, the teaching staff was less impressed. He was sent to Harrow in late summer, 1925, at the age of thirteen years. In the 1920s, schools like Harrow faced new challenges having just passed through a period of mediocrity with poor discipline and low academic standards.[50] While traditionally a great deal of latitude was extended to the sons of the English upper classes, at Harrow there had been a series of well-publicized scandals in which senior boys, including the head prefect, were in the habit of leaving the school on evening jaunts to London. They had been caught in compromising situations in several nightclubs. Within the boarding houses, "violence" and "vice" were rife as was the bullying of weaker boys whether for sexual or material favors. These unfortunate types of behavior had been passed over as accepted parts of the public school regimen. Before John arrived, Dr Cyril Norwood, a strong believer in the ethos of manly athleticism, had been brought in to clean up the school.[51] At this time, Leo Amery was on the board of governors and actively involved in the reform of curriculum and administration. A strong exponent of toughening up the standards at Harrow, he advocated getting rid of the "soft options" so that a boy could only win promotion to the next form after he had passed clearly defined academic benchmarks. Leo also had strong opinions about the importance of games—perhaps influenced by his own schoolboy enjoyment of physical activity—and at which levels rugby should be compulsory.[52] It was awkward that the Harrow ex-head prefect and academic star had a son in the school who was clearly an unenthusiastic participant, if not an outright failure at school life.[53]

Jack was, in his own words, "very unhappy at school." He found the discipline hard to take and was "ragged a lot" by other boys.[54] His parents worried greatly about him without knowing what to do. When he had to leave Jack at Harrow "looking sad in his room alone," Leo felt sorry. He knew that his son would far prefer to be at home rather than boarding. At first the parents hoped that this was homesickness that with time would subside. On one visit, when Jack was down with chicken pox, his father noted, albeit with amusement, that the patient was in high spirits in the school infirmary where he was delighted to have a few days respite and could legitimately escape schoolwork.[55] After a term break, as father and son traveled together on the train to take Jack back to school, Leo attempted to get to the bottom of what it was that made his son so unhappy.[56] Jack explained that he hated "playing footer in the rain." In fact he saw it as a "real grievance." Overall, what he "most disliked" about school was that students had to "do something continuously all the time whether it is work or games." They were never left alone with any time in which they could "do nothing." Leo, somewhat nonplussed, offered the advice that his own industrious self had always found useful. It was that "the only way to be happy is to enjoy the things you have to do because most of life afterwards will consist of things of that nature; as the occasions of really free choice are very few."[57] In order to cheer him up, Leo had Jack moved from a dorm into a "nice double room" where he would share with a boy who was, as Jack's father rather sadly noted, a "good fellow but low down in the school." It was hoped that this might make the son more settled.[58]

Jack continued to beg Leo and Florence to take him away to live at home and study with a private tutor. The parents steadfastly refused. Leo, with hardening heart, was sure that what Jack "really hankered for" was to enjoy "late dinner every night, plenty of opportunities for cinema-going and no doubt acquire a motorcycle to buzz about on in between." [59] As with many young men of his age, the motor car and the movies were the ultimate objects of Jack's fantasies and the main topic of conversation.[60] He had learned to drive on a holiday with Pipette in Brittany in the summer of 1925, just before his fourteenth birthday, and from then on pined to have an automobile or a motorbike of his own. Whether it was an indication of the son's powers of persuasion or the soft-heartedness of the parents, a month after Leo's vehement rejection of the idea of any kind of auto, he noted in his diary that John had ridden his motor scooter to Maidenhead. By July 1927, he had a "small car," a Morgan, in which he drove his father to Croydon airport and later motored the whole family down to Oxford to take Julian to prep school.[61]

Over the winter holidays in 1927, as usual, the family went for the skiing to a hotel in Switzerland. Leo was greatly annoyed by Jack's behavior, which he considered inappropriate in a fifteen-year-old. For example, Jack refused to enter a higher grade in competitive skiing even though Leo was sure that he could have succeeded. The conflict underlined the fact that the son did not share the father's passion for competitive outdoor activities. Similarly, when later on a trip with the tutor, Nock, Jack had shown his distaste for mountaineering, and had equally provoked adult irritation by insisting on wearing his bedroom slippers when taken to climb the Jungenfrau. In 1927 he preferred "fooling about" inside the hotel with a racy crowd that the parents disapproved of, instead of spending healthy days out with his father on the ski slopes.[62] And there was a girl with whom, in his father's greatly disapproving words, Jack had "had an affair."[63]

Back in London, with preparations underway for Jack's return to Harrow, he had an attack of a "panic terror." The father and son had been involved in acrimonious exchanges about what Leo considered to be the "ridiculous" width of Jack's baggy trousers. It seems that Leo caned Jack. Certainly, he warned his son that he had been "going beyond the limit in too many directions." Later the family had gone out to dinner and Leo was relieved that Jack promised to mend his ways: his appearance was "looking somewhat better in trousers of a reduced size and wearing a [more normal] hat."[64] However, the morning afterwards, when Florence woke early and checked that the boy was "properly covered up," she found that he had "decamped," taking money from his father's pocketbook and a service revolver. Equally worrying, in order to fetch a suitcase, he had broken into the locked pantry through a skylight. There was a dramatic note left behind that said that Jack had run away and would never go back to Harrow.[65]

Florence with MacLeod, the detective the government provided for Leo, searched Waterloo and Victoria Stations. As the day passed the parents became increasingly agitated. Florence's brother, Hamar Greenwood, tried to calm sister and brother-in-law with stories of his own youthful follies when he had run away to join the theatre. It was suspected that Jack might have tried to make his way to Brittany, where in Vannes he had spent several summers with the governess. Eventually, Scotland Yard was contacted, but with the strict instructions that "nothing should be done that would create publicity."[66] There was a tip-off that a young man had been seen boarding a train for Southampton. MacLeod went immediately and found that Jack had left his suitcase at the Great Western Hotel while he took in a matinee at the local theatre. The detective waited outside the cinema for several hours until Jack emerged, at which time MacLeod "duly put his arm around the boy's neck and gently conveyed to him that the escapade was over." The two arrived back at Eaton Square near midnight and, in his father's words, Jack was "surprised that he did not get another caning." All at home were relieved that the young man seemed to be "conscious that he had been very silly."[67]

In the meantime, Leo had been to Harrow to discuss with Norwood what should be done with the errant boy. Both men agreed that the best plan was for Jack to leave school for a term and work under a tutor. Officially, it would be said that he was taking time out for his health. Norwood promised Amery that if his son kept up with the schoolwork, he could return to Harrow the following term and be moved up into the next form. With the interview over, the ever-industrious Leo rushed off to London to address the Royal Society of the Arts on the virtues of using imperial sugar, though as he admitted with the turmoil he had been through that day he "was not sure whether it was sugar or salt that [he] was talking of."[68]

A tutor for Jack was found. A "sound young man" by the name of Leander Jameson who came with the reassuring colonial provenance that he was the grandnephew of "Dr Jim," the famous raiding Jameson. Equally promising, he had spent a childhood on the banks of the great Limpopo River.[69] In one of their first outings, and presumably in anticipation of a major change in Jack's interests, Leo took him, the tutor and the detective MacLeod to Twickenham to watch a rugby match between the combined English universities and a team of Dominion students. For a while Leo toyed with the idea of sending the boy with the tutor to some far-flung corner of the Empire where Jack could grow up in a healthy outdoor setting. Instead, tutor and charge spent some time camping in Norway, but as luck would have it, a German film company working in the area hired Jack as an extra. He was "film-mad" and the experience further fuelled his passion for a life behind the camera.[70] Jameson, who had hoped that riding lessons would foster his pupil's interest in the outdoors, concluded that the young man lacked confidence in himself and his abilities, and covered up this "ineptitude" with outbursts of bad temper. Much more to Jack's liking was their motoring about the countryside in the Morgan provided by his parents. They drove it all the way to Scotland, though in the tutor's estimation the boy was not a good driver and exhibited "bad road manners." When not so engaged, Jameson and Jack were expected to buckle down in the house of Florence Amery's sister at Berry Green where Jack was supposed to cram in readiness for the return to Harrow. In the meantime, his parents set off on a six-month jaunt through the Empire and the Dominions.

In April 1928, four terms after the original departure from Harrow, Jack was ready to go back to school. He promised his parents that this time he would try harder. His father offered the inducement that if Jack did well in the university entrance exams, he could take some time out abroad to study languages or filmmaking. Despite the upbeat talk about the future, Leo was fearful that, once back at Harrow, Jack would "relapse" into his old self, "especially if he did not meet with a kindly reception from masters and boys." And, perhaps predictably, this is exactly what happened. The school favored the practice of "tanning," whereby prefects and house captains could cane boys who stepped out of line. In Jack's case, his "backsliding" on the cricket field was seen to have let down the team, and for this reason the captain of cricket promised a "beating" and Jack ran away. This time never to return. Leo negotiated a face-saving compromise with the headmaster in which the caning would take place, but only in a "formal" sense—presumably meaning that Jack would not be "tanned" too violently. However, Jack simply would not agree to return to school and, as Leo sadly noted, since he would have to have been taken there "by force," his parents abandoned the idea.[71]

A psychiatrist, Dr Maurice Wright, was called in. He reported the dispiriting news to the parents that Jack "had no ambition to make a career for himself" and his condition was "incurable." During the consultation Jack had boasted with what probably were highly exaggerated stories about himself as a schoolboy. For example, he claimed that while at Harrow he had been a tout for rich men at a London nightclub, and he hoped that he could make this into a future career.[72] It may be that he had left school bounds in the evenings, or more likely he relished the stories that he had heard of the escapades of Harrow seniors a few years before his arrival at the school. In either case, Leo and Florence were greatly alarmed.

Other tutors were hired, one after another. None could galvanize John's studies or keep him on the schoolboy straight and narrow. In early 1929, he spent a brief period in Switzerland enrolled in a school for English boys where the curriculum focused on improving skills in winter sports. It was the sort of establishment in which the young Leo would have thrived as skiing and mountain climbing took up most of the school day. John was sent home. As his father carefully noted, it was "not for any particular offense," but for his attitude and his preference for "bar loafing" and chatting up local girls. The English headmaster feared that reports of such behavior would harm the school's reputation among the Swiss as it might suggest that this was what English education was all about. Another tutor, G. C. Nock, was found, but patently was not up to the mark. It was while in Nock's care that Jack went climbing in his slippers and, with much more serious consequences, visited a brothel or some such place. In any event, he contracted venereal disease and swiftly was brought home for treatment by a specialist in Harley Street.[73]

There was a final attempt to put Jack through a coaching course in Oxford for the university entrance exam. Very soon, however, the master bluntly informed the parents that, even with much luck, their son would have a very slim chance of passing. In Latin, the subject at which his father excelled, Jack had barely reached the level of a boy in "the common entrance" and his mathematics was extremely poor.[74] In any event, by this time, whatever interest Jack may have had in formal study had evaporated as he had set his heart on entering the exciting new world of cinema production. The parents soon came to accept what, all along, had been the inevitable end of Jack's scholastic career. They also came around to the view that a career in movies was the direction in which their son's future lay.[75] Leo, as ever planning for that future, carefully arranged for Jack to have some training at the British Instructional Film Institute at Welwyn. After six months he joined a small traveling film company as an assistant director, and it appeared that the problems of Jack's schooling were behind him. Leo and Florence were greatly relieved that at last their older son had discovered his real vocation.

CHAPTER 3

John Amery between the Wars

Like many people between the wars, John Amery was dazzled by the moving picture industry. Then, as now, the power of the medium was irresistible. Sitting in a darkened theatre watching the flickering images on the screen, a viewer could be transported from the humdrum of the everyday into a transcendent world of romance and allure. In the 1930s, traversing all nations and across the political spectrum, there was fascination with the movies and the potential of the medium. In England, the Conservative Party funded several ventures in moviemaking. The film unit of the Empire Marketing Board, perhaps reflecting Leo Amery's interests, put up money for an expensive spectacular that was to showcase the imperial vision. The movie tracked a small English boy as he traveled through the exotic settings of the British Empire searching out ingredients for the king's Christmas pudding. For a number of financial and technical reasons, not to mention the implausibility of the narrative, the film was not a commercial success.[1]

Leo Amery was enthralled by cinema. He went frequently, noting in his diary that stories from the classics could provide wonderful, cinematic subjects. After taking Jack to see *Ben Hur*, he noted that the Punic Wars and Herodotus easily beat the ersatz history he had just seen on the screen. And for narrative and adventure, Homer and the *Odyssey*, far and away Leo's favorite reading, would be sure-fire blockbusters. When asked to narrate a film about mountain climbing, Leo was flattered and keenly disappointed when his part in the final version was cut.[2]

Early on in John's fledgling film career, several newspaper correspondents remarked that the new cinema industry appeared to have a great attraction for the upper-class sons of English statesmen. In discussing the careers of Ivor Montagu and Anthony Asquith, the *Daily Herald* pointed out that, like John Amery, they were the film-struck sons of well-known fathers.[3] Both of these young men managed to break into the movie industry and went on to become serious filmmakers. Asquith's first film, made in 1931, was the superb *Tell England* that followed the experiences of two young friends at Gallipoli, a story from which Peter Weir's

Gallipoli heavily borrows. During the Spanish civil war, Montagu produced *Defence of Madrid* for the left-wing Progressive Film Institute. Shot in Spain in late 1936, the documentary made a powerful case for the Republican side. Jack Amery's ventures in moviemaking were not in the same league, his high point achieved in 1932. A year of considerable significance in the imperial efforts of the Amery family, it brought disappointments as well.[4]

The Ottawa Imperial Economic Conference of 1932 dominated most of Leo's activities.[5] Empire preference in trade was both his long-term goal and the particular area of his expertise. Though out of government, he traveled to Canada as a private observer, anticipating that the British and the Dominion delegates would call on his experience when the agreement on Empire and colonial trade was drafted. This was not to be. The representatives of Britain's ex-colonies were single-minded in pursuing their own national interests. Members of the British delegation, too, did not welcome Amery's intervention. Some blamed him for being too closely tied to Dominion politicians and several in the British team even suggested that he had white-anted the negotiations, particularly in the critical matters of British imports of colonial produce.[6] Excluded from the main event, Amery was frustrated and sharply critical of the caliber of the British delegation and the accompanying treasury officials. Writing twenty years later, Julian reiterated his father's position, reproving the delegations at Ottawa because, unlike Leo, they had "not come to the Conference table as missionaries of Empire." Instead, no great ideal drew them together, only the "ties of common funk."[7] In the government restructure that followed the conference, Leo was overlooked; his reputation as a spoiler in Ottawa probably cost him his place.[8]

John carried his own imperial vision in the field of British cinema by shooting a colonial blockbuster. It was to be a love story of high adventure set in the big game country of northern Tanganyika. Initially, his parents were enthusiastic about the project: delighted that Jack's energy at last was being applied to a productive endeavor.[9] In the intervening years between abandoning school at sixteen and starting off his own company at twenty, Jack had been "knocking around Worton Hall Studios." He also assisted in some way in the production of a couple of short films in France, but in these activities he was, as he said, "just Pooh-Bahing at the bottom rung of the ladder."[10] By 1932, he had formed his own movie company, John Amery Productions Pty. Ltd., and had raised the considerable sum of fifty thousand pounds for his first picture.[11] His business partner was a colorful identity in the city of London. Count John Edward Johnston-Noad, a solicitor and wealthy sportsman, had founded the Outboard Racing Club and attracted publicity when he won the Duke of York's Motor Boat trophy. The two men planned to produce two films a year. The first, a "super-talkie" to be called *Jungle Skies*, would be shot in "darkest Africa." On their books they had a second colonial spectacular set somewhere in the "beautiful locations available in the West Indies."[12]

In the beginning, the press was much taken with young Amery and his daring plans for large-scale extravaganzas. Florid reports in the dailies often referred to him as a "West End playboy" and a "real enthusiast with all the confidence of youth."[13] A newspaper piece, under the heading "John Amery and his Jungle Plans," described the young filmmaker as a "fascinating talker about pictures": one who "shows a rare combination of a fine imagination with a knowledge of cinema audience psychology."[14] In one interview, Amery modestly admitted that his father, too, was greatly interested in the movies and had helped him "facilitate" the project, especially in British East Africa, where such assistance would not have been extended to an American producer. Despite this, though, Jack stoutly maintained that he would "prefer to live by [his] own exertions and [his own] money." Henceforth, he would definitely be standing on his own two feet.[15]

Amery announced that *Jungle Skies* would be a mixture of *Hell's Angels* and *Trader Horn*.[16] These two films, made in Hollywood in 1930, enjoyed worldwide distribution. Both were romance-and-adventure epics set against exotic backdrops. With wild animals and sweeping jungle vistas, they were the most successful examples of the genre that had become enormously popular in the thirties and were made in great number by American and British filmmakers.[17] It is possible that Amery derived the main ideas about plot and location for his own films from the two outstanding examples. *Hell's Angels*, the personal project of Howard Hughes, plugged into the inter-war obsession of "air mindedness" and starred Jean Harlow in her screen debut: a vamp torn between her attraction for two American brothers studying at Oxford. When the Great War breaks out, both brothers volunteer for the Royal Flying Corps. The film made use of astonishing aerial footage; in one of the startling combat scenes there are thirty-one planes in the sky together. A smash hit at the box office, it continued to be screened for almost twenty years and made Hughes more than ten million dollars. The other movie that broke the box offices was the Hollywood-MGM production *Trader Horn*, a vast undertaking that required a huge technical team and an enormous cast, including two hundred pygmies. Filmed on safari in Nairobi and Kampala, it became a classic in the genre of imperial extravaganzas.

Amery's shooting plan replicated the form of these colonial adventures. The storyboard preliminaries included the following: "taking pictures from an airplane of animal life in the jungle; thrilling stunt flying by a famous pilot; engaging in big game shooting; and filming a duel with a lion."[18] To guarantee a surefire success, the plot would trace an unfolding love story among a group of Europeans who were surrounded in the jungle by wild natives and, in the nick of time, rescued by an airplane. The sequence of the narrative included "thrilling car crashes and stunt flying" and "great open spaces with colossal crowds of natives." In a breathtaking climax, "a native settlement would be blown up from the air."[19] The latter was an unusual twist, but not entirely new. At the Hendon Air Pageant in 1927, to which Jack may well have accompanied his father, the RAF had carried out a "mock bombing" of a native village in order to demonstrate the effectiveness of the "use of air power in colonial policing."[20]

Jungle Skies was shot on location, two hundred miles from any outpost in northern Tanganyika. An "African Sultan" who also played a minor part lent his village. The Earl of Lovelace, a British settler, offered the airstrip on his farm from where the planes would take off and land.[21] In the interviews before departing to Africa, Jack waxed lyrical about the beauty of colonial locations. Expressing a sentiment, which strongly echoed his father's enthusiasms, young Amery stated, "We have in the British Empire a colossal fund of natural scenery," and wherever possible he would exploit in his pictures. As he said, "One would be a lunatic to attempt to construct artificial settings when we have the real thing in such abundance in the Empire."[22] Though *Jungle Skies* might call for some shooting on location in Italy, he planned that all studio work would be carried out in London. And he would use an "all-British cast" because he considered England to have the "finest and most capable actors and actresses in the world." For reasons of commercial distribution into the United States, however, he had been forced to give the leading role to a Hollywood celebratory. It was hinted that the director was angling for Jean Harlow, by then commanding ten thousand pounds a screen appearance, and at the time starring in an American production of *Platinum Blond* on the West End. The columnist in the *Daily Film Renter* noted sardonically, "In this British East African epic none of the animals will strike much fear into the Platinum Blond who can hold her own anywhere."[23] The *Birmingham Daily Mail*, always a backer of an Amery enterprise, predicted that this would be "one of the greatest romance epics in the history of British films."[24]

On February 1, 1932, Amery and Johnston-Noad, elegant in fur coats and soft felt hats, flew out of Croydon Airfield for British East Africa. The crew had preceded them to set up camp and prepare for filming. On location the team experienced adventures aplenty, whose reports in themselves were the stuff of spine-tingling scripts. The directors' car became bogged in desert sand and had to be pulled by oxen. There was a "thrilling escape" from "one of the most venomous snakes in the world" which had insinuated its way under the car bonnet and had to be "plugged" by a revolver shot. There was also an encounter in a scene that sounded like a parody of imperial adventure in which five hundred spear-carrying native extras in plumed headdresses came over a ridge and instead of confronting the white actor speared the cameraman.[25]

Adventures aside, there were other problems. The Tanganyika Immigration Department issued an arrest warrant for Amery and Johnston-Noad because they had failed to land at the frontier and have their papers stamped. When Amery, with the sixteen thousand feet of shot film in his possession, eventually came "down country" he found that there were "police posses" out looking for him, and it took a good deal of persuasion to convince the authorities that he was not an ivory smuggler.[26] Even more seriously, perhaps, a group of local expatriates protested about the plan to bomb natives and blow up a village.[27] They claimed that the film misrepresented the relations between white settlers and black Tanganyikans. Amery dismissed these concerns, claiming that the film did not "interpret the relations of blacks and whites," but was "simply a story set in Africa." As he pointed out, he could have made the sets in a studio, but had come to Africa to obtain "the true atmosphere and correct background."[28]

On his return to Britain, the press was much less accommodating and he much more truculent. Amery blamed "certain sections of the white opinion" in Tanganyika for stirring up a storm in a teacup. The bombing was, he said, a "private affair" in which "the eggs were dropped by a moth," a very small plane, and therefore not part of "any military machine." As well, he insisted, the village had been purposely constructed in order to be blown up with dynamite. Now much less enthralled with imperial locations, Amery attributed the furor to the malign exaggerations of the "bush telegraph." The filmmaker claimed that what had happened was that when the explosion took place "about twenty natives were knocked silly for a bit; and then 500 miles away they were reported killed; and at 1,000 miles they had been dismembered." The Birmingham papers remained loyal, providing plenty of space in which to answer the critics. In these it was clear that Amery was decidedly less enthusiastic about the great outposts of Empire when they were peopled by thin-skinned locals. As he haughtily warned Tanganyikans: "If one brings things into the country and one is simply treated as a rogue and vagabond, one comes but once."[29] The Tanganyika government ordered an enquiry into Amery's venture, but it came to nothing.

In August 1932, Amery's film business broke apart to reveal a squalid core. The business partners had an acrimonious falling out over money. In fact Amery controlled five companies, each of which had run up enormous debts. It transpired that Jack Amery had raised part of the initial funding from two 250-pound debentures which he had sold to a father and son, the latter having come into insurance money after losing a leg in a car accident. They had received no return on the investment as the capital had been used to pay Jack and Noad's expenses. Almost as though young Amery's own life was a film script, it transpired that the father of the disabled young man was a retired police inspector who proceeded to sue for the loss.[30] After a drawn-out series of negotiations with the wronged father and son, by early September 1932, the Amery family solicitors had managed to "disentangle Jack completely"; though in Leo's terse words it was "naturally at my expense."[31]

It was not the end of *Jungle Skies*. According to Paul Rotha, later to achieve renown as a left-wing documentary maker, John Amery approached him at the end of 1932 for assistance to transform what Rotha said were "thousands of feet of almost useless film of wildlife in East Africa." Amery wanted the film made into a movie that could be cut in a studio and with the "wild animals interpolated."[32] Extremely hard up at the time, Rotha took the job and subsequently wrote what he described as "an appalling script, which Amery very much liked." When it was finished, however, the fifty-pound fee on which they had agreed was not forthcoming. In his recollections written forty years later, and in light of the knowledge of Jack's execution as a "Nazi traitor," Rotha described going to collect the check from Amery's "vast office" in Long Acre where on a huge desk were displayed "pictures of Mussolini and Al Capone." Very reluctantly, Amery wrote a check for the fee, but when Rotha was leaving, he threatened Rotha with a gun. He walked out with the check in his pocket, but when presented at the bank, it bounced. In an increasingly predictable finale, Rotha went to Leo who "embarrassed but not surprised by the story" paid the fee. The reels that had been shot in Tanganyika eventually were sold on to an American film entrepreneur in payment of debts run up in East Africa. They probably ended up as film stock for the backgrounds in another in the genre of jungle sagas.

In the same year of 1932, another series of crises in John's affairs caused embarrassment and heartache to Leo and Mrs Amery. At the end of that year, his father, much chagrined, noted that Jack's financial failures had sabotaged Leo's best efforts to "do something to mend [the family's] completely derelict financial situation." But even greater was the strain that Jack's escapades had placed on the parental bond. As Leo noted sadly in the very last diary entry for that year, "Jack has cost us both much, of which money has been the smallest item."[33] The exact details of some of the incidents are hard to piece together because Leo's personal contacts with editors and press proprietors meant that the newspapers downplayed the reports.

It was perhaps predictable that Jack's attraction to cars and girls would spell trouble. During a family conference to discuss what could be done for the shortfall in the film finances, Jack revealed that since starting to drive, he had received over eighty summonses, most of them for illegal parking in London. The latest summons was over an incident in the King's Road in August 1932.[34] A policeman, noticing that the registration on the car that John was driving was out of date, moved into the middle of the road and flagged down the vehicle. Instead of stopping, Amery had accelerated, driving straight at the officer, only at the very last moment swerving away. The policeman, in order not be flattened, had leapt to the pavement. Apprehended a few moments later at a nearby garage, Amery claimed, at first, that he knew nothing about what had just happened. His parents were "really alarmed." Leo and the family solicitor, Hutchinson, took advice from a contact in the Justice ministry over a lunch at Buck's Steak House. The "Police Authorities" were then "sounded out" and fortunately indicated that they were "not disposed to vindictiveness" if John's misdemeanors were properly dealt with.[35] The matter was brought before the Westminster Police Court, in John's absence. Hutchinson argued that "boys of twenty often do very foolish things," and though his client had behaved in a "disgraceful manner" it was the case that "most of the offenses were what might be called ordinary motoring convictions" and had not put anyone "in real danger." John was fined forty pounds with five pounds court costs and a disqualification from driving for five years. The magistrate observed that the "sooner Amery's career as motorist is checked, the better it will be for everybody."

Around this time, John had become involved with what the papers described as a "glamorous young film actress," but who was referred in a Special Branch report as a "common prostitute who frequented the West End."[36] Una Wing was good-looking and several years older than John. He was smitten and wanted to marry. She later claimed that she had only discovered John's real age when the application for the marriage was rejected. John applied at the Chelsea Register

Office for a license which was refused because he was underage and his parents withheld their consent. The young couple then set off for Paris. While all of this was happening, Leo was still in Ottawa and though Florence assured him by telephone that she and her sister Sadie Rodney had it in hand and there would be no marriage, Leo took the first passage home. He was greatly worried at "leaving B to deal with Jack alone."[37] When the parents reviewed the situation together, they decided that although the girl was "as bad as they had feared," there was nothing more they could do to stop the relationship. Instead, they provided the couple with a small allowance on which to live abroad.

The family maintained regular contacts with John. When he rang home ill in Paris, the British Ambassador to France was asked to send a doctor to check on his health.[38] Leo went to Paris on government matters quite frequently and each time saw John. During these visits, the father-son relationship was regenerated with man-to-man talks over lunch and in companionable walks in the Bois de Boulogne. Leo became more optimistic that "boredom and shortage of cash" would bring Jack to his senses. Thawing considerably, he helped Jack redeem some of his possessions that were in pawn. Somewhat incautiously, too, given the recent driving history, Leo gave Jack cash with which to get his car fixed so that he would be mobile and even be able to do some "taxi-ing" to earn a living.[39]

In May 1933, Jack and Una were in the headlines again. Through the good auspices of Sir Roderick Jones, the editor of Reuters and the father of Leo's godson Timothy, Jack was found a job in Shanghai.[40] He was to travel alone and, if he made a go of it, Una was to be sent for. At the very moment of departure from Marseilles, the two were unwilling to be separated and Jack abandoned the trip. Instead, on the spur of the moment and determined to marry, he and Una went to Athens. They converted to the Greek Orthodox religion and became man and wife according to the Eastern rites.[41] Even more controversy followed while they were in the Greek capital. Jack borrowed cash from an Athens moneylender on the strength of his own signature on a check, and he and Una had a fling in the best hotel in town. They also purchased jewelry, which later turned out to be worth a good deal less than they had paid. The check bounced, but by then Jack and Una had left for Paris. The Athens jeweler took out a warrant for their arrest and extradition. Sir Roderick Jones placed an embargo on Reuters reporting the whereabouts of the young Amerys, but instructed the agency's correspondent in Paris to keep the English couple under surveillance so that the details of their whereabouts could be phoned to Eaton Square.[42]

John and Una were taken into custody when they arrived in Paris and John, at first, called on his old film partner, Johnston-Noad, to serve as their legal representative. He showed his colors, however, by offering to give a scoop to the Reuters correspondent in Paris, who in turn was instructed from London that under no circumstances were there to be any dealings with Jack's erstwhile and disreputable associate. Leo was tremendously upset about the money, the couple's arrest and the publicity. Finally, the British Ambassador came up with an experienced French solicitor who argued that the young Amerys had been the unwitting victims of a Greek moneylender. They were released from custody on a bond and after many legal comings and goings the charges were dropped.[43] The quality press followed Reuters' lead, providing merely a few sober lines after the incident. The tabloids were inclined to treat John and Una as starstruck lovers whose romance had been thwarted by the stuffy Amery family.[44]

Between March and October 1936, John joined the editorial staff of Reuters in London. Again Sir Roderick had come to the rescue. Amery was taken on probation into the Mail and Features Department. With his poor writing and execrable spelling, he was not a strong candidate for a future in journalism.[45] Moreover, as he explained in a letter to Sir Roderick, he had no stamina for the humdrum and the clerical hackwork that occupy much of the journalist's time on the news service.[46] At that time he was living with Una in a villa at Maidenhead, though the notepaper for his Reuters correspondence came from a hotel in Mayfair. More often than not, Amery was tardy. There were mysterious accidents which prevented his coming in to the office for days on end: He fell down the stairs on the underground; he injured his back; called in ill; or, more frequently, did not call at all. Amery asked Reuters special leave to travel to Berlin where, he said, he had film business that needed winding up. Sir Roderick asked Dick Sheepshanks, an Old Etonian and a rising start in Reuters—tragically killed later reporting the Spanish civil war—to take Jack under his wing. Jack confessed to his mentor that he had "celluloid in his blood" and wished as soon as possible to get back to filmmaking. Having invited Jack for a drink after work to give him advice on how to manage life as a cub reporter, Sheepshanks was astonished when his protégé called for him behind the wheel of a "huge Hispano Suiza." As Jack airily explained it, there could be "no credit without flash."[47]

In May 1936, Amery offered Reuters a confidential scoop about an action in Palestine which was to be undertaken by an anti-Semitic group from Munich. In his words, his own principle was that he was happy to be involved "so long as it was not directed against the British Empire." Reuters noted the information, but did no more about it. In October 1936, Amery quit Reuters. He wrote to Sheepshanks to explain that he was on his way to Franco's Spain and that he and some associates had purchased eight thousand pounds worth of arms from the German government, and the Portuguese authorities would "put little difficulties in his way to run them into Seville." There was 100-percent profit to be made on the transaction. His longer term aim, however, was to "muscle in on the rebel racket to get a monopoly on the propaganda film market." Amery also asked Sheepshanks whether Reuters would be willing give him a letter of accreditation as a journalist that he could use in Spain. In terms of the latter, Sheepshanks pointed out that there was no hope of such an association, suggesting dryly that the *Daily Mail* would be a better bet.[48]

Early in November 1936, in London, bankruptcy proceedings were brought against John Amery. In court he was described as a company director and film producer. The Official Receiver reported that Amery had no assets and debts of more than five thousand pounds. These had been accumulated on visits to the Continent to raise capital for film companies. During the subsequent public examination of his finances, he was asked whether he had been "reckless and extravagant." Amery replied that "in the film business you cannot ride on a tram or travel third-class. You have got to dress your window, and it gave me no pleasure to entertain on this scale knowing the bills were running up." He explained too that lavish spending had been necessary in order to obtain contracts, and for the same reasons he had been forced to make presents of jewelry to various people. And he had also been obliged to visit Paris, Vienna and Geneva. Outside the court Amery stated that "for some time now I have been making my own way in the world and I hope to continue to do so." He also indicated that the reasons for his present misfortunes were that his creditors would not wait and that he "did not expect any family help in this business."[49]

In July 1938, Amery applied to have the bankruptcy order lifted on the grounds that he would never be able to make a living in film production until it was discharged.[50] According to his counsel he had "got in with a set when he was a minor who traded on his name and the name of his parents." It was significant, too, the lawyer argued, that "the largest trade creditor against Amery was a jeweler who had given him credit to the extent of hundreds of pounds when he was but 17 years of age." The Trustee in Bankruptcy, opposing the application, opined that although "the bankrupt was young he was no fool and had shown himself to be very quick-witted in embarking on this extravagant career at the expense of his creditors"; in Amery the court was confronted with a clear case of "heads I win, tails you lose"; and therefore in the "interests of the public he should be stopped." The judge agreed and rejected the application. In his summation, he found it unacceptable "these days that it was not uncommon for young men to indulge in heavy business transactions and, like the applicant, live lavishly." He recommended Amery reapply for discharge in three years, provided that his conduct in the meantime was satisfactory.

Franco, the Amerys and the Spanish Civil War

Within months of the failed bankruptcy appeal, John Amery was in Nationalist Spain. He may have been following in the footsteps of his brother Julian, who made three separate trips; or there may have been some other reason. What exactly John Amery did in Spain is not clear. He claimed later to have joined up with Franco's forces, but this was not the case. Nor, as was later suggested, is there a record of his enlistment in the Italian Divisions that Mussolini sent to Franco.[51] His passport shows multiple entries in and out of Portuguese and Nationalist territory, hardly the mode of an enlisted soldier. Much more likely, Amery was with the phalanx of foreigners, some loosely attached to Franco's overseas press corps, who were drawn to Nationalist Spain for ideological reasons and for the opportunity to pursue nefarious business dealings on the fringes of the war.

Tom Burns met Amery in Burgos at the Foreign Press Section of Franco's headquarters in September 1938.[52] An idealistic young Catholic who during the

Second World War was the British Press Officer in Madrid and eventually became the editor of *The Tablet*, Burns had given up his summer in 1938 to drive an ambulance in the British Medical Aid Unit sent to Franco by English Catholics. In Burns' eyes, John Amery was a "romantic young man" though "rather withdrawn." He noted too that the blond German, who was Amery's companion, wore a Nazi badge in his buttonhole and was jubilant when the Munich Agreement was announced because, in the German's words, his countrymen now would have the opportunity to "squash flat those Czech dwarfs."

In June 1939, John was in Madrid, probably having been there since early April for Franco's victory celebrations. He stayed at the Hotel Ritz and among his activities was engaged in selling the car that Julian had left behind when he had returned to his studies in Balliol. By January 1940, John was in Portugal and penurious. When Una wrote asking for money, Amery explained that his "little capital was exhausted" and he was "seriously perturbed" about his future. He told her to use her own initiative and sell the diamonds in her ring, if possible in New York. In order to do this she should make contact with a jeweler who was a regular visitor to Eaton Square. John also reassured his wife that she should take heart because it was very probable for the next few years at least that Leo would keep paying her allowanc.[53]

Whatever John's role in Nationalist Spain may have been there is no doubt that he was strongly pro-Franco and the other members of the Amery family shared with him a deep admiration for the Spanish caudillo. Julian, still a university student during the Spanish civil war, visited Nationalist Spain several times, describing the elation of being a journalist at the front.[54] Full of praise, too, for the "Nationalist Revolution," the youngest Amery passed over the fact that the Spanish Republicans were the legally elected government of Spain. Instead, he saw the Spanish Republic as no more than a feint behind which lurked the real adversary which was communism. Writing after the end of the Second World War, Julian conceded that it would have been in Britain's strategic interests to have favored the Republican government. However, in the long run, it was better not to have done so because a "Communist Spain in the post-war world would have presented a threat to the whole Western Alliance."[55]

Leo Amery harboured a similar perception that in the period leading to the Second World War, communism was an imminent danger to Western nations. The primary focus of the father's concern was the far reaches of Northern Europe where, between November 1939 and March 1940, Finland waged a defensive war against the invading Soviet Union. Leo, and the group of like-minded public figures who formed the Finnish Aid Bureau, saw "little Finland" playing the same heroic role in the Winter War that had been Belgium's lot in the First World War.[56] The members of the British committee raised funds, purchased uniforms and equipment, and recruited volunteers for a fighting force to stiffen the Finnish Army. Given the febrile state of international affairs at the time, members of the English committee studiously avoided publicity for their efforts. John Amery, living on the Continent and identifying strongly with his father's support for the anti-communist Finns, donated skis to a Finnish equipment fund which presumably were to be used in the snow-training that many of the volunteers undertook in the French Alps at Chamonix.

In March 1940 Leo and John met in Paris in what would be their last time together for several years. When France fell, the Amery parents were extremely concerned about how their elder son would manage if "isolated and perhaps stranded for some months." Leo contacted an acquaintance in New York who was reputed to have links into Europe. The family's fears were heightened when they received an urgent message on July 8 that John was penniless and had received no allowance since May. Faithful Leo headed off immediately to the Dorchester to speak to the Swiss Consul. He in turn contacted the headquarters of the Swiss Bank Corporation and arranged an immediate transfer of one hundred pounds to John in Southern France. Later that evening the Swiss Consul came in person to Eaton Square to devise a plan that would enable John to make his way into neutral Switzerland. Also, a few days later, the assistance of the Duke of Alba, Franco's ambassador in London, was enlisted to seek his advice whether it might be easier if the Amery's son came home via Spain and Portugal.[57] It very soon became clear, however, that returning to England was not the option that John Amery intended to pursue.

CHAPTER 4

German Wartime Broadcasting

Between the wars, governments had come to recognize the power of propaganda and the potential for radio in that process. In the new medium of radio transmission, the "microphone could be mobilized as a weapon."[1] By 1938, there were at least thirty European nations that had radio systems in place. A year later most of them had acquired the capacity to broadcast by shortwave outside their own borders.[2] And as war loomed, more and more ordinary Europeans became "avid listeners," having discovered that by twiddling the dials they could access an array of shortwave news and cultural programs. During the war, despite the concerted efforts of governments to discourage the practice, in many households of an evening with curtains drawn individuals surfed the airwaves for alternative information about the progress of the war.[3]

Prewar Germany had the best-developed radio infrastructure. In 1933, under the hand of Josef Goebbels at the Ministry for Propaganda, all German radio networks were brought into a single, centralized entity, the German Broadcasting Corporation, the RRG (*Reichs Rundfunk Gesellschaft*). In the subsequent years, Goebbels poured resources and manpower into expanding its capacity. Programs were directed specifically at German speakers outside the Reich. In a range of languages other than German, journalists and cultural commentators trumpeted the success of Nazism at home and abroad. Special broadcasts were carefully tailored to suit local tastes within Europe and the neighboring territories. In each of the events that marked Germany's foreign policy in the decade before the war, the German overseas network played an important role. For example, in January 1935, during the referendum in the Saarland, Germany transmitted over one-thousand separate programs encouraging Saarlanders to vote to join the Reich.[4] And in the series of crises leading to Austrian Anschluss—in Dollfuss' assassination in July 1934, in the months leading up to the proposed plebiscite in March 1938 and throughout the German occupation—Nazi broadcasts from Munich provided blanket coverage that was easily picked up on Austrian radio sets.

Within a very short space of time, after March 1938, Austrian national radio was absorbed into the German network.

A cluster of powerful transmitters, erected near Zeesen and Königs (south of Berlin) and a series of relays and transmitters on long, medium and shortwave beamed the voice of Nazi Germany across the Reich and abroad. In August 1936, in order to expand the capacity to broadcast the Berlin Olympics, eight powerful, new shortwave transmitters were brought into service. By 1939, the destinations of their emissions included the British Isles, the United States, South Africa, South and Central America, South East Asia and Australasia. By late 1940, the German Broadcasting Corporation employed about five hundred people in a Foreign Language Service that maintained, around the clock, one hundred and forty-seven hours of broadcasts in fifty-three languages.[5] The growth of German foreign-language radio created an increasing demand for commentators, broadcasters and translators fluent in the languages of the nations destined to receive these programs.

In Berlin, the buildings of the Foreign Ministry and the Ministry of Propaganda, both of which were concerned with overseas broadcasting, were located on the Willhemstrasse. The offices and studios of Broadcast house, the *Rundfunkhaus*, which included all overseas language departments, were in Charlottenburg, a twenty-minute trolley ride from the city centre. In August 1943, under intense Allied bombing of the capital, the radio studios and staff of German overseas broadcasting were moved to Königs Wusterhausen, a few miles from the transmission complex at Zeesen. Just before the end of the war, what remained of the English foreign broadcasting service was evacuated to Radio Luxembourg.

Despite National Socialist rhetoric about German unity and might, the Nazi state never functioned as an integrated system directed from the top. Rather, it ran within a polycratic structure whose parts resembled feudal fiefdoms. Players within the Nazi Party vied for control of parts of the state's terrain in order to exercise the power that such possession conferred. The institutions involved in radio propaganda replicated the character of the administration as a whole. The Foreign Minister, Joachim von Ribbentrop, was locked in permanent combat with Goebbels at the Ministry of Propaganda. Until 1941, the Foreign Office took precedence, responsible as it was for international negotiations around the signing of pacts with neutral nations and Germany's putative allies. As the military imperative came to the fore, however, the power of the Foreign Minister waned. In the galvanized conditions of wartime, international relations increasingly were governed by military success. At the same time, Goebbels strengthened his own power base by ensuring that the work of his department meshed with the objectives of the war so that as the German state became more militarized, the Propaganda Ministry grew in importance.

At all levels in the two ministries, the ministers' battles at the top were replayed down the line as departments and sections warred over administrative jurisdictions and the boundaries that demarcated departmental authority. As well as the overarching ministerial rivalries, internecine battles within the radio broadcasting sections were rife. Individuals and heads of divisions were at continuous cross-purposes, the contest more often about individual career aspirations than over ideology or strategy.

By the time John Amery arrived in Berlin, Hans Fritzche directed the Propaganda Ministry's broadcasting division. An experienced journalist and, prewar, a reputable radio commentator, he had joined the Nazi Party only after Goebbels appointed him to a senior post. Under Fritzche's supervision, the Foreign Broadcasting Service (*Auslandsdirektion*) was headed by Dr Anton Winkelnkemper, a "bull-knecked Westphalian" who was entirely devoted to Goebbels and the Nazi Party.[6] Within the sections of the foreign broadcasting service there were editors, translators and announcers, most of whom were native foreign speakers recruited within Occupied Europe or expatriates come home to support the war effort. Eduard Dietze, who ran the English language section, was born in Glasgow to a Scottish mother and a German father and held dual Anglo-German citizenship. A trained radio technician and a skilled broadcaster, Dietze in the mid-1930s had been the regular commentator from Berlin for the BBC and for the American NBC.[7] Dietze was brought to German government radio in an attempt to make the English propaganda broadcasts more acceptable to British listeners.

The Foreign Ministry ran a separate broadcasting division that was also concerned with overseas transmission. Von Ribbentrop had established a series of "target committees" reporting directly to him and focused on those countries that were in the Reich's sights for future conquest.[8] These committees included advisers from the rival Propaganda Ministry, and though their combined purpose was to map out future directions, in practice most of the time was spent untangling disagreements between the employees of the two ministries. The chairman of the England Committee, Dr Fritz Hesse, had been a German press officer in London before the war. His brief, directly from Ribbentrop, was to orient the committee's business with a view to bringing about a peace between Germany and Great Britain. Hesse worked diligently: Reading British papers; following the debates in the House of Commons; and, all around, becoming what he described as a "living dictionary" on British affairs.[9]

As the war effort geared up, the German broadcasting enterprise squandered more and more working hours in a gridlock of meetings. In the first months of the conflict, Goebbels had instituted a daily mid-morning conference at the Propaganda Ministry at which he and a small taskforce of key administrators were supposed to map out future propaganda initiatives. After a very short time, the gathering had morphed into a briefing for sixty or more, during which the participants sat silently through longer and longer ministerial monologues. The procedure was that after Goebbels had departed a second level of administrators prepared a précis of what they understood the minister to have said. It was then printed and distributed to the participants to be taken back to their individual departments. In turn, the summary of Goebbels' message was relayed in a new cascade of meetings and briefings that traveled down through all levels of departments engaged in news and commentary until the word finally reached the staff who were producing the day's programs.[10] Not infrequently, after the senior administrators had returned to their home bases, there would be an urgent phone call announcing that the précis of Goebbels' instructions had been overridden "On Higher Instructions" by a new order and the whole process would begin again.[11]

Despite the huge staff employed in the Foreign Language sections of the Propaganda Ministry and the Foreign Office, foreign nationals working as freelancers wrote most of the broadcast material. As well as John Amery and William Joyce, the latter the most senior British broadcaster in Berlin, there were thirty or so other English men and women actively engaged in making foreign programs.[12] The foreigners' scripts were checked by a panel of censors at Broadcast House and, from 1941, while the broadcasters were on air, a government employee sat in the studio following their words on a pre-submitted text. The foreign scriptwriters were never free to choose their topics, but worked around a series of themes that were provided in German government guidelines. These covered four predictable areas: The Bolsheviks would destroy civilization; world Jewry was an evil menace; Germany was the light of the future; and the Anglo-Saxon countries should join with their racial allies and bring an end to the war.

Amery's Participation in Pro-Nazi Affairs

Nazi officials lavished hospitality on the foreigners that they courted as potential German spokesmen. John Amery enjoyed a luxurious lifestyle once he was established as a figure on the pro-Nazi circuit in Occupied Europe. There are several versions, however, of the way that he achieved such a position. They all trace the steps that Amery followed from the declaration of the Second World War until November 1942, the first time that his voice was heard on the Berlin airwaves. The first, but not the most reliable narrative is John's own, written for the members of British Intelligence when he was arrested in Italy. Around the same time, when several of his associates in the Berlin broadcasting world were also arrested they gave detailed reports to their British interrogators. As well, Leo and Florence Amery left information in the trail of documents that were created as they sought to send money and comforts to their eldest son.

John's version is a long and ebullient statement that he typed in May 1945 while being held at the Terni internment camp outside Rome.[13] Convinced that his father would quickly extricate him from this latest scrape, the tone of John's narrative is upbeat. The sense it conveys is that the author is sure that the reader will share John's own sympathies. In a rambling disquisition on life and ideology, he harks back to the two core beliefs that he claimed had motivated his pro-Nazis stance.These were the defense of the British Empire and the defeat of communism. The narrative ends with a flourish in a reference to what he considers to be his crucial experience in the Spanish civil war. He vowed to continue to "serve his country" by carrying out the "life work" that had been "begun in Seville [at the time of the generals' uprising] in June 1936."[14]

In John's chronology of the first months of World War Two, he had been with his father in Paris, in March 1940 and they had discussed his enlisting in British Intelligence where his languages would be useful. Before being able to take this step, as John explains, there was film business to finish in the south of France, which is where he was when France fell. In the sequence that follows, he visited the Vichy government in June 1941 and, "finding it wanting," tried to contact Dino Grandi, a senior figure near Mussolini and the ex-Italian ambassador in London. When that produced no result, he then attempted to enlist in the Finnish Army, but was "politely refused." Again in John's version, he was interned in *Val des Bains* with a group of English people, but was soon freed by the intervention of Jacques Doriot, the leader of the French, Croix de Feu whom he had known in Spain, and by Amery's female companion, Jeanine Barde. While staying with Barde's family in Bergerac, he was invited to travel to Berlin by a German, one "Captain Werner" (presumably a reference to Werner Plack who became the minder of Germany's foreign propagandists in Europe). There are omissions and major irregularities in this chronology. For example the Winter War between Finland and the Soviet Union had ended with an armistice in March 1940. As well, the detail that John gives is at odds with other sources that document his movements and shed light on his defection to Berlin.

Leo and Florence pulled out all stops to help their son. Leo asked Sir Samuel Hoare, the British Ambassador to Spain, to use his best efforts to contact Jack in Occupied Europe. Hoare and Leo were friends, long-standing members of the Tory party and colleagues at the India office. During the Second World War, from the British Embassy in Madrid, Hoare supported an underground network that assisted downed Allied flyers to get back to Britain by crossing the Spanish border into neutral Portugal.[15] Through an intermediary who regularly crossed the border into France, Jack was located quite quickly and Lady Maude Hoare sent warm clothes and passed letters back and forth from Jack to his mother. When the Foreign Office warned sternly against the use of the diplomatic bag for personal correspondence, Sir Sam sent the letters to Leo.[16] The French papers reported that Jack had been critical of the British bombing of the Renault works at Billancourt, and Leo, apologetically, asked Sir Samuel to pass his own letter on to his son. In Leo's words, Jack was "often foolish and unguarded" and in need of a "stern reproof" to warn him to refrain from all public utterances.[17] In a familiar gesture, Leo also arranged to send Jack an allowance. The regular amount that the Foreign Office paid to British citizens in distress was ten pounds per month, however, through the United States Consul in Nice, the protecting power for Britain, Leo arranged that twenty-five pounds a month should be drawn against his Piccadilly bank, with payment to "continue for an indefinite period."[18] Wilfrid Brinkman, an Englishman employed at the American Consulate, recalled that he had had "considerable trouble" over the allowance payments to John Amery, who always expected to receive more than that to which he was entitled.[19]

In the communication to his parents after France had surrendered, Jack had greatly alarmed them by stating that he had been diagnosed with a serious lung disease and as a consequence was living in a sanatorium near Grenoble. (It is worth noting that the address he gave on his allowance payment was to the Hotel du Lac in Izère, and the autopsy after his execution showed no sign of damage to the lungs). A worried Leo, writing from the India Office, asked the American Consul to arrange with the Swiss to give Jack permission, on medical grounds, to cross the border and enter a Swiss sanatorium. Brinkman arranged the visa and called for help from the director of the English Queen Victorian Hospital in Nice, E. W. Ogilvie. An ambulance was found to transport the young Englishman but at the very last minute, when he discovered that he could not take his girlfriend and Sammy, the pet Pomeranian, Amery refused to go.[20]

In early 1942, British Intelligence noted that John was living at a hotel in Nice that was frequented by German officials. Around this time, too, he was caught up in a tawdry incident involving the German police and a stash of American dollars that the director of the English hospital had hidden. According to Ogilvie, Amery had importuned him to sell the dollars to a friend of Amery's who needed to pay a debt in Spain. At the point of sale, however, the German police had arrived and seized the money and the arrested Ogilvie spent several months in jail. In a postwar statement to British interrogators, Ogilvie swore that Amery had received a cut of the confiscated money.[21]

Hesse, head of the German Foreign Office's England Committee, managed the British broadcasters in Berlin and provided another version of the events around Amery's activities that offer the most plausible explanation of his joining the German propaganda mission. Previously, attached to the German Embassy in London, Hesse understood the significance of John Amery's family connections. By a curious coincidence, the German Ambassador's private residence was near the Amery's house on Eaton Square and during drawn-out renovations to convert the German Embassy into a suitably grand Nazi edifice, much German business took place at the Ambassador's home.[22] According to Hesse, Amery "fell into the hands of the Germans" in the summer of 1941, near the Spanish border.[23] While in custody and in order to prove he was not a spy, the Englishman offered to create a unit of English volunteers to fight with the Germans against the Russians in the East.

It is probably not surprising that this idea would be at the forefront of Amery's mind. At the time, the German invasion of the Soviet Union, bringing as it did an end to the Nazi-Soviet Non-Aggression Pact, had galvanized the extreme Right in Spain and France. Jacques Doriot, the founder of the Parti Populaire Français (PPF), along with Eugene Deloncle, Marcel Déat and Simon Sabiani in Marseille were addressing packed meetings calling for volunteers to support Operation Barbarossa by enlisting in a French Legion that would fight beside the German Army on the Eastern Front. Doriot and his supporters energetically lobbied at Vichy for approval of their Legion from a less-than-enthusiastic General Pétain. At the same time, they sought permission to recruit volunteers from among French prisoners of war.[24] Doriot's model, discussed below, was probably based on the French Joan of Arc battalion that Doriot and others had helped recruit to send to Spain to fight for General Franco. Amery's sketchy ideas to create his own unit of British volunteers, in turn, mimicked Doriot's project.

With Amery in custody, the German police had cabled Berlin for advice on how to deal with the prisoner and his proposal. Again according to Hesse, when the Foreign Ministry received the request, Ribbentrop sought his opinion, as the Nazi's British expert, on what should be done with this young Englishman. Advising that it would be highly damaging to German-British relations if the "son of a British cabinet member was executed for espionage," Hesse recommended that Amery be brought to Berlin to see whether the German government could use him in some way or another. Goebbels at the Propaganda Ministry and Ribbentrop as Foreign Minister both agreed. In addition, according to Hesse, the German military were decidedly cold on Amery's proposed foreign legion within the German Army, but Hitler saw it as having real propaganda potential.[25]

Ribbentrop still believed that a "peace offensive" towards the British was possible and with the Fuhrer's backing, proposed to offer some feelers across the Channel.[26] In this mission, Amery was the potential go-between. Therefore, Hesse arranged to transfer Amery to Berlin where he was to broadcast in a way that would encourage Britain to reach out to Germany. As outlandish as the scheme sounds, the degree of seriousness that was attached to the effort is attested by the seniority of the Germans involved. Professor Reinhardt Haferkorn, a senior member of the Foreign Ministry's division of English Language broadcasting, worked up several drafts of Amery's first talk. Dietze, the head of the entire English Language Broadcasting service, personally devised advertisements and the publicity for the programs; and Ribbentrop himself vetted the final content of the broadcast.

Predictably, Amery's call for an "end to an unnecessary war"—which finally went to air in November 1942—drew no discernible response from the British government though several of the British tabloids referred to the speech as a "peace-feeler."[27] The Japanese government, though, complained. According to Hesse, they feared that the "political tendency" of the talk signalled a reconfiguration of the Anti-Comintern Pact that had been signed between Japan and Germany in Spain in November 1936. Once the broadcast had been transmitted, Amery and his female companion were accompanied back to France where they were to await a future summons.

John Amery Broadcasting in Berlin and Paris

While John Amery was in Berlin, he was a guest of the German Foreign Ministry and enjoyed the capital's finest hospitality. There were three great hotels in the city whose names since the early twentieth century had been synonymous with luxury and service. The Adlon, a five-star beacon of light opposite the Brandenburg Gate, was the hotel of choice for rich foreigners and the Third Reich's valued visitors. It was Amery's destination on his first trip to Berlin. Until Pearl Harbor, it was also a home away from home for the American press corps, though by 1941, in the jaundiced view of one of them, the Adlon's foyer had become the gathering place for all the "flotsam and jetsam" of proto-fascists and foreign Nazi camp followers in the capital. The Kaiserhof, further down Unter den Linden, had accommodated the Duke and Duchess of Windsor in fine style when they came to meet Hitler in 1937, and on a number of occasions was host to Amery. The Hotel Bristol in Berlin's posh West End shared with the other two a reputation for impeccable service. The Bristol's namesake in Paris was the haunt of high German officials and, during the Occupation, ran two dining rooms—food and wine was in abundance for the Germans and their guests—while in the other strict rationing was the norm. Favored by the Amery family before the war, the Bristol became John Amery's primary residence in the months that he spent in the French capital.

The other watering holes in Berlin for the foreign press corps were the two press clubs run by the Ministry for Propaganda and the German Foreign Ministry, respectively. Each outdid the other in hospitality for foreign journalists and broadcasters, their rivalry reflecting the competition between Goebbels and Ribbentrop. In 1933, as soon as he had been made Minister of Propaganda, Goebbels had taken over the old Foreigners Club on Leipziger Platz and lavished millions to transform it into a "palatial refuge for journalists."[28] Despite rationing everywhere else, within the Foreign Press Club's large and ornate restaurant guests enjoyed one of the best tables in Berlin. The bar served the latest "American" cocktails at ridiculously low prices.[29] In a suite of comfortable reading rooms where the thick carpets muffled all sound and shaded lights stood behind deep chairs, daily papers from around the world were laid out. In quiet alcoves there were ample desks with typewriters and the telephones provided immediate access to a switchboard that connected overseas calls.

The Foreign Office Press Club off the Kurfürstendamm in West Berlin was set up in 1938 by Von Ribbentrop when he became the Reich Foreign Minister. Smaller than Goebbels' establishment, the premises were equally luxurious, providing excellent service, real coffee and fine dining at subsidized prices. There, too, the latest foreign papers and efficient, around-the-clock communication technology were available in well-appointed reading rooms. Ribbentrop's club also boasted a games room with Ping-Pong and pintables where journalists who felt the need could let off steam. In both places a "throng" of dateable blond-haired girls hovered at hand.[30] The convenience meant that a number of foreign journalists forewent the expense of setting up their own office. For the rest, the German press establishments doubled as private clubs for the foreign news and radio journalists in the capital. Senior Nazi Party officials took the opportunity of these venues to rub shoulders with the foreigners in the hope that the stories that were sent abroad would show Germany in the best possible light.

John Amery was a regular at the press clubs. According to Reinhardt Spitzy, who had been a First Secretary in the German Embassy in London before the war, Amery and his "French lady friend" spent a great deal of their time socializing there. They were especially frequent visitors at Ribbentrop's establishment. On one memorable evening, at a reception hosted by the German Foreign Minister,

Spitzy observed Amery "absolutely paralytic," so intoxicated that he was "incapable of making any coherent conversation."[31]

The German government, with a view to eliciting a favorable view of the Nazi state, went to elaborate lengths in other ways to make as comfortable as possible the lives of those associated with foreign press and overseas broadcasting. Howard K. Smith, the Berlin correspondent for American United Press, pointed out that in their "private lives" journalists were "smothered with favors and special privileges" from arranging the lease of large apartments to the easy provision of opera and theatre tickets or vacation trips around the Reich. Otto Dietrich, the Reich Press Chief, frequently hosted banquets for the foreigners at which officials and guests "feasted on foods and drinks that were denied other people." At a typical gathering that Harry Flannery attended in 1942, he was served "Brussels sprouts and cauliflower," their disappearance from Berlin tables having transformed these humdrum staples into sought-after delicacies. There were also large portions of roast beef that, if it had been available, would have required weeks of food coupons. Fine French wines accompanied each course, Flannery assuming they were part of a huge shipment of French wine he had seen being unloaded from trucks a few days before, outside the Propaganda Ministry.[32] As well, foreigners in press and broadcasting received extra clothing rations and were issued with a special red card that could be used for quick and cheap transport on taxis, trains and buses. Each fortnight, after the daily foreign press conference at the Propaganda Ministry, Goebbels' officials handed out extra ration cards for food. Not surprisingly, these press conferences were well attended and Goebbels used them to announce news items that he particularly wished to be reported abroad.[33]

The German Foreign Office covered Amery's expenses. Unlike the other English-speaking broadcasters in Berlin, he received neither fixed salary nor appearance payments. Instead, the Foreign Ministry paid all his bills.[34] Even more, Ribbentrop had ordered that because Amery was the son of a British government minister, it was only fitting that he should be permitted to "live at a certain scale" which translated into a lavish lifestyle, on top of the already generous privileges extended to the German government's favored guests.[35] Hesse, who met these costs from a special account, often looked with a jaundiced eye on Amery's extravagances.

Von Ribbentrop also provided Amery with the minder, Werner Plack, who chaperoned important English-speaking collaborators on Radio Berlin. He kept a weather eye on his charges while smoothing out the details of their travel in Europe. In the 1920s, Plack had run a German wine business in Los Angeles and had been a figure on the Hollywood scene. Back in Germany, he enjoyed some connection with Frau Ribbentrop's family, the Bavarian wine producers.[36] Acquaintances in Berlin, described Plack as a "playboy" and "Hollywood-wise," someone who used the opportunity of travel with the German collaborators in neutral Europe to stock up on scarce goods, silk stockings, soap and cigarettes that could easily be sold back in Germany.[37]

In whatever guise, the bills that Plack picked up, as he squired John Amery around Europe, were for staggering amounts. According to Amery's own computations, he clocked up in expenses 346,000 francs—or the equivalent of almost two thousand English pounds—between November 1943 and early March 1944, paid for by the German Embassy in Paris. From March to June 1944, Amery received 270,000 francs in expenses, or one thousand, five hundred pounds plus one thousand, two hundred and twenty-two francs in a hotel bill at the Bristol in Paris. There was an additional five thousand francs, about twenty-eight English pounds, claimed for the tips he had made to the hotel porter.[38] It is perhaps ironic that in a speech at the Gaumont Palace cinema in Clichy, on May 7, 1944, Amery reassured the audience, in response to what he claimed was the question everyone wanted to ask—which was how much he was being paid by Germany—that the Germans were not interested in supporting a traitor. And besides, he had a "large personal fortune." A good part of this, he said, had been saved, and though the rest had been "seized by Churchill" Amery looked forward to getting it back, presumably when Germany won the war.[39]

In Paris, the lives of those who collaborated with the Germans revolved around the activities and institutions promoted by the German Embassy and its ambassador, Otto Abetz.[40] Apart from the embassy functions, there were the social and cultural gatherings at the German Institute that showcased German and pro-German culture in France. The German government, through the Propaganda Ministry, also sank a great deal of money into the *Propaganda-Abteilung*, the propaganda initiative that included the replacement of prewar French publishing houses with those that were pro-German. The Rive Gauche bookstore, close to the Sorbonne on Boulevard Saint Michel, distributed French translations of German books and the new French releases by the pro-Nazi intellectuals who had remained in the capital. The Germans also funded Radio Paris, the pro-German station, whose lively programs drew listeners away from the staid music and moralizing lectures that were typical fare over Radio Vichy, Pétain's mouthpiece in the southern zone.

Abetz was open-handed with German funds for sympathetic French writers and journalists. He sent them off to Berlin and around major cities in the occupied countries to attend a never-ending merry-go-round of literary conferences, symposia and cultural gatherings. These promoted what the Nazis dubbed as a "new intellectual order in the New Europe." Amery and his female partners, with Plack in tow, were recipients of this largesse. As they sped from public podium to radio talk in Belgrade, Prague, Vienna, Berlin, Stockholm, Brussels, Paris, and various pro-German venues in between, they amassed stacks of bills for rooms and suites in the best hotels, food and drink in the finest restaurants, dry cleaning, car rentals and even doctors' bills. All were paid without quibble by Abetz in Paris or via Hesse from Von Ribbentrop in Berlin.[41]

Amery's companion, Jeanine Barde, was a French woman and, until her death in April 1943, accompanied him on his peripatetic adventures through Occupied Europe. Like him, she broadcasted over German radio. Born in Bergerac, Barde was twenty years of age with a five-year-old daughter who remained with the child's grandmother during Barde's absences. In the view of a German employee of the Foreign Ministry, Reinhardt Spitzy, who first met the couple at the end of 1942 on the train from Berlin after Amery's first broadcast, Barde was "vivacious," "witty" and "well endowed."[42] Over sandwiches and copious amounts of champagne provided by Amery's minders, the three made a convivial journey. The German found his traveling companions fascinating: Amery "frail, intelligent and typically English"; Barde, "half gypsy" and with good nature, acceded to Spitzy's requests to sing "Sur le Pont d'Avignon." From time-to-time Amery and Barde "discreetly retired to their sleeping compartment from whence they emerged after a short while, she evidently refreshed and he looking rather exhausted."[43]

Barde succumbed to a squalid death in the Kaiserhof in Berlin. After a night of heavy drinking at the Foreign Office press club, she and Amery had returned to their hotel room and passed out. The next morning, when Amery woke, Barde was dead. An autopsy showed that she had choked on her own vomit.[44] Her distressed partner brought her body back to Bergerac and for the rest of his days continued to speak about her as the great love of his life; several of the collections of his speeches are dedicated to her memory. Within a fairly short time of her death, however, Amery met a sultry twenty-six-year-old Parisian, Michelle Thomas. She too was a "good looker" with "plucked eyebrows, very red lips and fingernails, raven hair and wearing a lot of imitation jewelry and a small gold chain around her right ankle." The two went through a marriage ceremony in October 1943 at the German Embassy in Paris.[45]

Barde had been an *habitué* of Cagoulard circles, either as a result of her own background in the south of France, or, equally likely, from her association with Amery. The *Comité Sécrète d'Action Revolutionnaire*, or the Cagoule—called after their symbol of the hood—were part of an efflorescence of groups on the extreme Right that had spawned in France in the turbulent period of the Popular Front. Strongly based in southern France, and with cadres later in Parisian collaborationist circles, the clandestine organization carried out assassination and sabotage against what in their parlance were referred to as "France's enemies": Jewish citizens, suspected Freemasons and anyone of communist sympathies. During the Spanish civil war, Cagoulists claimed that they provided the "link in a chain between Franco's Spain and Mussolini's Italy."[46] Between 1936 and 1939, and carrying over into World War Two, their networks connected senior members of Mussolini's inner circle with the leadership of the Spanish Falangist movement. Among the latter was Franco's brother-in-law, Ramón Serrano Suñer. A Falangist ideologue and an admirer of Mussolini, he pushed a pro-Axis foreign policy while he was Franco's Foreign Minister between 1940 and late 1942 and remained at the core of the Falangist movement in Spain. Serrano Suñer certainly knew John Amery. Indeed, when Julian Amery approached the Falangist for assistance in 1945, Serrano Suñer went so far as to arrange the forgery of documents to prove that in 1937 John had become a Spanish citizen. On the same visit, Julian reported that other leading Falangists—like General Muñoz Grandes, the leader of the Spanish Blue Division that fought beside the German Army on the Eastern Front—had spoken of John as a "Byron-like figure" who cared as deeply for another country as he did for his own.[47]

The region on both sides of the border on the Spanish and French Atlantic Coast and across into southern France provided the staging area for much trafficking between Franco's Spain and Occupied France.[48] Similarly, during the Spanish civil war, certain key French figures had crossed back-and-forth, in supporting Franco's movement. During World War Two, in ultra circles, those who had been in Nationalist Spain enjoyed the cachet of having been present at what rightist ideologues heralded as the first victory in the predicted worldwide success against "bolshevism and international Jewry."

A number of Frenchmen who fought for Franco in the Spanish civil war crossed Amery's path in Occupied Europe. For example Jean Hérold-Paquis, originally a volunteer in the Jeanne d'Arc battalion in Spain, transferred to the German-supported Radio Saragossa after a combat injury and from 1941 in World War Two, like Amery, was a regular commentator on Germany's Radio Paris.[49] The journalist Jean Fontenoy was another veteran from Franco's Spain with a high profile in Germanic circles in Paris. As a volunteer in a list of conflicts that might have pleased both generations of Amerys, Fontenoy had volunteered with the Jeanne d'Arcs for Franco and in early 1940 signed up with the unit of foreign volunteers for the Finns in the Winter War against the Soviet Union.[50] Although he suffered horrendous frostbite in Finland, it did not prevent Fontenoy from heading off in late 1941 with Doriot's volunteers in the Légion des Volontaires Français Contre le Bolchevisme (LVF) for several months in subzero conditions to fight the Russians on the Eastern front. Later, appointed director of Germany's *Agence Française d'Information et de Presse,* which managed collaborationist journalism in Paris, Fontenoy was, in the words of the admiring German Ambassador, "the most meritorious among those in the struggle against international Jewry and Bolshevism."[51]

Most significant of all the characters that Amery met in Nationalist Spain was Jacques Doriot. The founder of the right-wing Parti Populaire Français (PPF), Doriot crossed the Pyrenees several times during the Spanish civil war to visit party members who had volunteered to join up with General Franco. His followers provided the majority among the French fascist volunteers in the Joan of Arc Battalion.[52] The unit was created to aid Franco's victory because it was believed that in striking a blow against the Spanish Republic, the Jeanne d'Arcs would damage the hated Popular Front government of "the Jew Blum and his communist confreres" to use the graphic fascist language. As well, it was hoped that Nationalist Spain would provide the training ground for a future French insurgency that would follow the lines of Franco's uprising against the Spanish Republic. The French Jeanne d'Arc battalion in the Spanish civil war was the prototype for Doriot's LVF formed in 1941 to fight beside the Russians on the Eastern Front.

The actions of the charismatic Doriot were the inspiration for Amery's hare-brained and unsuccessful attempt to form a British legion that also would fight on the Eastern Front. Equally, it was probably the excitement surrounding Doriot's departure for the Soviet Union—taking a second cohort of French volunteers—that prompted Amery's impulsive visit on April 20, 1943 to the British internment camp at Saint Denis in the hope of recruiting British prisoners of war. In the month leading up to the departure of the French Legion, Doriot and Déat had held mammoth rallies, haranguing their anti-communist followers to show their mettle by enlisting in the French Legion and fighting in solidarity with their German comrades in order to defeat the Soviet Union.[53] Saint Denis was Doriot's home ground. It had provided the base of his electoral success in his previous life as a Communist Party mayor and remained a stronghold of the PPF which he had formed in 1936. It was as well the site of the party's animated rallies. It was also in Saint Denis that the Germans had set up an internment camp for prisoners of many nationalities,of which the largest contingent were three-hundred British internees.

The Foreign Ministry and the Propaganda Ministry in Berlin both denied any part in Amery's half-cocked attempt to recruit British volunteers at Saint Denis.[54] Nor did they accept any responsibility for the posters and the extravagant proclamation that preceded Amery's arrival at the camp.[55] Amery had been fired up by the charismatic Doriot and the thrilling speeches that roused the crowds at his huge rallies. Probably, the Englishman and the sidekick Plack had come up with the plan themselves, assuming that in mimicking Doriot's iniative it would find favor with him. And with a camp of British POWs nearby, Amery and Plack imagined that it would be easy to find enough recruits to form a legion from those prisoners willing to volunteer in return for their freedom.

On April 20,1943, about thirty British prisoners were brought by the camp administration to the visitors' hut to hear Amery speak. He laid out the benefits that a POW could obtain in joining what he claimed was the growing English opposition to the war and volunteering for the British unit that would fight on the Eastern Front. The volunteers would wear German uniforms, with a British shoulder flash, and while they would be led by German officers, there would always be British NCOs on hand. Most of the POWs summoned for Amery's lecture were unhappy at being selected because their presence suggested they were potential collaborators, which would mean later that they would be on the receiving end of rough treatment from other prisoners. A single, very young, merchant seaman seems to have been the only volunteer that Amery managed to recruit.[56] By an extraordinary coincidence, Walter Brinkman, previously employed by the American Embassy in Nice, was interned at Saint Denis and having seen the posters for Amery's talk, forced his way into the hall and loudly heckled the speaker. When Amery and Plack left, a crowd of shouting English prisoners gathered at the gate and "gave them the bird" until the German guards were called out and forced the prisoners back into barracks.[57] Months later and without Amery's involvement, a unit of British volunteers was formed, but when it proved to be ineffectual, it was merged into the Waffen SS.[58]

In November 1944, as the Allies were closing in, Amery with Michelle Thomas crossed the Alps to make several broadcasts over German-sponsored radio from the Republic of Saló. The couple was warmly welcomed into Mussolini's inner circle, seeded as it was with individuals who were Doriot supporters and those from Cagoule backgrounds. With the diehards of the PPF, Amery traveled to Mengen in southern Germany in February 1945 for Doriot's funeral, killed when an Allied plane strafed his car. At Lake Garda, Amery met the Duce several times and was part of the entourage that accompanied Mussolini when he traveled to Milan in April 1945. At around this time, Victor Barthélemy, a founder of the French Legion (LVF) and Doriot's representative to the Republic of Saló, passed what he described as an "extremely interesting evening" in discussion with John Amery and "his charming young French wife." Well aware of the Englishman's family connections, Barthélemy and the other Doriotists shared Amery's belief that an alliance between the "two racial cousins" Britain and Germany could wipe out the "communist menace" of the Soviet Union.[59] The brother and sister of Mussolini's mistress, Marcello and Maria Petacci, were also part of Amery's inner Italian circle. In the last letters that he sent from Wandsworth Prison, John urged Michelle Thomas to make all effort to get to Spain where she could count on the help of close friends, like the Petacci family, who immediately after the war had fled with a cavalcade of European fascists into the bolt-hole of Franco's Spain where they were guaranteed sanctuary and protection from Allied post war prosecutions.[60]

John Amery remained in Occupied Europe throughout the war. The family name coupled with his previous contacts smoothed the way for the life of a pro-German foreign propagandist. In the French and German capitals, with sweeps across Europe, east to west and back again, Amery was the recipient of a level of largesse only accorded to the most desirable of the foreign nationals at the Nazi court. A number of people may have found Amery insignificant, even unpleasant,[61] but in collaborationist circles he was someone to be reckoned with. As described by a Nazi insider, Amery was a "real catch in propaganda terms" and someone who could make a "real stir."[62] At critical times throughout the war, for example in the first year of the conflict and again at the time of Operation Barbarossa, there were many Germans who assumed that Britain would never risk an all-out war and certainly not one in alliance with the Soviet Union. In late 1945, too, industrialists and politicians in both Germany and at the Republic of Saló were keen to negotiate a separate peace in order to salvage their countries' infrastructure. The remnant ultra-right in Europe, even in the hour of defeat, hoped that Britain finally would throw its weight behind Germany in a final showdown with the Soviet Union.[63] Within these circles and as the putative facilitator of an Axis-England rapprochement, John Amery was guaranteed a welcome. His previous involvement in Franco's Spain gave him both the credibility and the contact with many of the important figures on the European extreme right who after Franco's victory re-emerged as enthusiastic partisans in pro-Nazi Europe. The ties between Nationalist Spain and Axis Europe, reflected in the trajectory of Amery's own doings, highlight a distinct strand of the history of the European fascist movement.

CHAPTER 5

Amery's Reception in Britain

In Berlin, at 9 P.M. on November 19, 1942, John Amery made the first of the seven broadcasts that were beamed on shortwave directly to Britain. In the course of World War Two, he gave a great many talks at public meetings and over the airwaves: In English on German radio in Belgrade; in Italian from Radio Milan; in French from Radio Paris and from the Danish and the Belgian capitals. In all of them he lauded the virtues of the Nazi's "New Europe." Equally, he castigated the evils of communism and the folly of the British government in entering an alliance with the Soviet Union. Amery's voice on-air was not unpleasant, though it was pitched in a slightly high register and revealed a distinctive speech pattern whereby the "th" sound was articulated as a "vee."[1] This linguistic propensity was particularly noticeable when he pronounced the word "father." And, in the son's broadcasts, the real-life Leo Amery was frequently invoked. Even when Amery *père* was not named, he was never far from mind.

Always introduced as the son of Leo Amery, John's style on-air was strongly reminiscent of his father. While many of the other English-language broadcasters raved and ranted, John adopted the guise of the serious British commentator, very much in his father's manner. If the virulent anti-Semitism is set aside, John's polemic carried the hallmarks of Leo's world, in particular the abiding belief in the British Empire and a deep distrust of the United States and its no-holds-barred free trade. Always and overridingly, there was the visceral hatred of communism. In both cases the Amerys underlined the urgency of a solution to the position of world Jewry—the consequences for the father were his backing a Zionist homeland while the son embraced the exclusion of Jews from civic life. But it was their common view that in the twentieth century, Jews could not be ignored. The store of references that leavened John's broadcasts strongly recalled Leo's rhetoric. Magna Carta and the English yeomen were favorite examples as were the "liberty-loving Finnish people," dear to Leo's heart and in John's speeches, the very model of the anti-Bolshevik resistance.

The Broadcasts

The themes of Amery's broadcasts, reiterated over and over, were published in several collections. The fullest exposition appeared in *England Faces Europe* which originated in Paris in 1943 under a Franco-German imprint and was reprinted in shorter French versions that later were translated into the languages of Occupied Europe.[2] With a single exception, most historians faced with the ugly anti-Semitism in Amery's writings have passed over them as not worthy of much attention. More usefully, Nigel Copsey has analyzed Amery's writing in light of British anti-Semitism. However, an even more powerful insight into the provenance of Amery's ideas is available when they are set against the background of the French anti-Semitic polemicists that were enjoying a heyday in Occupied Paris.[3]

The bibliography in *England Faces Europe* lists the sources that were influential when Amery was putting his ideas on the page. Gibbon's *Decline and Fall* offered a model of the *longue durée* and *Seven Pillars of Wisdom* by T. E. Lawrence, an old friend of the Amery family, is referenced in bibliography and text. Not surprisingly, John paraphrases Leo's essays on the British Empire. The anti-Semitic material is lifted directly from Louis Céline's *Bagatelles pour un Massacre* and from Lucien Rebatet's autobiographical *Les Décombres*. Both were considered classics in anti-Semitic circles in the 1930s and were re-issued in Occupied Paris by the same Nazi-funded French press that was responsible for Amery's publications. In *England Faces Europe* and the shorter versions, Amery attempts to glue together the material that he had taken from the English and French sources that provided the inspiration.

The British Empire and the malevolent Jew are central to the analysis. In Amery's view, these two have set the trajectory of Western civilization up to 1943 and, will determine the outcome of the war. In the discussion of Britain and the Empire, it is Leo's voice that comes through loud and clear though the detail is larded with anti-Semitic examples. John states that British power rested on the strength of the Empire which in its heyday could boast that there was "no country in the world that was not in Britain's debt," and nowhere a class that was "freer and happier" than the English yeoman. The supremacy of the British navy quarantined the British army from engagement in continental wars, protecting British merchants and explorers while "the Clives, Warren Harley, Raffles and Captain Cook" opened new lands for imperial expansion. At crucial points in history, Britain failed to maintain the "national position" that is in the tradition of the East India Company, in which Empire trade was privileged over any with Europe. Using analogies that recalled the Empire Food Movement, John argued that eating and cultivating only within the "garden of the British Empire" would benefit the empire family as a whole. John's ideal future for England was one in which British sterling provided the currency of an Empire trading bloc in which the Dominions and an independent India, as equal participants, were joined with the British motherland. In a spirit of reciprocal loyalty, the Dominions would buffer England whereby low taxes on all the necessities for the English workingman's table would hold down British prices and ensure a high standard of living. As a final flourish, in John's ideal world, the English King would rotate around the Empire to spend a year in residence in Britain and in each of the far-flung imperial outposts.

This happy domain, according to John, had been corrupted by the evil figure of the Jew. He had infiltrated the British merchant class, leading them away from their proper imperial vocation. At particular historical moments English merchants and the aristocracy, whose impoverished members found Jewish cash irresistible, turned away from the Empire and the Dominions to trade with Europe. The pernicious effect was that British wage rates were forced down in order to compete with the low standard of living in places like Poland and Czechoslovakia. So misled were British merchants that it had come to pass that they were no longer willing to finance imperial migration schemes (these one of Leo's pet projects) even though they would have taken British working families to a healthy life in the Dominions. Instead English money was put into "hare-brained schemes" in Eastern Europe.

As evidence of the power and vindictiveness of Jewish capitalists, John offered what he claimed were his own father's experiences when he had opposed sanctions against Mussolini over the invasion of Abyssinia. According to the son, when Leo "upheld the justice of Italy's claims" and in the House of Commons showed up the "barbarity of the Negus and his nigger dictatorship," the "Jewish newspapers" refused to publish his speeches and "mysteriously none of his directorships was renewed." Only after "several years of humiliation" was his father "allowed back into the fold" and only then after he had had to support Chaim Weizmann and the Zionists even though his "public utterances were far from what he really thought." John's interpretation of Leo's position stretched the facts. His father, outside the cabinet, was opposed to sanctions against Italy because he doubted the League's capacity to enforce them and he saw Britain's interests best served by maintaining ties with Italy, rather than pushing Mussolini towards Germany. And of course, Leo's stout support of Zionist efforts for a Jewish homeland were sincere and unequivocal.[4]

In John's view, the only resistance to the machinations of the groups of the Rothschilds and the Disraelis came from Edward VIII (among Europeans of all political persuasions sympathies ran strongly with Edward and the romance with Mrs Simpson versus the British Parliament and the royal family). However, in Amery's narrative, the Honorable Edward was quickly removed from the throne and "replaced by a king who is utterly incapable of any action, positive or negative." British leaders turned away from the last possibility of a future when they rejected Germany's peace offer in July 1940. As a consequence, England's allies, in 1943, were the "Judeo-Plutocrats in Washington" and the "Judeo-Mongolese in Moscow."

In the course of Amery's historical narrative, world Jewry, the Americans and the Bolsheviks became morphed into a single configuration of evil. Against them stood only the principled and hard-working German nation. The conceptual problem in this schema, which is that Germans are continentals and in allying with them the British would be turning away from the "East India Company option," is never confronted. Instead, as the chapters unfold, the Germans more and more come to resemble citizens of the Dominions. Germans and Britons, we are told, have the same sorts of things in common as are shared by the colonial cousins. In eating habits, both like beer and tea, sausages and potatoes, ham and eggs; and they hold dear that quintessential English quality, a "love of the home."

Amery's anti-Semitism, and the language in which it is expressed, paraphrase exactly the words of Louis-Ferdinand Céline and Lucien Rebatet. Core members of the French intellectual set in Paris during World War Two, they were "fervent ideological collaborators" with Nazism.[5] Like John Amery, Celine and Rebatet also admired Jacques Doriot and his fascist Parti Populaire Français. In *Bagatelle pour un massacre*, published in 1937 and reprinted during the Occupation, Céline rolls out elaborate statistics to prove the growth of Jewish influence in France and the rest of the world, and Amery cites these exact figures as fact, though (given his own preference for a tipple) he eschews Céline's conclusion that alcoholism is the ruination of the health of French people and the final proof of the influence of the malignant Jew. In *L'Ecole des cadavers*, Céline argued that if the Aryan was not to disappear, Jews and Freemasons must be expelled and Europe must become fascist. John endlessly repeats this exact scenario. Rebatet, a French fascist and contemporary that John draws on, wrote extensively for *Radio Journal* and, like Amery, was a frequent commentator on Radio Paris. As well, a journalist on the radical rightist *Je Suis Partout*, Rebatet edited several issues of the newspaper that were entirely devoted to the Jewish question and in which he expounded on the corruption that he claimed Jews had brought to Europe. In *Les Décombres,* amongst the ruins that Rebatet claims to foresee is England as the "New Carthage." Rebatet's concepts and his precise expressions are seeded throughout Amery's published writings and leaven the speeches on the airwaves.

The language that Amery employs in his talks in person is much more robust and vulgar than that which he puts on the page. European monarchs come in for particularly scathing comment. On-air and in speeches he referred to that "fat old cow Queen Wilhelmina" and her "silly motto" which was "I will maintain." As Amery tells us, when put to the test it meant nothing because she "packed up at the first alarm" and left the Dutch people in the "mess she had created." England is led by the "stuttering half-wit that has had the insolence to be crowned King of England when we had a perfectly good Socialist patriotic king." And British citizens live in the "filth and misery" that has not changed since the time of Charles Dickens. Priests in The Church of England "stink of stale gin" and give "hypocritical blessings" while they "drape their altars in red flags and lick Stalin's boots" despite the fact that just before the war they "prayed to the Almighty God for the victory of Finland against Bolshevism."[6] The English elite, following the lead of Churchill as he heads off to see "his syphilitic boyfriend" Roosevelt, go to Washington with their foxhounds and their mistresses because they feel more at home with the "plutocrats in America and the boys of Harvard and Colorado" than they ever felt in the "home of an English working man." Over and over Amery warned that if the nation continued in this manner, England's history would be no more than that of "politicians, homosexuals, bankers and bourgeoisie, priests and prostitutes" because what comes over the BBC is "not English opinion but that from Radio Synagogue." As Amery intoned in pamphlets and talks, the "barbarism of the steppe is hammering with its enormous fist on the fortress of Europe," and within six months of Germany's defeat a Bolshevik revolution would "break out in London."[7]

The style of broadcasting, in which John spoke with an informal directness to the audience, recalled his father's most engaging presentations. Leo, conscious of the potential offered by the new mediums of radio, worked hard at public speaking. On-air and on the electoral hustings, in the latter particularly when confronted by hecklers, Leo's strategy of addressing the audience directly was very effective.[8] In the same mode, the beginning of John's first broadcast could easily have come from his father's rhetorical armory. He said, "Listeners will wonder what an Englishman is doing on German radio tonight. You can imagine that before taking this step I hoped that someone better qualified than me would come forward."[9] There are many examples where father and son approached similar topics, though with a different slant. In Italian to Italian listeners, Leo spoke on the BBC about why Britain had declared war, while John, over Radio Milan, expounded on the wrong-headedness of Churchill's war strategy. Or, on March 17, 1941, speaking in Serbo-Croatian in a BBC shortwave transmission to Yugoslavia, Leo urged the population to stand firm against Germany. In a tone personal and direct, he said, "I speak to you as an English Minister, but not, I hope, altogether as a stranger. It is more than forty years since I first wandered through your beautiful Yugoslav lands." John, over Belgrade radio in November 1943, urged Yugoslavs to remain on the side of the "revolutionary Germany of Adolf Hitler," explaining that "the ties between my family and Serbia date back far into the past" and at his father's knee he had heard "stories about the days of Serbia's liberation from the Ottoman Empire."[10]

Without doubt, in all John's interviews, the question of his father hovered in the background. As part of the campaign to publicize the first series of radio talks, a German journalist interviewed John in Berlin, painting a picture of a young man intrepid in pursuit of his ideals, but also a regular fellow "with his pet dog Sammy curled under the chair." Amery explained that he had become an "anti-Semite at Harrow" and had seen what communism meant firsthand in the Spanish civil war. In answer to the inevitable question of what his father might think of his political activities, Amery stated that "you cannot expect an old man and a Right Honorable to be able to break out of the old rut." Despite this, he had just received a "cordial letter" from Leo and was able to maintain good contact with his family through the efforts of his "godfather, the British Ambassador in Madrid." (Amery's godfather in fact was Sir John Simon.)[11]

In much the way his father monitored the potential electoral impact of his public utterances, John kept tally of the responses to his talks as he travelled through Europe.[12] For example, Yugoslavia had been a success with "fifteen hundred people at the university to listen" and news of his visit and speeches "held the headlines on all columns of the front pages of all the Serbian papers for four days." John "left Norway in a storm of applause" because he had given "heart and courage to the Quisling Party." As an "Englishman of a well-born family" he had been able to "bring to our side many neutral persons among the ship owners and herring kings" and Quisling himself had presented Amery's partner with a "superb silver fox." In Belgium, where he spoke in person and over the radio in English for the Flemish population and in French for the Walloons, there was an audience of seventeen hundred in Antwerp, a thousand in Ghent, seven hundred in Liege and over twenty-five hundred in Brussels and the "press gave a good reception." As well his book was sold out. In Prague he spoke to members of the Czech elite including seventy representatives of the local press and made "good contacts for future newspaper articles." Overall he assessed that in the effect of his communications, the "credit of [his] name, position and [his] family" carried more weight when he spoke to Europeans in Europe than when he spoke to Englishmen in England.

The Amery Family Listen in London

In London, the day before the first broadcast, Leo received "unpleasant news" from an American wire service reporter that John was in Berlin. The next evening, November 19, at 8.30 P.M., Leo and Bryddie faced the "miserable ordeal" of listening to the transmission over German shortwave. The parents were "stunned." They were convinced that it was neither their son's voice nor his manner of speaking. Julian, who listened to the repeat broadcast at midnight, agreed that it did not sound at all like Jack, but more like a professional broadcaster.[13] Leo, writing to Hoare in Madrid about "this sorry business," stated that he held the "gravest doubts that it was Jack who delivered the speech."[14] He repeated his suspicion to Churchill.[15] Florence wrote to John's friend in Lisbon, noting that it was not her son's voice, and confessing that she was worried that "heaven alone could know to what use his father's honored name will be put."[16] Again to Hoare, Amery confessed that the family was "distressed" that the "Germans have got hold of my son whether by cajolery or intimidation."[17] Lord Beaverbrook, having listened carefully to one of the Berlin transmissions, opined that it had been "done under some form of duress."[18] When a journalist from the *Daily Mail* buttonholed Amery about what his son was doing in the German capital, adding that young Amery had an "unfortunate and much-to-be pitied father," Leo explained that John was an "invalid" and it was "just possible that he asked to go there for treatment of his lung trouble."[19] In general, people in England were very kind. Leo, noting that several colleagues in the House went out of their way to greet him warmly, was grateful for the attention of good friends during the "recent trouble."[20]

What John said in the broadcasts undoubtedly embarrassed the family. His father dismissed it as the "ordinary anti-Semitic tripe that is poured out by German propaganda headquarters, and by Mosley."[21] It may be true, as W. D. Rubinstein has argued, that Leo Amery's own Jewishness added weight to the burden that the broadcasts brought.[22] Certainly Amery *père* was an important public figure in Britain arguing the case for a Jewish homeland in Palestine, and therefore would be chagrined at the filial affront. However, the evidence suggests no more than that. To have a son visibly and actively working against the Allied war effort was pain enough. In Leo words "there was nothing to be done but to shut one's mind to the degradation of it all and steel oneself to going on as if he never existed."[23] In mid January 1943, the Amerys made new wills in favor of Julian as sole beneficiary.[24] In John's absence, the younger son became the apple of the parents' eye. And with good reason. They took pride in Julian's successes in British intelligence and as a courageous member of the S.O.E.[25] Indeed the younger brother was in the mountains of Albania liaising with the resistance at the same time that the older brother was consorting with the Ustashi in Belgrade.

Leo's dearest hope had always been that father and son would be in the Commons together. The prospect was improved when the Conservative Party sought out Julian among young men with war service as a candidate in the first peacetime elections. And even more promising, the Preston electoral committee invited Julian and Randolph Churchill to stand together on the Conservative ticket. The poll was slated for early July 1945. In April, when John was captured in Italy, his father's first thought was for the effect it would have on Julian's campaign. Leo made a tentative approach to see if there was "any chance" that the "wretched Jack might be tried out in Italy." When it was not, he hoped for a quick election before the trial.[26] There were some rumblings among the Conservative Party members that Julian's brother might hurt Tory chances, but in the event, Leo was glad to note that only once on the hustings when a reference was made to Jack's fate it had "produced a storm of disapproval."[27] In the overall swing to Labour, "the terrible twins," as the press called Amery and Churchill, were defeated, but made a very creditable showing.

Under the MI5 code name "Warble 869," John was brought back and arraigned in London on July 7, 1945 at the Bow Street Magistrate's Court. Leo engaged J. E. Lickford and Sons who retained G. O. Slade as senior counsel. The legal team conferred with Julian, Leo and Mrs Amery about John's defense. The original idea, that John simply should plead an obsession with communism, was set aside when John raised the fact that he had acquired Spanish nationality during the Spanish civil war. This became the defense strategy though it was a curious decision because Slade already had had indications that this defense would fail, as indeed it did, when he pursued it in William Joyce's trial.[28]

Julian Amery was untiring in his efforts for John. If he had found distasteful his older brother's activities during the war, or resented the awkward situation in which they had placed him and the family, it was not evident in any flagging in commitment to Jack's case. Julian worked closely with the legal team, nutting out defense strategies, visiting his brother in prison and writing long minutes based on notes from their discussions. In early October, Julian travelled to Spain chasing what turned out to be the red herring that Jack had become a Spaniard. The Duke of Alba, Franco's Ambassador in London, promised the Amerys that he would "do what he could to make people produce the documents." In letters to colleagues in Spain soliciting their assistance, he described Leo as a "conservative commentator and a long-time friend of Franco's Spain."[29] In Madrid, Ramón Serrano Suñer and senior members of the Falangist Party, never renown for their commitment to the rule of law, signed documents that purported to prove that John had joined the Spanish Foreign Legion and by the end of the civil war had been promoted to the rank of captain. As well, on March 19, 1937, either in Murcia, Saragossa or Burgos, he was supposed to have renounced his British citizenship and his name had been entered in the Municipal Register of the Madrid district of Chamberí in July 1939 which, it was claimed, sealed his Spanish nationality. Julian also brought back evidence that at some time or other his brother had become a lieutenant with the Italian Blackshirts in Spain and as a consequence had been decorated for bravery.[30]

The Director of Public Prosecutions, Theobald Mathew, accompanied by MI5's Lieutenant Colonel Cussen and Major Burt, travelled to Madrid in order to ascertain the authenticity of the claims for Amery's Spanish nationality. The Spanish Ministry of Justice, after a request from the British Ambassador to the Spanish Foreign Ministry, provided the legal opinion that even if the municipal registry inscription had taken place as the defense was claiming, it was in itself not sufficient to ensure Spanish citizenship. In any case, MI5 (with meticulous sleuthing through shipping records) had established that John had been onboard a Dutch ship between Lisbon and Genoa in March 1937, including the date on which he was supposed to have renounced his British citizenship. A careful scrutiny of the original legal register in Madrid also indicated that the Spanish judge had added John's entry at the time of Julian's visit to Madrid. Faced with the evidence that there had been "considerable skullduggery" among the judges responsible for the "bogus entries" and that Serrano Suñer was "implicated," the Department of Public Prosecutions in London indicated that they would "air in court the very strong presumptive evidence that the entries were procured for the defense by fraud." Unbeknownst to the defense, the prosecution also had up its sleeve the receipts for the payment of John's allowance in Nice in the early 1940s on each of which he had sworn to his British citizenship when he had collected funds.[31]

Apprised of the core facts of the prosecution, Amery's defense team changed tack. It was decided that John should plead guilty. It saved the embarrassment of a drawn-out trial with evidence from the thirteen sworn witnesses giving the prosecution the opportunity to comb through Jack's nefarious doings in Occupied Europe. And there would be no opportunity for the Spanish lawyers, whom the prosecution had already brought to London, to reveal Julian's involvement with the disreputable crowd of fascists and Nazi exiles in Madrid.

The trial on November 28, 1945 lasted less than ten minutes. Before a packed courtroom, when John was asked how he responded to the charge that "Between 22 June 1941 and 25 April 1945, while owing allegiance to His Majesty the King of England, he had adhered to the King's enemies in parts of the Continent controlled by the King's enemies," he replied that he was guilty. The efforts of the family to invoke a pardon based on insanity, as we have already seen, were unsuccessful. Their only consequence was to leave to posterity a cache of carefully constructed documents that attested to John's "moral abnormality."

When Jack was first brought back to England, Leo had rallied the defense team, but had been unwilling, himself, to meet his son face-to-face. He noted in his diary that the whole business was "terribly hard on B" though for himself he had "long since lost any feeling on the matter."[32] When the Tories were defeated in the elections in July 1945 and Amery had gone to Buckingham Palace to hand over the seals of office, the king had "murmured a few words of sympathy" about the Amery's "more domestic troubles." And in Churchill's retiring list of honors in standing down as prime minister he recommended Florence for the Order of the Crown of India, a distinction rarely given to a woman other than a queen consort or the wife of a viceroy.[33] When she was awarded her honor, in November 1945, she "took her courage in her hands" to speak about her wayward son to the kindly king.[34]

Florence Amery's devotion to her son never flagged. The first to see John on the afternoon after he arrived, Florence was overwhelmed with gratitude that her son, "quiet and affectionate" had been returned to her. It is worth noting though that Una Wing, who also had been admitted to see her husband, from whom she was not divorced, reported that he was "almost insane" and seemed to be "completely caught up in the Nazi-fascist mania" and quite "incapable of realizing that Nazism and communism are the same thing."[35] Often accompanied by her sister, Sadie Rodney, Florence visited her son in prison as often as possible. She worried about his pallor and his emaciated state, which she took as proof of serious illness. Her support, also, was highly practical. The day John returned to London, the housekeeper was instructed to gather up a parcel of clothes and deliver them to Scotland Yard for him to wear for his first court appearance. The family and Lickford had been perturbed by John's intention to be arraigned in black shirt, jodhpurs and high black boots.[36] She also wrote letters to everyone she could think of who possibly could assist. When Viscount Fitzalan, who had been a member of Leo's committee to raise volunteers for Finland, sent sympathy, she urged him to write to Chuter Ede and explain that her son was "brave and utterly sincere," and that his illness had kept him in France and stopped him joining Fitzalan and Leo's Finnish legion.[37] To Beaverbrook she wrote sweetly asking that he correct a comment made in the *Sunday Express* that she and Leo had not been regular visitors to Wandsworth in case it might "count against John." And after her son's execution, she again begged Beaverbrook to use the photograph of John she had enclosed instead of the "dreadful untrue photograph" taken just after his arrest in Milan, and in which he appeared ill and disreputable.[38] Above all, Mrs Amery peppered the Labour Home Secretary, Chuter Ede, with requests to give her son another chance. She explained that he had been "so ill in the beginning" and had had to "struggle with weakness and hunger to defend his anti-communist convictions." And she asked for "mercy in his judgment" and that he remember her husband's "years of service to the Empire." Her tone became more beseeching as the date of execution drew closer.

Mrs Amery also sent warm telegrams to Michelle Thomas, still interned in Italy. It was probably through the mother's persistence that arrangements were made to bring John's de facto by military plane to London on December 13 so that he could bid her farewell.[39] The distressed family took the young French woman to their heart. Conversations at home and at Wandsworth henceforth were in French, and in Leo's words, the Amerys found Thomas "warm-hearted and sweet."

Leo and his son were reconciled in the fortnight before the execution. Until then the father had "not felt able" to see the son who had "made us all suffer so terribly." At their first meeting after more than five years they talked about the "big political issues," public affairs and international events. Leo was impressed by Jack's sagacity, noting that his son was "no longer a playboy" but had grown into a "real man." Leo noted that there was a side to his son's character that he was sure would have impressed the Germans and made him a convincing lecturer. He was also moved by the "touching devotion" between his son and his "little French wife." At the same time Leo saw the "cheery naturalness" of the "old Jack" who could never realize that he had done anything wrong and therefore was never burdened by the "shadow of remorse." At subsequent visits, father and son spoke about international leaders with whom both were acquainted, like Subhas Chandra Bose and Mussolini. In relation to the latter, Jack passed on Mussolini's "kind words" that if only Leo had been "Foreign Secretary a rational peace might have been possible." The father agreed that even if Mussolini "went under" it was certain that "fascism was bound to come again possibly under another name."[40] Sadly, Leo noted too that "these petty traitors, [like his son] whether sincerely misguided or just out for the comfort or the money, hardly seem deserving of the same fate as those who butchered or tortured to death millions."[41]

According to Leo, the final gathering at Wandsworth where Mrs Amery, her sister Sadie Rodney, Leo, Julian and Michelle Thomas had their "last glimpse of Jack" was "full of charm, gaiety, whimsical humor and philosophical detachment." Speaking in French, John gave instructions to Michelle to write about her experiences and asked Julian to assist in the enterprise. In a tender letter to "Micky," Jeanine Barde's daughter, John described her mother's courage and encouraged the child to turn to Thomas for care and advice in the future. John also charmed the visitors with his observations about national cultures and international relations. In prison he had come to see the similarities between Britain and Germany, which were "cleanliness, good treatment but inflexible regulations," but that for himself he was more comfortable with "Latin slovenliness" and a "sense of the easy-going." He confessed that at heart and for whatever reason he "only felt at home when he crossed the Channel." Perhaps in deference to his father's industry and sensibilities, before the family left John declared that he had "done his work" which he hoped eventually would be recognized. As they each said their final goodbyes and Leo praised the courage with which Jack faced death, he was heartened by Jack's reply: "But I am your son."[42]

In prison, Amery changed the terms of his will. In May 1943 in Paris, he had named Jeanine Barde his beneficiary and Werner Plack the executor. In the new version, Thomas became the beneficiary and Julian the executor. Jack also requested that there be no religious service after his death and that his body be cremated and the ashes returned to the Bergerac cemetery where Jeanine Barde lay.[43]

Very late in the evening before the fateful morning, Julian with Michelle took Sadie's car and drove down to Wandsworth to spend the night, near Jack, outside the jail. As a mark of respect for his brother, though perhaps a curious one given that they had been on opposing sides during the war, Julian wore his military uniform. The Amery parents rose early on December 19 and gathered with the servants upstairs in Florence and Leo's apartment. Leo read a few verses from Corinthians in the Bible, and together they said the *Lord's Prayer* and then "waited in silence" until nine o'clock had passed.[44]

Leo and Florence Amery photographed by Cecil Beaton in the study of their home at 112 Eaton Square in November 1943. Courtesy of The Cecil Beaton Studio Archive, Sotheby's Picture Library.

John Amery addresses a pro-German rally in Antwerp, April 1944. Courtesy of The United Kingdom Public Record Office, Kew.

John Amery with Michelle Thomas on a lecture tour in Antwerp in April 1944. Courtesy of The United Kingdom Public Record Office, Kew.

John Amery taking tea in Antwerp in April 1944 with German officers and members of the pro-Nazi Flemish nationalist movement the Vlaams National Verbond. Courtesy of The United Kingdom Public Record Office, Kew.

Mrs. Cousens driving Charles Cousens home after a day in court in Sydney, July 1946. Pic. News Ltd / historical / GAL. Courtesy of The Newspix Collection, News Limited, Sydney, Australia.

Charles Cousens at the time of his trial in Sydney in July 1946. Pic. News Ltd / historical / GAL. Courtesy of The Newspix Collection, News Limited, Sydney, Australia.

Iva Toguri taken outside Radio Tokyo in December 1945.
Courtesy of The U.S. National Archives and Records Administration, San Bruno.

Iva Toguri faces the American press corps at the Bund Hotel in Yokohama in September 1945. Courtesy of The U.S. National Archives and Records Administration, College Park.

PART II

Broadcasting to Australia and the United States from Wartime Tokyo

CHAPTER 6

Japanese Wartime Broadcasting

The Japanese government was firmly convinced that political propaganda, what in local terminology was called "winning the thought wars," would help clinch military victory. And of all the available mediums, radio possessed the greatest potential. Carefully chosen programs would showcase the imperial enterprise while promoting Japanese cultural hegemony in the captured regions.[1] As a consequence, during World War Two, the Japanese government sank considerable energy and resources into building a shortwave service that came to occupy a large band of the shortwave radio beamed into Asia and the Pacific. A great many English speakers were needed to sustain such an operation and in order to do so the Japanese military made use of prisoners of war with previous experience in radio. Japan's expanding overseas network also provided employment for English speakers of Nippon descent who were stranded in Japan during the war.

There were many shortwave services competing for the listener's attention across Asia and the Pacific. By 1940, Deutsch Radio transmitted to South Asia and Australasia on a powerful wattage.[2] In Shanghai, there were three Axis radio stations; a German outfit had been set up in 1933, as soon as the Nazis took over. It broadcast in German, English and French as well as in a number of Asian languages. Italy and Vichy France both ran radio stations from their Shanghai legations. These three broadcasters, however, paid little attention to the war in the Pacific, favoring instead an upbeat stream of news chronicling Axes successes in Europe.[3] The Allies, too, had raised the volume and the wartime coverage. The BBC Empire Service, Radio Australia and Radio New Zealand transmitted full throttle, as did the American programs emanating from San Francisco. The Voice of America broadcast loud and clear, from February 1942, later to be joined by American Armed Forces Radio targeting American soldiers on the front line.

The Japan Broadcasting Corporation, known as NHK (Nippon Hoso Kyokai), had begun transmitting overseas on shortwave in 1935. The news programs came from Domei Tsushin Sha, the new Japanese agency that had been created in early

1936 to break Reuters' traditional hold over news from the Far East. NHK set about providing news and current affairs from a Japanese perspective. Created by private shareholders, NHK functioned always under strict government control that was exercised through the Ministry of Communications.[4] Some of its earliest shortwave programs, in English and Japanese, were beamed to Hawaii and the West Coast of America to listeners who predominantly were Issei and Nisei, that is, first- and second-generation Japanese who were permanently settled in the United States. In a surprisingly short time, Japanese broadcasting had expanded along a finely tuned net which stretched to the outer reaches of the areas of Japan's influence. In the flowery rhetoric of the Empire, it was on the way to bring the "eight corners of the Japanese world under one roof."

When the Imperial Army invaded Manchuria in 1937, broadcasts to and from Munchuko were stepped up, with new programs directed at Thailand, French Indo-China, the Dutch East Indies and the Philippines. After Pearl Harbor, Japanese overseas broadcasts on shortwave were expanded to ten transmissions in sixteen languages, twenty-four hours each day. In early 1942, programs to Italy and Germany were added, and by the end of 1943 shortwave was transmitted to Papua, New Guinea and Australia.

In the first months of war, as increasing amounts of territory fell to Nippon, it seemed that the Japanese army was unbeatable. Guam, Wake Island and Hong Kong surrendered in December 1941. By the end of February 1942, Australian and British troops had been defeated in Malaya and thirty thousand fighting men herded into the prisoner of war camp on the Changi Peninsula. By May, the Dutch East Indies had fallen and, by the end of the month, the one-hundred-and-seventy-thousand-strong American army was routed in the Philippines with many taken into captivity. As troops of the victorious Japanese army spread out across the Pacific and Southeast Asia into what Japan described as the Greater East Asia Co-Prosperity Zone, NHK went with them. Japanese engineers took over captured radio stations and repaired existing transmitters and buildings damaged in the fighting. As well, and with all speed, new studios, substations and relay equipment were erected to carry forward the voice of Nippon into the conquered territories. By 1944, Radio Tokyo was transmitting more than thirty-five hours of programming a day in twenty languages. There were also innumerable Nippon outstations relaying Tokyo programs and transmitting their own local productions.

Radio Tokyo, located in Broadcast House in the centre of the capital, was the nerve center of broadcasting operations. Three transmitters were located on the Japanese mainland, at Nazaki, Yamata and Kawachi. In the occupied territories throughout South and East Asia, a plethora of local stations were controlled by the Japanese forces and made programs to be transmitted to the immediate surroundings through a series of Japanese quisling stations and broadcasting services.[5] To take an example, in 1944, NHK in Tokyo transmitted programs to Formosa, where the Taiwan Broadcasting Corporation broadcast some locally and relayed others on shortwave to the Philippines, Malaya, the Dutch East Indies and

Singapore. The Korean Broadcasting Corporation transmitted throughout Korea in the Korean language and in Japanese. In China, the Manchurian Telegraph and Telephone Service Company transmitted in Japanese, Mandarin, Cantonese and five other languages and was in close contact with German and Italian radio corporations. Also, North China Broadcasting organization emitted programs in Japanese and Chinese from Beijing and from Nanking. In Manila and Hong Kong, the main stations received Tokyo broadcasts as well as producing some of their own programs, which, in turn, were relayed in Japanese, English and Spanish to their hinterlands. Saigon received and transmitted by short and medium wave from Tokyo to India, Burma and Australia. In Singapore, the Japanese built a five-hundred-watt shortwave station in March 1942 and subsequently six more were set up on the Malay Peninsula that eventually were broadcasting in seven languages. When the Singapore signal was strengthened, at the end of 1943, it had the capacity to transmit in a broad sweep through India, Burma, Chunking, Australia and the Pacific islands, and as far a field as North and South America, for the latter using both Japanese and Spanish as well as English. There were also transmitters, stations and relay towers in the Celebes, Borneo, Rangoon, Jakarta and Bandung, which, with the high power capacity added in January 1943, drew listeners in India, Australia and North America.[6] From the first successful flush of quick victories, however, Japan began to face shortages of qualified broadcasters, especially those with a facility in English or in the local languages.

Japanese mass media was under the control of the Cabinet Information Bureau (CIB) that had been reformed in December 1940. The bureaucracies it spawned would have warmed the heart of Gilbert and Sullivan. The CIB consisted of five divisions and seventeen sections employing five hundred and fifty officials. A group including representatives of each government ministry, newspapers, motion pictures and Japan Broadcasting Corporation oversaw all operations. Those responsible for overseas broadcasting functioned in a labyrinth of competing and countermanding authorities. A committee from the departments of the army, the navy and the foreign and home offices and the divisions of the Greater Asian and the communications departments as well as representatives from NHK and the Domei news agency met every morning under the auspices of officials of foreign affairs to determine the news reports for that day. As the war progressed, overseas broadcasting within NHK expanded greatly and by mid-1942 overseas operations were restructured into four sections that represented the various areas of overseas activity. The American section was in charge of broadcasting directed at North America and at the Allied soldiers at the front, as well as handling anything dealing with prisoners of war. The programs discussed below, which used prisoners of war as broadcasters, fell under the purview of the American section.

There were other competing players in the field with an input into Japan Broadcasting or they controlled alternative, and often conflicting, operations of their own. The Japanese Imperial Headquarters, the Daihonsei, maintained an active propaganda and information section, as did the information departments of the army and the navy, which, in turn, held separate responsibilities that often were in competition with each other. For example, the Navy Information Department oversaw the planning and execution of military propaganda; the army did likewise, but in a different carve-up in which its Information Department dealt with the actual execution of propaganda.[7] These webs of propaganda and the creation of programs that each spawned produced endless red tape, and it is no surprise that often the outcome was total paralysis.

Censorship was very strict, though its application was erratic given the labyrinthine authority structures. The Ministry of Communications was responsible for the censorship of all overseas broadcasts and kept their transmission under close surveillance. Official censors monitored every program. The radio transmitters for both domestic and overseas stations were equipped with circuit breakers that allowed the censor to interrupt transmission within a split second. In the case of the overseas section, a direct phone line linked the Ministry of Communications with the studios at Broadcast House, so that, on hearing an offending statement, a Ministry official could telephone to have the transmission shut down. The secret military security police, the *kempetai Seguradai*, were active also in rooting out infringements of censorship. Those suspected of violating the rules faced swift and often arbitrary punishment.[8]

The General Staff, Eighth Section, of the Japanese Imperial Army was responsible for the important parts of overseas broadcasting administration. Every foreigner involved in broadcasting was kept under surveillance and the *kempetai* kept a close eye on the several hundred Nisei, mostly American and Canadian-born, who monitored foreign news broadcasts. As the war progressed, the Japanese army took over more and more aspects of Japanese life and the military department that was responsible for "psychological warfare" expanded along with the powers of the security service.

To begin with, the Japan Broadcasting Corporation had seen its mission as providing serious programs. The initial Japanese broadcasting charter emphasized the need to foster the true spirit of the Japanese nation. At Radio Tokyo, in the early days, serious talks and formal lectures were the norm. When there was music, it was invariably Japanese folk songs or classical performances. Before the war what was seen as the formal mode of presentation, used on the BBC, was much admired. Entertainment of the sort favored by commercial broadcasters in the West, particularly the United States, was eschewed. Jazz and "sensual music" were specifically prohibited in both domestic and overseas broadcasts. Once the Japanese army became dominant in the Imperial administration and the winning of the war took overriding priority, there was a shift in attitude towards broadcasting. Because victory in the "radio war" was perceived as integral to military victory, Army representatives increasingly urged the Japan Broadcasting Corporation to adopt a more "westernized" mode of presentation because it would draw greater numbers of overseas listeners to tune in to Japanese programs.

There were also calls to smarten up the announcers so that their on-air presentations would be more engaging. As early as July 1940, two NHK senior staffers had pointed to the drawbacks of the stiff style of Japanese broadcasters. Sent on a radio reconnoiter through Australia, New Zealand and the South Pacific, the NHK managers noted that among the shortwave listeners they met, the BBC Empire Service was preferred.[9] Its reception was better, and its content and presentation more appealing. Similarly, a fact-finding tour to the West Coast of the United States and Canada, in March 1941, brought back criticisms of the stuffy Japanese on-air manners. Among the generations of Japanese origin, the reporters found a large audience for Radio Tokyo, but one that would appeal to even more listeners if Japanese announcers could improvise on-air in the informal manner of American presenters. North American listeners also criticized the awkward and heavily accented English of Radio Tokyo announcers.[10] John Morris, an English resident in Tokyo who always listened to Nippon radio, recalled that the microphone techniques of Japanese broadcasters left much to be desired. Nearly every talk "opened with a burst of thunder" as the announcer cleared his throat on-air prior to beginning to speak. Frequently, too, the crackle of "pages being turned," bouts of coughing or the noise of the studio next door "warming up" interrupted broadcasts.[11]

There was a widespread belief among Japan's military and broadcasting circles that the key to attracting non-Asian listeners was modern American dance music. Information about Allied prisoners of war, later to provide such listening bait for POW families at home, was introduced on-air in 1942. Originally and indeed throughout the history of Japan's shortwave broadcasts in World War Two, it was understood that American music was what Anglo-Saxon listeners—civilians and soldiers—wished to hear when they tuned in to shortwave. American music enjoyed great cachet in Japan in the 1930s, especially among the young avant-garde. In the Tokyo teashops catering to students, American jazz and swing was played with the volume at full blast. Even after western music was officially banned, it continued to be played in many student haunts because it was known that few in the *kempetai* could distinguish Duke Ellington from Wagner.[12] In early 1942, Radio Tokyo attempted to modernize itself by commissioning "The New Order Rhythm Orchestra" and "The Japanese Swing Singers." These instrumental groups performed live on-air, but the music was not always recognizable as swing or jazz. The frequently played "Nihonbashi in the Edo Period," for example, simply grafted a modern beat onto traditional melody and lyrics. Others, such as "The Japanese Sandman," were awkward adaptations of well-known American pieces.

Foreign Broadcasters on Japanese Radio

From very early in the war, Japan faced a shortage of qualified broadcasters, especially those who were native English speakers. And as the networks expanded, the demand for English speakers became even more pressing. In Tokyo alone, staff with a capacity in English was needed at Domei, at Imperial Army headquarters, at the Nippon Board of Information and at the Japan Foreign Office. In all these places, foreign wire service news was first transcribed into English before being translated into Japanese for distribution. The stations and relays in the areas of Japanese occupation required similar English-language services. In many parts of Southeast Asia, English was already established as the second language and remained so despite Japan's best efforts to promote intensive Japanese language teaching. Japanese is difficult to learn and very few Japanese were fluent in other Asian languages, therefore those running the outrigger radio stations used English as the language of communication.

From the first days, Radio Batavia in Indonesia drafted-in English-speaking prisoners of war and locals who had English as a second language. Many regular Indonesian radio staff, on what previously had been a Dutch network, were favorably disposed towards Radio Tokyo staff, arriving with the Japanese army, because it was believed that Japan would bring liberation from Dutch colonialism. By and large, Indonesian radio personnel were quickly disabused of such ideas. However, Radio Batavia retained a degree of independence from Tokyo in certain areas of broadcasting, and in turn Tokyo came to adopt Batavia's strategy of deploying announcers from among the community of captive English speakers.

Initially, Japan Broadcasting tried, though without success, to attract broadcasters from the English-speaking foreigners living in Japan. The tactics of recruitment varied. John Morris, Cambridge-educated and employed as an English lecturer at Keio University and in the Japanese Foreign Office, was "very affably" approached about becoming a broadcaster. When he refused on the grounds that he did not wish to become "Japan's Lord Haw Haw," he was able to leave Japan unmolested.[13]

By contrast, many western journalists in Tokyo received abrasive proof of Japan's interest in them as potential English-speaking broadcasters. Immediately after Pearl Harbor, foreign reporters in Japan were interned, the majority being held incommunicado in the Sugamo Prison where some faced rough handling by Japanese officials. The American correspondent for the *New York Times*, Otto D. Tolischus, who had been expelled from Berlin as an anti-Nazi, spent several months in Sugamo Prison and was savagely beaten by a team of interrogators, one of whom spoke "fluent Americanese."[14] In August 1942, foreign journalists were included in a prisoner exchange for Japanese diplomats in the United States. A couple of days before departure, the journalists were taken from detention to the Sunno Hotel in downtown Tokyo for what was billed as a farewell luncheon. After nice food and cordial speeches, the military head of Japanese propaganda, Lieutenant Colonel Tsuneishi, asked the correspondents to broadcast a greeting to their families at home. Most declined. Each then was asked to write a story about their experiences in Japan for distribution to the foreign media. When the group again refused, individuals were taken under guard into separate rooms, where a typewriter and table had been set up, and were ordered to write five pages in English about the war and Japan. Those who were reluctant were roughed up by guards. In the hotel lobby before a crowd of gaping Japanese guests the Associated Press correspondent had his teeth smashed by a powerful punch to the jaw.[15] Facing the possibility of being denied permission to leave Japan, all the correspondents produced the required pages, some taking heart by writing in a facetious manner that would not escape anyone familiar with idiomatic English.[16]

In the end, the main source of English broadcasters for Japanese overseas radio came from the overflowing numbers of captured Allied soldiers crammed into swollen prisoner of war camps across Japan and East Asia. It is perhaps curious that the Japanese broadcasting service would choose to use prisoners of war as announcers when there were so many native, English-speaking Japanese Americans—that is the Nisei—already in Tokyo. In fact, a good deal of use was made of English-speaking North Americans of Japanese descent particularly as clerks and transcribers. For example in 1942, within NHK, the overseas broadcasting section employed around one hundred American-born Japanese as typists, clerks and transcribers. The Overseas Monitoring Centre used a further two hundred Nisei as transcribers of the English broadcasts that were monitored around the clock. As well, the news service, Domei, used Nisei transcribers and clerks. Overall, though, prominent in program production and as announcers over the airwaves were the Allied prisoners of war.

NHK's preference for foreign POWs over North Americans of Japanese descent was a consequence of several factors. It reflected the common Japanese disdain for foreign-born Japanese, who were seen as poor relations, uncultured and without education. It is likely, too, that the Japanese military had learned from the British example in World War One.[17] In that conflict, Britain, seen to have won the propaganda war, employed a strategy of using broadcasts by German prisoners in English prisoner of war camps. These POWs were given food and extra comforts in order to encourage them to send word to their German families about the kind treatment they were receiving at the hands of the British. Early in the Pacific war, the Japanese went to great lengths to collect stories from captured Allied servicemen to document that the Japanese were benevolent masters. And as we will see, the Imperial army reasoned, correctly, that POW families were ready listeners to any information that was broadcast about their captive men folk.

At the end of November 1941, a lieutenant colonel in the Imperial army, Shigetsugu Tsuneishi, was put in charge of Japanese Psychological Warfare.[18] A graduate of Tokyo Military Academy, he had little previous experience of propaganda or broadcasting. Indeed, Tsuneishi's first foray into the subtle world of indoctrination was to order a set of leaflets to be dropped on American soldiers in the Philippines that carried images of busty blondes in diaphanous gowns that were supposed to make the recipients pine for what they were missing at home. According to reports, the GIs who picked them up were highly amused.

In the area of broadcasting, Tsuneishi's main project was to expand the short-wave radio network in order to attract western listeners. Their attention, once caught, could be redirected to Japanese propaganda. The draw-card in the new operation was to be revamped programs of modern American music: foot-tapping jazz and the languorous notes of popular dance music and with English-speaking announcers using the most engaging and up-to-date presentations. Tsuneishi sent word to Imperial army commanders across the Pacific that they should comb the camps and pens in which the captured enemy were being held in search of Allied prisoners who had previous broadcasting experience in the fields of music or entertainment and even anyone who was identified as possessing a "good voice." Interrogators were also asked to keep a lookout for individuals among the enemy who were "anti-war or anti-Roosevelt" as they too could be useful in some way or another for broadcasting propaganda overseas.[19]

The selection process that the Australian prisoner John "Tim" Dooley followed from Burma railway laborer to Radio Tokyo announcer is fairly typical.[20] Dooley, forty-three years of age in 1943, had been a secondary school teacher in the inner Sydney suburb of Redfern and had enlisted in the Australian Imperial Force in a transport unit. After the British surrender, he had been in Changi and then sent with "D" Force to Thailand in a labor team to build the Thai-Burma railway. In February 1944, Dooley and nineteen fellow prisoners were informed that they had been chosen to audition for the Japanese radio and if successful there would be an opportunity to send a message back to their families in Australia. In the camp, an ex-announcer for Radio Normandy offered training, fashioning a dummy microphone from wood with which each practiced making a broadcast from a makeshift stage. From the initial group, the final broadcast party was reduced to six. All, with one exception, were well-educated and had good speaking voices. Major Francis Page-Goulay was named leader. A member of the London Stock Exchange and apparently well off, he struck Dooley as "very aristocratic." When asked his address, for example, he gave the name of the Bath Club in London. Another of the six was an Indian teacher at one of that country's best colleges, who spoke a number of languages as well as several Indian dialects. Dooley spoke German as did another Australian, Hal Hart, who had been educated at the University of Sydney. There was an Englishman with a degree in chemistry as well. The odd man out was a Gordon Highlander, a regular soldier with little education and a Scottish accent so broad that no one could understand anything he said. He had given his occupation as "scholar," meaning "student," which probably was the reason he had been singled out.

Other prisoners in the Thai camp gave the six putative broadcasters a great sheaf of messages to read to the families at home if there was an opportunity. They were taken first to Bangkok and interviewed by Japanese filmmakers and broadcasters and then sent to Singapore where they spent a few weeks locked up in the Cathay Building where Japan Broadcasting had set up a radio station. Here, they were paraded before a press conference of Japanese journalists from *Nippon Times*, *Asahi News* and Domei, who asked questions about the progress of the Japanese railway to Burma. According to Dooley, the journalists were taken aback at the stories of the deaths and cruel hardships that prisoners were facing in that hellish place. While in Singapore, the Japanese broadcasting staff played the prisoners a recording of a British and Australian concert party in Changi that had been sent out on shortwave along with a brace of Changi POWs reading letters home. Dooley and his comrades made a program about the Burma railway, cobbling as many prisoners' names as they could in to a rambling narrative, the

Japanese having refused to allow a straight reading of a list of names. Dooley himself sent a message home, framing the greeting in the form of a joke so that anyone hearing the message would realize that what he had said about his wellbeing in captivity was risible.

After the Singapore sojourn the men were put on a train and sent back to the camp in Thailand. Dooley was surprised when a few days later he was called out and told he was being sent to Tokyo. Again, when word went around the camp that he would be making further broadcasts, a great many prisoners gave him messages in the hope that he could send them home. Put on a plane in Bangkok, he made the flight to Tokyo in a series of hops that took in Saigon, Hong Kong and Formosa.

The steps that the Japanese American Frank "Foo" Fujita took prior to his becoming a radio broadcaster were not so easy. As an American with Asian looks and a Japanese name, he constantly attracted the attention of his captors. Fujita's father had been born near the port of Nagasaki and had left in 1914 for the United States, where he worked across Texas in a series of jobs, eventually marrying a woman from Oklahoma. A patriot, firmly committed to the United States, though not permitted to take out citizenship, Fujita senior raised his children to speak only English and to hold the United States dear in their hearts. "Foo" joined the Texas National Guard as soon as he was of age and immediately after Pearl Harbor was drafted for the Pacific, sent with the first American units to land in Australia in World War Two. Stationed during Christmas 1941 outside Brisbane, the capital of the northern state of Queensland, the Texan drank a lot of beer and let off steam slogging it out in fistfights with Australian servicemen bivouacked nearby. As Americans, they were horrified at the Antipodean diet—meals of "link sausages, foul-tasting coffee and very bitter marmalade"—and when Christmas dinner of roast mutton and hot tea was served, the whole unit rioted.[21] They were shipped out to east Java where they were captured by the Japanese and eventually arrived in Changi. In Singapore, probably, Fujita's most outstanding achievement was to kill, cook and eat the canine mascot of the British regiment whose officers were camped beside the hungry Texans. From Changi, he was sent to a "horror camp" in Japan that provided slave prisoner labor to the shipbuilding industry.

Fujita's obvious Japanese looks constantly caused problems. There was a brief period during which he was taken out of the POW mainstream by a prison commander, determined to restore a lost son to Nippon. Unnerved even more by this prospect than by his fate as a prisoner, Fujita played dumb to all efforts at Japanese language instruction. Much more commonly, however, Fujita attracted negative attention and suffered terrible beatings—one while in Nagasaki left him with a lifelong disability. After a succession of camp assignments, he was picked out as suitable to join the broadcasters in Tokyo.

The majority of the prisoners who were brought to work on Radio Tokyo had been processed through the same funnel. Once identified as potentially useful, they were sent to Omori, the headquarters of the network of POW camps in the Tokyo area. Located just south of the capital, on the western shore of Tokyo Bay, the prison occupied a small island linked to the mainland by a single wooden bridge. In late 1943, an overflowing Omori boasted more than six hundred prisoners, mostly English, who provided work parties for the Japanese docks and nearby industry. The fifty-five potential broadcasters from the trawl across the occupied areas were kept in a separate pen. Each was put through an intensive interview to establish civilian background and skills. A few of them were told that they were being considered as broadcasters and they would receive special privileges if chosen. On the POW grapevine, too, some had heard that Tokyo broadcasters "got the best treatment of all the prisoners."[22]

Most of the selected POWs, however, had no idea why they had been sent to Omori and, even after they had survived the final cut, were no more enlightened. The Australian Kenneth Parkyns and Fujita both recalled that they had an inkling that they had been assessed for a special task, but only discovered what it was after they had been paraded before a senior Japanese officer in Tokyo. As a result of the sweep and the final selection, some thirty prisoners were drafted into broadcast work in Tokyo. There were also prisoners, both civilian internees and captured military personnel, in Indonesia, on Radio Batavia and in the Philippines on Radio Manila. As well, there were English speakers in all of these places who had sought employment as regular members of radio and relay stations producing and transmitting Japanese programs overseas.

Tokyo's Australian Broadcaster Charles Cousens

The first Allied POW to be brought to Japan was Charles Cousens, an Australian serviceman who had been identified in Changi as having been a leading announcer on prewar commercial radio in Australia. He arrived in Tokyo towards the end of July 1942 and made his first broadcast over Radio Tokyo on the last day of that month. Between then and the end of the war, he wrote hundreds of radio scripts and continuity pieces, most of which were read on-air by other broadcasters. During later interrogations and throughout the preliminary hearings in his Sydney treason trial in mid-1946, Cousens maintained that he had no choice as a prisoner of war but to do as his Japanese captors ordered and that, within these constraints, he had tried to send information over the airwaves that would be useful to the Australian military command.

Charles Cousens and Life before the War

Cousens had been born in Poona, India, in 1903 into a British military family. Educated at Wellington School and Sandhurst, he had taken a commission in 1925 with the Sherwood Foresters Regiment in India, where he reached the rank of lieutenant. He was an outstanding cricketer and golfer; he won several prizes in military sporting events and was an amateur boxer of some note. In 1927 he resigned his commission, possibly because he lacked the private funds expected of British officers in those days in order to maintain their lavish lifestyle.[1]

With scarcely a penny to his name, Cousens landed in Sydney sometime in 1928. He immediately found work in pick-up shifts on the wharves and in small-time professional boxing, ultimately securing a position at radio station 2GB selling on-air advertising. Quite soon, probably because of his mellifluous voice, Cousens became an announcer. In 1929 he married Dorothy Allan and fathered a child; after a divorce, he married Grace James in 1938. Their son Robert was born in 1940. Grace Cousens' father, William Dettman, was a wealthy property owner and welcomed the new son-in-law into the family.

Cousens struck many of his acquaintances as the "quintessential Englishman." In Australia this meant that he spoke with a "fruity" British accent and had good manners. In 1942, after his capture by the Japanese, one of his former colleagues, Adele Shelton Smith, wrote a profile of him for the Sydney *Sunday Telegraph* in which she recalled that he was the sort of soldierly figure that Yeats Brown might have written about. Yeats Brown's books, particularly the *Bengal Lancers*, wildly popular among interwar middlebrow readers, chronicled the military adventures of the British army as it upheld the values of Empire at the furthermost corners of the earth. Shelton Smith noted that, as a soldier, Cousens was a "bit of a disciplinarian and very keen about saluting and maintaining appearances."[2]

Certainly, Cousens held strong ideas about correct behavior and dress. There was also a large component of the amateur enthusiast in his persona. An active Christian Scientist, he conscientiously followed Mary Baker Eddy's pronouncements that the power of the self should never be underestimated, and that health and success were a sign of God's approbation. In Cousens, these beliefs were manifest in an enthusiasm and a commitment to whatever enterprise engaged his attention. Another former colleague, J. F. Barnes, who had employed him in the mid-1930s, reported to Australian Military Intelligence before his trial that Cousens was a "man's man" and an "outstanding personality," but with a "butterfly character," by which was meant that he was bluff and gregarious, but his interests and understanding were shallow.[3]

Australia, supposedly, was a land of opportunity, a place where a man could make his mark, and Cousens attempted to recast himself into the sort of person who possessed what he saw as the essential Australian qualities. He called himself "Bill," which he considered a more suitable, knockabout Australian name. After the war, when his younger brother, Tim, arrived from England, Cousens gave him instructions on how to become a full-hearted local. He should "adopt the bush as his muse" and permit no backward looks towards Britain. Suggesting perhaps that he was not fully converted to the bushman's mien, Bill also recommended that his brother's minimum wardrobe should include a dozen pairs of shoes, as many shirts and two very good suits. In the same correspondence Cousens noted that, during his absence at the war, his small son had developed a "foul Australian accent," which his father certainly would have to eradicate.[4]

From the mid-1930s, he ran an extremely popular children's program on 2GB. *Charles Cousens Children's Newspaper* came on-air every weeknight at 6 P.M. The station boasted that it had fifteen thousand young reporters on its books, all of whom had qualified by sending in a piece of their own news writing. In an interview in July 1939 for *Radio Pictorial of Australia*, Cousens explained that the young reporters were encouraged to phone him with potential news items and that, through them, he had been able at times to scoop the newspapers at breaking stories. As well, he ran a series of children's essay competitions on-air, which, he claimed, drew from eight hundred to twelve hundred entries. The topics he set for these essays, perhaps, reveal his own inclinations; certainly he endorsed the children's choices. On the questions of whether Russian ballet or wood-chopping was a better form of entertainment for Australians, and whether in modern life it is the Thinker or the Doer who is more important, Australian children overwhelmingly opted for wood-chopping and doing.

The voice was undoubtedly Charles Cousens' most notable feature. It was the quality that brought him career success on Australian radio and that, equally, when he was a prisoner of war, triggered the attention of the Japanese. A cartoonist in the mid-1930s drew him in evening clothes swaying with a sexily dressed microphone-like partner, describing him as "the honeyed wooer of mistress mike."[5] Cousens himself had lofty ideas about the role of the human voice as the instrument of thought, but in his view, though a good speaking voice was essential, it was "not worth a row of beans without the grey matter behind it."

He had a well-elaborated theory about the mode a radio broadcaster should adopt in order to build a loyal following. The announcer should "aim for a voice that shows fairness, sincerity, a good clean articulation with an absence of an accent." He also judged "temperamental announcers" to be the "best sort." His definition of temperament was not in the sense of "hysterical people, biting their nails and revealing bad manners," but in their being sensitive to subtlety and able to respond instantly. They also must be capable of intense concentration. In his own case he explained that after he had completed his roster on-air, he was "wrung out, emotionally exhausted and craving solitude." The latter he satisfied in extended periods of fishing.

Commercial radio was a new and expanding medium in the 1930s and Cousens took his role as a public announcer very seriously. His ideas are interesting in light of how effectively, later, he carried out the task the Japanese set him of training Japanese announcers. To a reporter seeking the secret of good broadcasting, Cousens revealed his own clear conceptions of how the medium worked and what part was played by the studio announcer. The best were those who appealed to the "emotions of the listener not just their reason." And in an era in which "the public has discovered the entertainment value of news," the announcer must "dramatise his subject matter." Cousens explained his mode of broadcasting as one that relied on constructing a very particular frame of mind. The announcer must mentally place himself in the listener's lounge room, never where the broadcast was being recorded. Those announcers who speak as though they are in the studio, he said, are "utterly useless." Expressions such as "listeners wishing to purchase" should never be used because they break the intimacy between speaker and listener. As an example of the need for subtlety and a quick response—of which many "phlegmatic people" were incapable—he described a situation in which he had been given a "blunt script," in which an advertisement for pills was scheduled between two ten-minute music slots. Because it would be "obscene" to simply announce the advertisement after the sublimeness of the music, Cousens would ignore the copy in front of him and say instead, "Do you mind if I speak to you about your ailments for a minute?" This would make a comfortable transition and retain the listener's attention. Whatever the secret to Cousens' on-air techniques, they were very successful, and his voice came to be associated with advertisements for all kinds of products, from Vincent's APC and Bonnington's Irish Moss to Bundaberg Rum.

In September 1935, Cousens left 2GB for a year to work for an Australian advertising company, Samson Clarke Price-Berry Pty. Ltd. The agency had accepted a commission from a Japanese account to produce a book that would promote Japanese and Australian trade. When it was ultimately published, it included essays on Australian exports, wool and the BHP steel industry. The English editors of the Japanese daily *Osaka Mainichi,* had conceived the idea of this volume to complement an exhibition of Australian goods that was to take place in Tokyo. Kennoske Sato, the editor of the paper's English edition, spent several months in Australia and New Zealand lining up the contributors to the volume and getting to know the local scene. He spoke excellent English and in speeches to several chambers of commerce around Australia, energetically promoted the idea of an expansion of Japanese-Australian trade. Cousens was placed in charge of the account and there exist a number of letters between the Japanese Consul and the advertising company, and to Cousens, dealing with matters to do with this publication and with Sato's business contacts.[6]

Singapore Surrender and Changi Internment

Cousens' military record was straightforward. In July 1940, after an initial rejection based on age, he had enlisted in the Australian Imperial Force (AIF) and, as a captain and adjutant of the 2/19th battalion, was sent to Malaya in January 1941. There he was promoted to company commander, was injured slightly in the Malaya rout and by the time Singapore collapsed in February 1942, he was second in charge of his battalion, carrying the rank of major.

The British Malaya Command's surrender to the Japanese brought administrative chaos and profound psychological shock. British and Australian soldiers considered themselves racially and technically superior to Asian troops. The idea had been sustained by a potent myth—that the power of the British Empire rested on British naval superiority and on an army that was second to none. Australian soldiers also were deeply imbued with the story of Anzac, at the core of which was the belief that Australians might not be given to the ornamental formalities of saluting and marching in step, but once in battle they would stand fast by their mates brave, fearless and never surrendering.[7] The Malaya command had been ramshackle and muddled and the swift defeat showed that notions of an impregnable Singapore as the lynchpin of the Far East defense was a house of cards. It was also abundantly clear that British and Anzac soldiers were as able to be defeated as were the footsloggers of any other nation. The disorientation within the Allied forces was cruelly exacerbated by the knowledge that the defeated army had lost contact with its home headquarters, and that in Britain and Australia military families had no idea what had happened to the men folk.

The psychological shock of swift defeat was manifest in a number of ways. Many of the enlisted men who found themselves, suddenly, to be prisoners of war were "dazed," overcome with "lassitude of the will" and feelings of "stupor."[8] As well, in Singapore, a number of them felt deep resentment towards the British army, which they believed had abandoned Australia's defenses. There was also disillusionment with the imperial mien; the "preposterously spoilt and artificial existence in an outdated atmosphere of Kipling" as one soldier described it.[9] Among Australian soldiers the shock of defeat often brought to the surface an incipient and traditional distrust of commanding officers. These symptoms were real; though they may have been less apparent at first in Singapore where Allied troops were marched into captivity with their formations intact. In Changi, too, the Japanese military initially behaved in a circumspect manner, dealing only with the British and Australian command, leaving them to run their own affairs within the camp compound. Though this remained the structure throughout the war, it came to matter less when the officers were removed to a separate place of detention, Changi becoming the staging post for prisoner labor drafts. In Indonesia, where from the beginning the situation was much more chaotic, Allied soldiers, without clear direction, were left to deal with the captors as best they could. In both places, the Japanese army set about collecting detailed information on every individual soldier taken into captivity. Names, regiments and serial numbers were recorded as well as the details of their previous civilian occupations and the addresses of their families at home. This information would be useful later when the Japanese were actively seeking Allied prisoners with experience in entertainment and radio work that could be drafted into Japan's overseas broadcasting network.

In Changi, almost as soon as the captured troops had been interned, a Japanese mobile sound truck turned up at the gates. The technicians were looking for stories to broadcast about the captured prisoners of war and their good conditions under which the Japanese were holding them. Speaking educated English, the Japanese approached several officers for interviews, among them Colonel James Thyer, the senior intelligence officer for the 8th Division. He immediately saw the possibility of getting word back to Australian families that their men had been taken safely into captivity.[10] The divisional headquarters discussed the idea and agreed that a broadcast to Australia should be made and, given his previous radio experience, Charles Cousens was the man to do it. Either Thyer or Colonel Wilfred Kent Hughes wrote the message and Cousens read it over the air. It indicated that the British Malaya Command had surrendered, the men were in good health, and they were being well treated by the Japanese.[11]

The Japanese command in Singapore sent word to the Allied command that a number of officers were required to write "theses" about the war and the treatment they were receiving at Japanese hands. General Callaghan, passing on instructions from Allied command in Changi, directed that officers asked to produce essays should not resist, but in carrying out the Japanese order they should reveal nothing that might be important to the enemy. Though the Allied officers were not aware of it, the supreme military command in Tokyo had sent instructions into the field that suitable captured individuals should be identified so that they could be used as writers and broadcasters on Japanese shortwave radio.

Cousens, already having made a broadcast to Australia, was asked to write an essay about Australian defense. Instead, he offered to write about possible future Japanese-Australian economic cooperation in the Pacific after the war. He claimed, later, that he had described a hypothetical situation which could bring an end to the conflict between the two countries, and that in any event, he had lifted the material from an old *Readers Digest* that was lying around in the barracks. He carefully made a copy of the essay and brought it to his superiors to file with the battalion papers. The essay shocked the Intelligence Officer, Thyer, who had previously been impressed by Cousens' "knowledgeability on international affairs." He concluded that "Cousens was a fool," or was suffering from a misguided belief, which he noted was shared by a number of soldiers in the AIF, that "some effort on his individual part could help bring about the cessation of hostilities." Kent Hughes, interviewed about the incident at the end of the war, recalled that he, too, had been "dumbfounded" by the suggestion that contact between the Nipponese and Australians might end hostilities. He could not imagine that any individual might believe that he could "settle the peace of the world" let alone that a member of "AIF Malaya," interned in Changi, in 1942, could "ever suggest any such course of action to the enemy."

Much as had Thyer, Kent Hughes observed that at the time, many men struggling to accept the reality of defeat and their own imprisonment had "definitely become mentally unbalanced." Again, according to Kent Hughes, among the enlisted men in Changi there was constant speculation about the possibility that they would be rescued and what action they could take to assist this outcome. He noted the poignant fact that when the first "Burma Party" was shipped out on the way to become laborers on the Thai-Burma railway, "many individuals were firmly convinced that they were not going to Burma, but were to be repatriated or exchanged and sent home to Australia." Kent Hughes did not see Cousens again until the end of the war, but in Changi in July 1942, he knew that prisoners listening on a secret radio set had heard a Tokyo broadcast by Charles Cousens and it had "caused considerable resentment among the men."[12]

It was in Changi that Cousens met Takafumi Hishikari, a war correspondent for the Domei news service in Tokyo. It is likely that Cousens' broadcast, the subsequent essay on postwar relations or that the Japanese had discovered that the Australian previously was a radio announcer had alerted Hishikari. The journalist was in Singapore as part of a sweep through Japan's newly occupied territories documenting Japanese military success. Oxford-educated and well mannered, Hishikari invited Cousens, very pleasantly, to write some stories about his experiences of the defeat, or to come to Tokyo and make a broadcast.[13] Equally politely, Cousens refused.[14]

At the end of April 1942, when "A" Force, the first group of three thousand prisoners to be shipped north to the Thai-Burma railway, left Singapore, Cousens was with them. Both he and his senior officers considered it wise that he should be removed out of sight of the Japanese. But in early June 1942, when the group arrived in Mergui, the port on the west coast of Southern Burma, he was picked out by the Japanese officers and informed that he was to be returned to Singapore and sent to Tokyo. When he asked whether his batman could go with him, Cousens was told that he must go to Japan alone.

Wilfred Thompson, who was with "A" Force and previously had been Cousens' orderly room sergeant, had a precise recollection of the event.[15] According to him, Thompson, Cousens and Phillips, who would assume Cousens' rank as second in charge of the hundred men from the original battalion, had discussed the ramifications of the Tokyo trip. The three of them felt that "it would be all right if [Cousens] went to the Japs with the idea of his getting information through to the Japs" about the lack of housing and scarce food for Allied POWs. Once in Japan, Cousens would be able to "make representations" to improve the lot of the prisoners of war and creating the opportunity to send a list of those in captivity back to Australia. Given the subsequent Japanese treatment of prisoners of war, these concerns are touching, but totally unrealistic. In the discussions before Cousens left, evidently, he and his colleagues canvassed the possibility that if he broadcast for the "Japs," it would very likely be misunderstood in Australia and diminish his later "standing in the broadcasting world." Therefore, in what was a rather theatrical gesture, Thompson called onto parade the hundred men of the remnant 2nd 19th Battalion to explain that Cousens was leaving the next morning, under duress, and would use all his powers to get word about the men back to their families. Cousens, himself, then made his farewell, assuring the men on the parade ground that he had always had their best interests at heart and that he would "not broadcast anything detrimental to the Allied cause." In a final emotional flourish Cousens took off his wristwatch and gave it to one of the officers announcing "it was to be disposed of for the use of the men he was leaving behind."

Before Cousens left Burma in June 1942, he wrote a letter to his old boss at 2GB, though H. G. Horner did not receive the letter until after the end of the war.[16] In it, Cousens described a cordial meeting between the Australian and the Domei correspondent and that, in traveling to Tokyo, Cousens "hoped to do something worthwhile for Australia and ensure that the peace we get is worth the lives of the splendid men we lost in Malaya." There is a Yeats-Brown-like bravado to the patriotic sentiments expressed. In Cousens' words, "whatever happens in the Japanese capital they will at any rate know and remember that they've met an officer in the AIF" and though he did "not anticipate any undue trouble" it was the case that "you never know in wartime." The letter concluded: "I would like it to be known at 2GB, if I don't come through, that I went out as a man should." There is also another letter, also upbeat and in hindsight equally naïve that Cousens wrote to Colonel G. E. Ramsay on June 19 from the steamer returning to Singapore. He reported "very pleasant journey so far" and "bad conditions at first are improving." As well as sending "compliments" from the ship's captain, Noguchi, Cousens noted with satisfaction that he had made some headway with improving the conditions in the prison camps, having "impressed very strongly the importance of health and food relationship."[17] In Singapore, he collected a tin trunk containing warm clothes, was escorted to get replacements for the spectacles that had been broken in Burma, and was taken onboard the *Arabia Maru*, a Japanese steamer, headed for Tokyo; the "only white man" among the two thousand Japanese soldiers.

Viewed with the knowledge of POW treatment under Nippon, there is a poignant innocence in the response that Cousens evinced to the events he experienced in the first stage of captivity. Just as Kent Hughes and Thyer suggest, it is likely that the defeat, so quick and unanticipated, caused profound shock among the troops and no less so to Charles Cousens. As well, the documented recollections by Australian soldiers at this time reveal that they were unequipped to deal with defeat and unprepared for captivity. Presumably, armies avoid encouraging enlisted men to contemplate defeat lest they choose it over the danger of combat.[18] Military training aims to build discipline, obedience and the sense of an invincible spirit, but the consequence, in early 1942, after the collapse of the Malaya campaign was that Allied soldiers and their military leaders were disconcerted. And of course, there were few who could have foreseen the terrible years ahead in which almost a third of the prisoners under Nippon would perish and the lives of the remainder in captivity would be reduced to unimaginable levels of brutality and despair.

Broadcaster in Tokyo

Cousens arrived in Tokyo on the last day of July 1942 and was immediately set to work on programs that were designed to be beamed over shortwave into the Pacific. At the treason committal in Sydney four years later, both the Crown prosecutor and Cousens' defense expended much energy in trying to establish precisely what happened during the initial days that Cousens spent as the first Allied prisoner of war assigned to the Japan Broadcasting Corporation.[19]

Cousens and his defense claimed that at every opportunity he had tried to speak about the terrible conditions in which Allied prisoners were being held; and at the initial meeting at Imperial Army headquarters, the Japanese head of Psychological Warfare, Lieutenant Tsigetsugu Tsuneishi, had threatened him with execution if he did not broadcast as he was ordered. Subsequently, at Broadcast House, Japanese staff reassured the Australian that he would not have to broadcast anything that he found unacceptable, but later he was ordered into the studio and given a script that was very critical of Roosevelt's Pacific policy. In his narrative of events, Cousens explained that when he had refused, Tsuneishi had come to the station, five feet three inches, in full military dress, with a three-foot sword dangling from his belt, and had threatened to kill the Australian if he continued to disobey orders. In sworn testimony Cousens stated that at this stage he realized that he had few options and that further refusal would mean that they would "give him to the *kempetai* to play with for a few days." Therefore, he had agreed to read the script.

In refutation, the prosecution produced several Japanese who claimed to have been present at the incident. Foumiko Saisho, a Japanese staff member who checked the political content of broadcasts before they were aired, recalled Cousens shaking hands with the radio staff when he was introduced as a "radio expert" come to give announcers advice on how to improve their microphone technique. She also recalled that he was reluctant to broadcast and when Tsuneishi had insisted that the prisoner must do as told, he had bowed, but later the broadcast Cousens made was in a voice that was "flat and monotonous" and clearly not like his regular, engaging performances. And according to Saisho, as a consequence, he was transferred into commentary and scriptwriting that had made him "much happier."[20] The three interpreters present on the fateful day each in sworn testimony offered slightly different recollections. Yuman Ishihara, Tsuneishi's interpreter, agreed with the defense that when Cousens had shown himself to be reluctant to broadcast, Tsuneishi had been summoned to the station. Ishihara was sympathetic to Cousens, a man he claimed to respect a good deal, and recalled that on the day the POW was "very nervous" and his face was "pale under the sunburnt complexion" as he confronted the Japanese commander. The three interpreters agreed that the Japanese officer had read a statement to Cousens that indicated that he was a prisoner of the Japanese and therefore under orders of the Imperial Japanese Army. But, in their versions, Tsuneishi also had read out the conditions relating to the Australian's tenure in Tokyo. These were that he would be paid at the rate of a Japanese officer of equivalent rank, would be accommodated in a comfortable European style hotel and was obliged to obey all orders.

It may never be possible to establish beyond doubt what precisely happened at this time. Both versions agree, more or less, though the sequence of events in each is different, as is the emphasis on the threat of violence. Tsuneishi maintained that the three Allied broadcasters, that is including the two new broadcasters who arrived three months later, had come to Tokyo with the understanding that they were being used as advisers to raise the level and quality of the broadcasts being made for overseas transmission. As part of this arrangement, they were encouraged to wear civilian clothes, were provided free accommodation in good Japanese-European hotels, and were paid at the equivalent rates of their Japanese officer counterparts. When he appeared in November 1949, for the prosecution in the treason trial in San Francisco of Iva Toguri, Tsuneishi was an unconvincing witness who claimed under cross-examination that he had never heard of a single occasion on which the Japanese military had behaved in an untoward manner towards enemy prisoners of war.[21] However, as we shall see, this did not mean that he was entirely unsympathetic to POWs, and Cousens in particular.

Cousens was lodged in comfortable accommodation at the Dai Itchi Hotel, about fifty yards from Radio Tokyo. Western-style and reserved for officers in the Imperial Japanese Navy, the hotel had set aside a floor in an upstairs wing for foreign broadcasters resident in Tokyo. The other radio announcers, none of whom was a prisoner, included Dutch, Arab, Spanish, French, Latin American and German nationals. Cousens had a room to himself with a bath. At first, an interpreter from Broadcast House, Ken Oki, was assigned to accompany him back and forth to work. Before long, however, the Australian was permitted a good deal of liberty. He could walk to Broadcast House alone, make purchases at stores in the city, and take his meals in the hotel dining room. At least once, he ate dinner at the Imperial Hotel, the finest in Tokyo, as a guest of a Frenchmen involved in some way or other with Japan's economic expansion into China. Also, Cousens was permitted to return to the radio station in the evening, though his own programs were not on at these times. At some stage, while the Australian was still alone in Tokyo, a Japanese naval officer living in the Dai Itchi complained about the presence of a prisoner of war dressed in enemy uniform. As a consequence, Cousens was given coupons and used his pay to have a tailor make up a civilian suit in conservative grey.

Two more Allied prisoners of war arrived in Tokyo towards the end of October 1942. The American, Wallace Ince and Norman Reyes, a nineteen-year-old Filipino, had been captured at the fall of Corregidor. Both had been involved with Voice of Freedom, a clandestine radio station that continued pro-American broadcasts until the Philippines were overrun by the Japanese army. Reyes had read the station's last message, which was the American surrender. When Cousens met them they were emaciated, with hair cropped to the scalp and deeply sun burnt faces; the previous months in Japanese detention had taken a heavy toll. Ince and Reyes were placed with Cousens at the Dai Itchi. Some time in March 1943, a Japanese naval officer complained about sharing a hotel with enemy POWs, and as a consequence, the three were moved to the Sanno, a Japanese army hotel. Though further away from the radio station, their new quarters were comfortable. They remained at the Sanno until the end of 1943 when they were transferred into Bunka camp, a prison that had been created in Tokyo to hold the growing number of POWs being brought to broadcast in the capital.

Cousens' first broadcast from Tokyo was heard in Sydney on July 31, 1942. As the months passed, Cousens seems to have settled into a routine at the studio whereby he wrote broadcasts and news items, and advised Japanese broadcasting staff on how to improve their microphone techniques. Until mid-1944, when he became very ill with beriberi, he wrote radio scripts and continuity pieces that were heard on-air. In his own voice he read a great many POW messages, including a number to his wife in Sydney.

Allied prisoners, when working at the radio station on programs that were to go on-air, behaved in a professional manner though within a setting over which they had no control. Broadcast House, with studios, production rooms and offices, hummed with activity day and night. Though English broadcasting occupied most airtime, there were also programs in a whole range of languages: Spanish, Arabic, Hindu, Indonesian, German and Italian, Chinese and Russian, transmitting on a twenty-four-hour schedule that fitted the peak listening times of the destination audiences. The foreign staff working in these areas were not prisoners of war. Within the sector of English broadcasting overseas, Cousens, Reyes and Ince were the moving spirits behind *Zero Hour*, the first and most successful of the Japanese English-language variety programs that were beamed on a wide arc to Allied soldiers and their home fronts around the Pacific. Later several spin-offs from *Zero Hour* were produced and, though never as popular as the original program, commanded an enthusiastic audience.

The broadcasting outfit at Radio Tokyo's Broadcast House was highly professional. The staff was committed to making successful programs, and most of these individuals, whether devoted to Japanese victory or not, were glad to be working in the industry. In all of the radio processes, the Japanese broadcasting service operated along the same lines as any other large radio station. The Japanese staff, who subsequently talked about their experiences in wartime shortwave, appear to have been keen to produce high-quality programs. In this sense they were very much like broadcasters and technicians elsewhere in what was the new, burgeoning field of radio. Similarly, contemporaries at Broadcast House noted that in general the Allied prisoners of war working on Radio Tokyo invested their expertise in the productions to which they were assigned even though they had little choice in what that assignment might be. Cousens, Ince and Reyes, for example, were exercising the prewar vocation in which they had excelled. The professional engagement of all these people, Japanese employees and prison broadcasters alike, probably was a response to the medium itself. It is part of the tragedy of war that, under normal peacetime conditions, the Allied radio professionals and the Japanese NHK staff would have had much in common. As it was, few among the Japanese that Cousens met at Broadcast House could have imagined that the war, once begun, would generate the unstoppable energy of a whirlwind and draw everything into its violent vortex.

Allied prisoners who made regular broadcasts on Axis radio assumed (though it was rarely the case) that the government monitors and family members whom they hoped would be their audience would be sensitive to every implied nuance in the messages they sent. The reality was that even if the messages were heard and understood, and that was not always the case, POW families held no purchase with the wartime governments in Australia or the United States. Indeed the official purpose in setting up homefront listening posts was not to sift out the variation in detail in POW messages, but to collect evidence that could be used if charges were later laid against those whose voices had been heard on Axis airways.

It is not at all surprising that prisoners of war had little idea of the progress of the war, completely cut off from combat and from news at home, as they were. Nor did they know that in the larger scale of things, elliptical messages sent under enemy sponsorship were small beer, no matter how earnestly they may have been dispatched. The priority for Allied governments was to tool-up industrial production and recruit more enlistments at home while maintaining oversight of fighting forces spread across the globe. Equally, it cannot be overemphasized that ordinary prisoners of war never had the choice of resisting their Japanese captors. An individual like Cousens might exert some small influence at Radio Tokyo where the radio station was keen to acquire his broadcasting skills and in order to ensure his cooperation provided him some leeway at work. The space in which he could only ever operate, however, fell within the narrow and immutable boundaries of the POW caste. Also it must be remembered that many prisoners were psychologically unprepared both for the violence of life in captivity and their own physical and mental deterioration as the years dragged on. Again, to use Cousens as the example, nothing in his previous life experiences or his intellectual models provided preparation for what was ahead. Neither the shallow solipsism of a Yeats-Brown nor the can-do individualism of Baker Eddy was much help. As a prisoner of war in Tokyo in 1942, he was separated from his comrades, cut off from all contact with the family in Australia and isolated from outside news, which, according to many POW narratives, was the only lifeline that might bring sanity.

Like many others who shared his situation, an emotional, even naïve man like Cousens was out of his depth. He described his own state of mind in these early days in Tokyo as "weak and disheartened." He had suffered severe dysentery on the boat to Tokyo and his desperation had shocked some of the English-speaking staff at Broadcast House when he threatened to commit suicide.[22] At the end of 1943, Cousens and Ince were moved into a regular prisoner of war camp. Reyes was freed when the Philippines became part of the Japanese Empire but chose to remain in Tokyo working for Japan's overseas radio service. In Bunka camp, the conditions of life were much harsher and took a great toll. As before, Cousens continued working at Broadcast House until mid-1944 when his health collapsed, brought on by beriberi, exhaustion and neglect.

CHAPTER 8

Allied POWs
Broadcast from Japan

In late 1943, faced with the flagging military initiative, the Imperial Army ordered that overseas radio propaganda should be stepped up by bringing in an expanded staff of POW broadcasters. In Tokyo, a designated prison, Bunka Camp, was created to house them. When Charles Cousens and Wallace Ince arrived in mid-December, Bunka held a dozen Allied prisoners. In the first week of January, four more were sent and by mid-1944 another half dozen, until in total there were about thirty men. They included three Englishmen, a couple of Australians and a Dutch citizen from Java. The remainder were captured Americans. All in some way or another were involved with radio broadcasting though most of their work was carried out in the camp under the supervision of civilians hired by the Japanese military. When required, on-air the prisoners were taken to Broadcast House.[1]

Although Bunka prisoners spent the rest of the war together, they were never in harmony. The range of nationalities, ages and backgrounds, not to mention their captive status, precluded the possibility. As one of them explained, much as they might "encourage each other in a bleak and dismal existence" there was always a tendency, "as a measure of self-preservation to hold a certain something back."[2] The urge to survive made prisoners wary of each other, and of forming close relationships that could make for vulnerability.[3] Deep disagreement about what was the correct stance for Allied servicemen when dealing with the Japanese further divided the community. Despite the special status of prisoners in Bunka as broadcasters on Nippon overseas radio, it provided them no protection from the violence that civilian overseers and guards meted out to the prisoners in their control.

Bunka Prisoner of War Camp

The Bunka compound occupied a small block between two streets in the Tokyo suburb of Surugadai, in the Kanda District. It was three miles from Broadcast House and about eight blocks from the Imperial Palace. From the upstairs windows, looking south, the peak of Mt. Fujiyama rose majestically behind the city skyline. Before the war, the Women's Higher Normal School had occupied the site. The three-story buildings at the front and back were constructed around a small open square that had been the playground. The structure facing the street was of solid brick and a brick fence, low at the front but rising to nearly thirty feet behind the compound, enclosed the whole perimeter. A wide front entrance was boarded up, and people came and went through a small door cut in the main gate. The guardhouse stood inside the entrance so that from the street there was no indication that the walls enclosed a prisoner of war camp.

The civilian employees of the military and the Japanese guards who ran Bunka Camp occupied the building that looked onto the main road. The prisoners referred to it as the "Front Office." Uniformed members of the Imperial Guard manned the gate and the perimeter at night. Japanese civilians, in ordinary street clothes, ran the Front Office and the shortwave receiver that was located there. They also were responsible for overseeing the prisoners' scriptwriting in the back building and for making sure that the prisoners who were needed at Radio Tokyo were taken there on time. In the first months, the men were driven to Broadcast House, but later they went on foot, accompanied by a Bunka interpreter and a *kempei*. Within the front section of the complex, as well as dormitories, there were meeting rooms and even a small theatre where films could be screened on portable movie equipment. For example, a captured copy of *Gone With the Wind* was shown several times in 1944 to a mixed group of Japanese and prisoners of war, ostensibly so they could use the material for several shortwave broadcasts. As with all who saw the movie, the Bunka audience responded enthusiastically, though a number of the Japanese were disturbed by the scenes of Atlanta burning, perhaps a prefiguring sign for the fiery Hiroshima that would bring an end to their own war.

The quarters for the prisoners were at the rear of the compound. On the third floor, in the middle, there was a workroom with tables and chairs. There was also a small library of "looted literature" and books in English on Japanese culture and history that were supposed to prompt the POW scriptwriters to produce their daily quota of broadcast material. When Cousens arrived, all the prisoners slept in one room, but, always a stickler about rank and correct behavior, he insisted that enlisted men and officers were separated. Henceforth, the officers slept in a room to themselves on the east corner and the NCOS and the enlisted men bunked in together. In a parody of racial hierarchy, two unrelated Mexican Americans, Ramon and James Martinez, were quartered in a small room on their own. Perhaps not so curiously given that the prison was Japanese and ruled by Japanese guards, Frank Fujita, a mixed heritage Japanese American, was accommodated in the large room with the enlisted men. A long platform at about knee height ran the length of the dormitories, covered by a tatami straw runner. On it, prisoners lay side-by-side wrapped in whatever coverings they could scrounge.

The floor below consisted of a workroom and a dining room; the latter furnished with two rows of tables the full length of the room. Officers sat separately at the end of one row and the men filled up the rest. The bottom floor, part of which was below ground level with covered windows, provided secure storage areas for supplies and old school equipment. An aged Japanese couple, the caretakers, who came to treat their upstairs neighbors with kindliness, occupied one ground-floor room. The cookhouse functioned in another at the very end of the building. The *benjo*, with a few squat toilets, was at the opposite end at the back of the building and there was a row of washbasins at the entrance.

The prisoners ate together. The guards took their meals in their own quarters. The rations were prepared for everyone in the cookhouse under the charge of Warrant Officer Nikolas Schenk.[4] A large fair-headed Dutchman with a limp, he had been a journalist in civilian life and had been brought from Java when his reserve unit of the Dutch East Indies Army capitulated. His first assistant, Kenneth Parkyns, was an Australian, the single prisoner of that nationality when the first group of POWs had arrived. Later, in September 1944, another Australian, John Dooley, arrived. Parkyns had been assigned to the galley because during the final selection at Omori Camp he had claimed, falsely, that he knew how to cook. The provenance of Schenk's mastery of the cooking pots was no more certain. It was several months before he managed to cook rice that did not resemble "raw dough," and to use vegetables or whatever else he could scavenge to create a semblance of soup. The absence of salt, constantly mentioned in prisoner writings, did little for the overall flavor.

The preparation of meals was soured by the acrimony between Schenk and Parkyns. Keeping control of rations, constantly in short supply, was Schenk's most arduous task, and Parkyn's activities tried the cook's patience. For example, around February or March 1944, the Australian "pinched a large number of spuds from the store" and distributed them to his mates, who furtively and at great speed demolished the lot. Finally the relations between cook and helper degenerated into a full-on, knockdown fistfight which was ended only by the intervention of the guards. Henceforth, Parkyns was placed on outdoor cleaning duty, swabbing out the latrines and sweeping the courtyard, activities that enabled him to "snoop around" the compound while using his bucket and broom. Although two new American assistants, Joseph Asterita and James Martinez, were sent to the kitchen, Schenk's burden became no lighter. When he complained about the Japanese quartermaster stealing prisoner rations from the kitchen, the guards with kendo sticks beat him into unconsciousness until he had to be carried upstairs to the dormitory. A continuing source of grievance for the prisoners was that whenever the radio station needed extra English voices, the galley staff was pressed into service. With nobody in the cookhouse, food went unprepared and mealtimes were simply passed over.

Bunka prisoners never had enough to eat. Cats that strayed into the compound were added to the pot. As the war went on, the portions diminished. Charles Cousens noted that when he arrived at Bunka the rations had been "good," but as the time passed quantity and quality "declined steadily." Rice disappeared from the menu altogether, to be replaced by a grain substitute mixed with ground wood fiber. Fish, which became increasingly rare, always smelt of the ammonia in which it was preserved. It is worth remembering, of course, that Japanese citizens were experiencing the same shortages, and like the prisoners, struggling to manage with fewer and fewer supplies.

The guards' treatment of the prisoners added the ingredient of malice to what was eaten. When the first group of POWs arrived, the Camp Commander, Lieutenant Junichi Hamamoto, asked Parkyns and an American, George Henshaw, how the Bunka rice ration compared with what they had received in Omori Camp. Applying the ineffable POW principle, which was never to attract attention by making any statement to a Japanese person without knowing what answer was required, the new arrivals had given the noncommittal reply that the rations were "about the same." At this, Hamamoto flew into a rage, claiming that the men were lying because broadcasters officially received 20 percent more rice than did ordinary POWs. The punishment for this perfidy was that all Bunka prisoner rations were cut by 20 percent. The reduced amount of food lasted until there was a change of guard in the camp management.

The Bunka Guards

Daily life in Bunka—what the prisoners ate, how they were treated and their chances for survival—was entirely in the hands of the Japanese running the camp. The military top brass in the Eighth Army Section, men like General Asune and his next in command Lieutenant Colonel Tsuneishi, oversaw propaganda production. Tsuneishi's attitude to the prisoners was contradictory and often hard to fathom. It helped the positive perception of Tsuneishi among some prisoners that his interpreter, Tomatsu Muryama, who spoke fluent English, had attended an American university and been an English language correspondent in Tokyo.[5] Several POWs recalled that Tsuneishi treated them as decently as was possible in the circumstances. Fujita, for example, noted that quite soon after their arrival, Tsuneishi had paraded the prisoners and asked about conditions. He listened carefully to their complaints and seemed to have made some effort to deal with them, even if it was not very effective. He provided blankets and a small hibachi, a portable firebox half filled with sand in which coal could be burnt. Two coal heaters were also brought into the recreation area, though during the course of the war they were never hooked up.

Cousens' assessment of Tsuneishi was that the Japanese was a military man who did not enjoy the task he had been assigned of overseeing a propaganda unit. Despite their abrasive encounter when Cousens had arrived alone in Tokyo, it was Tsuneishi who was responsible for having Cousens moved to the Shinagawa

Military Prisoners of War Hospital in mid-1944, after he became very ill. And again, when faced with the Australian's seriously failing health, Tsuneishi had him moved to a private civilian hospital near the camp. The intervention to assist Cousens may not indicate humanitarianism as much as a commitment to carry out the army's policy of raising the levels of Japanese broadcasting, in which policy Cousens' role was central. During the interrogation in Yokohama in October 1945, Cousens also indicated that Tsuneishi had been a "considerable help" in getting rid of "Buddy" Uno and several other civilian Bunka guards whose behavior to the prisoners was particularly objectionable.[6] Similarly, it was through Tsuneishi that Kaji Domoto, a Japanese American and a graduate from Amherst College who was helpful to prisoners, was promoted to main interpreter and finally placed in charge of the entire camp. It is equally the case, however, that Tsuneishi constantly reminded the prisoners that "nothing could be guaranteed" (this precise term appears over and over in POW recollections of the time). Those who heard the statement read it as an unambiguous threat of execution for anyone who disobeyed.

An incident that occurred in the very first days after the prisoners arrived in Bunka evokes the prevailing malevolence and Tsuneishi's part in it. It also underlines the sheer powerlessness of prisoners in their surroundings. On December 10, 1943, the prisoners had been mustered in the courtyard to hear Tsuneishi explain that they had been brought to Tokyo under the orders of Imperial Japan and must obey all orders as given.[7] The words were translated by the interpreter, after which Tsuneishi asked whether anyone present was not willing to broadcast over Japanese radio. A civil servant from the Gilbert Islands, George Williams (British, though sometimes described as a New Zealander) stepped forward. While the rest of the prisoners watched in horror, Tsuneishi shouted that anyone else with similar ideas should also come forward. The POWs stood in frozen silence as Tsuneishi, in full fury, ordered Williams to be taken away. He was dragged off between two guards to the front administration building. The POWs knew that he would be beaten and in all probability would be executed, an impression that was strengthened by the sight of Williams' personal belongings that remained in front of his bunk rack for several days. The guard who eventually took them away told the prisoners that where Williams had gone he would have no more need of such possessions.

What had happened stood as a mordant example of Japanese brutality, etched on the consciousness of all the prisoners who had seen it, or who later heard the story. It became part of the collective memory of Bunka inhabitants and is cited in a great many recollections, both Japanese and European. It provided living proof of what would happen if anyone was foolish enough to step out of line. In fact, Williams had not been executed, but had been sent back to Omori and reassigned to labor underground in a mine in northern Japan.[8] Remarkably, he survived the war.

In the camp setting, day-to-day dealings were in the hands of those with power on the spot. Face-to-face relations between individual guards and the men in captivity were conditioned by the particular personality of the guard. The interpreters were very important figures. Because so few prisoners spoke Japanese, the interpreters mediated the contact between Japanese giving orders and prisoners carrying them out. In Bunka, only Private Fred Hoblitt and John Provoo spoke good Japanese, Provoo having studied as a Buddhist convert in Japan before the war and Hoblitt, a young American Marine corpsman, had a flare for languages. Cousens and Parkyns acquired some facility in spoken Japanese as their years in captivity went by.

The Japanese administration of the camp passed through two stages. The initial regime was very harsh, relaxing only in September 1944, by which time Japan was losing the war and a new set of military and civilian administrators were appointed. In the second stage, the camp was run in a more humane manner, which lasted through the last months of the war, though by then shortages had bitten very hard. In these final months, too, Tokyo was under constant bombardment and Japanese civilians and military alike looked upon the prisoners of war with real hostility because it was widely believed that the Allied countries had started the war.

In the beginning, Lieutenant Hamamoto was in charge of Bunka. A man with a violent temper and the habits of the old school, he struck prisoners and subordinates on the face at the slightest provocation. The practice of *binta*, the face slapping of subordinates, was a long-standing Japanese custom that shocked non-Japanese, and has remained a strong collective memory for POWs and Asians in the occupied areas. It was particularly offensive to Buddhists for whom the head is sacred. The slapping was no mere symbolic gesture, but was delivered with real force. A British teacher in a Tokyo school, whose windows overlooked a military parade ground, regularly saw senior officers knock conscripts unconscious for tardiness in obeying an order.[9] According to an Australian prisoner, regularly on the receiving end of such treatment, "every Japanese soldier was entitled to bash a fellow Japanese soldier of a lower rank; colonels bashed majors, majors bashed captains and so it continued down the line" with prisoners the lowest on the pecking order.[10] In Bunka, as in camps elsewhere, guards carried sticks of solid bamboo or wood in the shape of an elongated baseball bat with which they hit prisoners. The climate was one in which bashing was common and unrestrained. In January 1944, Hamamoto beat Wallace Ince with a wooden stick until the prisoner fell unconscious on the ground. Although a very senior broadcaster, the POW supposedly had shown a lack of enthusiasm for the physical training session in the courtyard that Hamamoto was supervising. Ince was unwell for a long time afterwards and seems not ever to have left the compound again. The beating ended his participation in programs at Broadcast House.

Among the senior civilians employed by the military to oversee the preparation of broadcasts in Bunka, in the first period, were Norisane Ikeda, an aristocratic Japanese educated in Oxford at Balliol, and his brother Kuchiki. Ikeda, while a member of the Imperial diplomatic corps, had been posted in Australia. When war was declared he was interned and only returned to Japan after a diplomatic exchange of officials had taken place. The Australian Parkyns was surprised when being interviewed by Ikeda in Omori that the interrogator seemed to have a great familiarity with Australian affairs.[11] At morning muster, while prisoners stood at attention in a corridor outside the Bunka dormitory, Ikeda often bragged about his understanding of the English and mimicked a perfect Oxford English accent. He also, from time to time, regaled the POWs with unnerving renditions of western opera. In February 1944, Ikeda was replaced by Joe Tadaichi, who came to be remembered in a more kindly light by the POWs, even though it was he who turned a blind eye to the quartermaster's looting the Red Cross parcels and warm clothes intended for the prisoners.[12]

The other key figure was George Kazumaro "Buddy" Uno, a Japanese American who had lived in Japan, off and on, since 1937. A complex character described by the American war correspondent Carl Mydans, in Shanghai, as "one of the most tortured souls" he had ever met because he was an "American trapped in Japanese uniform."[13] A more accurate description of Uno, perhaps, is as a "marginal man." He was never at home in the United States where he had suffered scarifying racism as a boy growing up in Salt Lake City—excluded from the swimming pool, even when he was with his Boy Scout troop, and forced to sit in segregated seating at the movies. Nor was he entirely accepted in Japan where his Japanese language was not strong though he had carved out a media career, interpreting America to the Japanese.[14] In the middle of 1939, Uno was attached as civilian journalist to the Imperial Army in Shanghai. In March 1942, he was with the Japanese army at the fall of Corregidor where he interviewed captured American GIs for a volume of pro-Japanese testimonies published by the Japanese Press Bureau. Later, in Tokyo, he was attached to Bunka Camp, supervising the POW scriptwriters and broadcasters.

Several Bunka POWs described him as having established a "reign of terror" in the camp and "having no time for white men." Others claimed that Uno was "particularly obnoxious" to American GIs. In Cousens' view, he was a "menace" to the prisoners' safety. In Sydney, in 1946, however, Foumy Saisho testified that she had observed that Uno's antipathy to Cousens came only after the Australian had moved from Sanno Hotel to share the living arrangements of the other POWs in Bunka. Before that, Uno, who wished to be assigned to Radio Tokyo as a broadcaster, had sought Cousens' assistance. In the autumn of 1944, Uno was transferred from Bunka Camp to oversee the NHK shortwave in Manila.

In his own testimony after the war, "Buddy" Uno claimed that he had overseen a mild prison regimen.[15] The routine, between seven o'clock rising and ten in the evening when the electric lights went off, consisted of work and leisure and was alternated by meals and a stint at the radio station, to which they were driven in "chartered automobiles." Sundays were given over to recreation. As Uno explained, on this day and "in groups of four or five, escorted by [Uno] or another Nisei interpreter, prisoners in civilian clothes visited parks, art galleries, museums, department stores, strolled along the Ginza, Tokyo's main street, and did shopping for personal needs."

Clearly, Uno exaggerated. However, it is true that all Bunka prisoners received wages—not always paid regularly—to the equivalent of payments made to Japanese of equal rank. Cousens noted in his interrogation that on several occasions the Bunka prisoners were taken by truck out of town for a picnic. They were also permitted to buy food from the small shops they passed as they walked back to camp from Broadcast House. Common purchases were synthetic coffee, curry powder and pepper, the latter presumably to spice up a bland, grain-based diet. Parkyns and Cousens both bought English books at a downtown bookstore, the latter making purchases at least four or five times. As well, he was able to use his own funds to pay for a civilian suit. While these activities might suggest conditions that were more comfortable than those endured by many POWs, Bunka was no holiday camp.

An American-educated Japanese, Domoto, took Uno's place and in early 1945 became the senior Japanese civilian in Bunka Camp. Sympathetic to the POWs and increasingly convinced that Japan would be defeated, Domoto struck up a friendship with Cousens and, with the limited means at their disposal, the two attempted to create a noticeably less harsh regime.

Resistance in Captivity

The prisoners in Bunka, in Cousens' words, were a "mixed group" and divided into two "factions" over how to deal with the Japanese.[16] Everyone distrusted the two prisoners who were "pro-Nip." Mark Streeter and John Provoo were suspected of being in cahoots with the Japanese and whenever the guards in the Front Office had knowledge of what was being said and done in the back building, these two were blamed. Streeter, forty-four years of age and a civilian, had been a broadcaster on an Axis network in Shanghai since 1939.[17] His pro-Japanese feelings were clear from the start. One of his earliest broadcasts was entitled an *Ode to President Roosevelt* and described the American leader as the "wily, oily, double-talking politician whose personal ambition was to become the Alexander or the Napoleon of the twentieth century." On-air and in Bunka, he trumpeted a new world order of "Energocracy" that he had invented and which would bring together world technocrats of all nations to solve the world's problems. Prone to self-aggrandizement, he boasted that he had been an editor and a publisher of thirty magazines in America and had a court case pending against President Roosevelt before the United States Supreme Court. Henshaw noted in his diary that Streeter was a person to be careful of because he was "loco in the co-co." Probably in response to his complaints about cold-shouldering from other prisoners, in November 1944, the Japanese moved Streeter into quarters in the Front Office and later that year they moved him out of Bunka to board with a private family.

John Provoo was a twenty-five-year-old GI who spoke fluent Japanese. A former bank clerk from San Francisco, he had spent time in Japan in the 1930s at a Shinto monastery studying Japanese and Buddhism and later enlisted with the

American army, in the Philippines achieving the rank of staff sergeant. According to testimony at his treason trial after the war, when the Japanese arrived in Corregidor, Provoo had shaved his head, donned the garb of a Shinto priest and greeted his captors in Japanese. Because so few understood Japanese, Provoo was favored and used his position to lord it over other prisoners. In a reprehensible incident at Corregidor, Provoo had been directly responsible for an American officer's execution by the Japanese.[18] His Tokyo program *The Voice of Greater East Asia*, featuring news about the glorious victories of the Imperial Army, carried his stentorious signature call: "Japan, Strong, Determined and Ever Victorious."

Even though none of the other prisoners was pro-Japanese, they were never united over how to deal with the enemy. George Williams' bravado was favored by no one: immediately on arrival in Bunka Williams had declared he would openly resist the Japanese though his comrades urged him to adopt the prevailing POW position which was that it was "foolish to risk your neck." In his diary Henshaw's view was "why get yourself shot" when the "Japs" would simply bring in "other poor bastards" as replacements. After the guards hauled Williams away, there was admiration for his "remarkable courage," but the unanimous judgment among the prisoners was that "sacrifice of that order was not required."[19]

The two senior camp figures, Charles Cousens and a young American Air Force major, Williston Cox, profoundly disagreed over the way in which patriotic POWs should sabotage the enemy. Cox, who had been shot down over Rabaul in New Guinea, became the senior officer when he arrived in Bunka. He outranked Cousens, who saw the machination of "Buddy" Uno behind Cox's appointment and complained that the flyer was "too young, too inexperienced and too American." By this the Australian meant that he disapproved of Cox's democratic approach to the enlisted men. The American airmen were wary of the POWs already in Bunka. They scoffed at the antiquated military hierarchy that Cousens had resuscitated and the idea that military discipline could be enforced in the uncongenial conditions of captivity.

Cox argued that a loyal Allied prisoner confronting the Japanese enemy from captivity should attempt continuous resistance to their orders. Prisoners of war should do what they were told, for example when instructed to broadcast over Japanese radio, because to openly disobey would endanger prisoners' lives. But such prisoners should comply as slowly and as incompetently as possible in order to sabotage the enemy war effort. In strong contrast, Cousens argued that a strategy of negative resistance towards the Japanese was ineffective and demoralizing. Instead, he proposed that POWs become actively involved in the broadcasting enterprise. Later, under interrogation, Cousens explained that his plan had "crystallized" in his first days alone in Tokyo.[20] In his view, captive broadcasters and scriptwriters should get on with what they were told to do as smartly and efficiently as possible. At the same time, they should devise alternative messages in code to include within the broadcasts that the Japanese demanded. For example, when asked to write commentaries—in Cousens' case he wrote more than two hundred between the end of July 1942 and the Japanese surrender in

August 1945—the programs should be as professionally produced as possible while containing double messages with information that would be useful to the Allied war effort.

The clear advantage of Cousens' approach was that it demonstrated compliance with Japanese orders and therefore ensured the prisoner's safety, or as far as that was possible within the volatile and uncertain environment of Japanese captivity. Equally importantly, the Cousens strategy raised POW morale. It kept the men busy and absorbed. And, because many of them came from radio, journalism, or the entertainment industry, in making programs they were drawing on professional skills from previous professional lives.[21] As in Cousens' own example, he exercised his considerable expertise on the airwaves, while taking comfort that he was sabotaging the scripts that came his way.

The problem with ostensible compliance, as was immediately apparent once the war was over, was that it could equally be interpreted as collaboration. It seems that a number of Bunka POWs were aware at the time that they were running the risk that they could be accused of aiding the enemy. In subsequent sworn testimonies several Bunka inmates indicated that Cousens had assured them, if they followed his strategy, he would take full responsibility to explain to the authorities at home that Bunka POWs had operated under his orders in response to a situation of intolerable duress.

When Cousens returned to Bunka after a stint in Tokyo hospitals in late 1944, Tsuneishi's interpreter Murayama had replaced "Buddy" Uno in the important position of chief camp interpreter. He demonstrated a good deal of sympathy for the plight of the POWs and seems also to have realized that Japanese defeat was inevitable. Friendly to Cousens and supportive of the approach that encouraged prisoners to comply with Japanese directives, Muraya was probably motivated by self-interest in that active compliance made for little confrontation between the Japanese and their captives. At around the same time, Cousens attempted to manage the content of the Bunka programs going out on shortwave in order to stymie the exaggeratedly pro-Japanese material produced by Provoo and Streeter. For a very brief period, around February or March 1945, Cousens established a "Loyalty Group" that vetted scripts written within the camp before they were sent on to Broadcast House. Cox and Parkyns were in the group as, oddly enough, was Provoo. Predictably, word soon reached the Front Office, either via Provoo (according to Parkyns) or Streeter (in Dooley's assessment) and the Japanese put a stop to the operation.

Cousens claimed consistently in all his statements that he had played a double game of sabotage. The clear drawback in his defense was the difficulty of providing proof that it was a strategy that harmed the Japanese war effort. A good example of this problem related to Cousens' training Japanese announcers. NHK, actively seeking to make their radio broadcasts more attractive to western listeners, viewed Cousens as a radio expert who could transform the on-air techniques of Japanese broadcasters to make then more appealing to western listeners. For his part, Cousens claimed that he had misled Japanese NHK. To hoots of laughter in the Sydney courtroom, he described how he had made his Japanese trainees sing Grey's *Elergy* to lay down habits of mis-intonation that would render unintelligible Japanese microphone deliveries. Also, according to Cousens and contrary to his own practice, he had encouraged the Japanese announcers to ignore careful word articulation and put plenty of personal expression into their deliveries.[22] In very marked contrast, however, the Japanese whom he trained, including the chief of the English section, Mr Hirakawa, and the announcers Igaraghi, Niino, Yoshii and George Noda, attested that they had derived great benefit from the Cousens method. After a few sessions with the veteran Australian broadcaster, the Japanese believed that they were more effective, comfortable and convincing on-air. Certainly, under his tutelage, Iva Toguri, who had never stood before a microphone, mastered an on-air delivery that was able and memorable.

Two of the Bunka POWs whom Cousens took under his wing also found remarkable success with the Cousens system. For Parkyns and Joseph Asterita, their "manner of speech and vocabulary" had been improved as had the quality of their "voice culture." In the Australian's case, the positive outcome was demonstrable. A bricklayer who had lived his entire life on the outskirts of Sydney, Parkyns, by the end of his imprisonment, "spoke like a gentleman." Indeed, in October 1945, his rounded vowels aroused deep suspicion in Allied military interrogators, who kept probing Parkyn's claim that before the war he had been a manual laborer and had never lived outside Australia. The other Cousens protégé, Joseph Asterita, possessing what his voice coach called a "dead-end Brooklyn accent," was similarly transformed. Both Bunka pupils testified that they had been made to read poems aloud and articulate words distinctly, and Cousens had helped them expand their "grey matter" by discussing the emotions the poet was attempting to convey. All in all, Cousens' two POW pupils estimated that they had "raised their own self-presentation and become more powerful."

In the last months of the war, when it was clear that the Allies would win, Cousens set his closest supporters the task of collecting information that could be useful for victory. His fellow Australian Kenneth Parkyns adopted the habit of rising at four in the morning in order to scout around the Bunka buildings while the Japanese staff was asleep. As well, he sought out sympathetic pro-Allied employees at Radio Tokyo, climbed the perimeter wall at night to meet informants and, whenever possible, pumped information from a typist at the radio station who was, to use Cousens' description, a "half caste lass." Her Portuguese father was the principal baker at the Imperial Hotel, the top meeting place in Tokyo, so that if the baker reported that he had a special order, Parkyns took careful note in case it indicated that an important meeting was about to take place.

Undoubtedly, the constant activity in gathering information raised the soldierly spirits of the prisoners involved, even though it had no effect on the outcome of the war. On August 8, the atom bomb was dropped on Hiroshima and three days later another on Nagasaki. And on August 18, Emperor Hirohito announced over the radio that his loyal subjects must "endure the unendurable and accept the unacceptable." Japan had surrendered.

After the Surrender

When news of the Japanese surrender came through to Bunka, Cousens and Cox placed Provoo and Streeter under arrest as suspected traitors and, once it was possible, handed the two suspect Americans over to the U.S. Marshals. Bunka prisoners were evacuated to the collection centre at Omori, from where most were transferred by American hospital ship to Yokohama. U.S. Military Intelligence put POWs in Japan through an intensive interrogation. The Australians were dealt with by George S. Guysi with the assistance of Australian Army Intelligence. In the very last days of captivity, the indefatigable Parkyns had hidden radio scripts, documents and several POW diaries in the safest place he could find—within the ceiling in the Japanese officers' quarters. Alerted to their existence, Guysi had retrieved the materials from Bunka Camp. The three Australians were sent on to Manila where Cousens was arrested while Parkyns and Dooley were dispatched home to Sydney by plane to the joyful welcome of family and friends.

On November 13, 1945, under close arrest, Cousens was flown back to Australia. In order to avoid the press, the plane touched down outside Sydney at the small military air base at Richmond. From there, he was taken to the Concord Military Hospital and admitted, under guard, for medical treatment. It was here that Charles Cousens was re-united with his wife Grace and their son Robert, now almost six-years-old. After three weeks, with strength regained and the Sydney solicitors McFadyen & McFadyen providing advice, Cousens was permitted to live under open arrest with his family in Mosman. At first this necessitated daily trips across town to report to military headquarters at Victoria Barracks. After the solicitors petitioned that their client, still very frail and suffering acute anxiety from years in captivity, found it a great strain to deal daily with city noise and traffic, the army allowed Cousens to report by telephone from home.

CHAPTER 9

POW Families Listen to Radio Tokyo

The Asia-Pacific region was crisscrossed with competing shortwave grids as the airwaves hummed with the din of call signs and the crackle of transmission. It is impossible to know for certain the size of the audience that tuned in to this babel of radio, news, music and features. Nor is it clear what it was that was heard, let alone whether the exposure to radio propaganda changed individual opinions.[1] What is certain, however, is that radio listening was widespread even in countries where listening to foreign radio incurred a heavy penalty, and all governments, no matter their political hue, actively discouraged shortwave listening. Amongst the great array of programs that were available on Axis and Allied airwaves, those that carried information about prisoners of war were assured of an audience.

Belligerent nations, knowing the strength of the appeal of POW information, made it regular fare. The BBC broadcast news into Occupied Europe about the capture of European soldiers indicating the identity of those who had been taken into British custody. These broadcasts sometimes had an unpredictable outcome. For example, among a list of new prisoners in February 1940, the BBC gave the name of a recently-downed Luftwaffe pilot. In Berlin, eight German listeners wrote to the pilot's mother with the good news of her son's survival. The mother immediately denounced them to the Gestapo for the crime of listening to a foreign broadcast. All eight were arrested.[2]

Similarly, German shortwave stations made a practice of reading out, at random times, the names of prisoners of war. By 1944 a daily segment, *Forces Hour*, was beamed to Britain carrying Allied prisoner of war greetings to their families. As well an announcer from the station read lists of names of Allied POW casualties and those killed in action.[3] Another German program, *Anzac Tattoo* with the call sign *From the enemy to the enemy* and the signature hit tune "We'll Meet Again," was broadcast to troops in North Africa, predominantly Australians and New Zealanders. It gave details of prisoners' names and addresses. From mid-1943 every Saturday morning, "Axis Sally," the radio name of Mildred Gillars—an

American attached to Goebbels' department—interviewed two or three prisoners of war who had been captured by Germans or Italians in the Mediterranean theatre. A wisecracking vamp with a sexy voice, Gillars was sarcastic about what her subjects' wives and girlfriends were doing at home while these fighting men were forgotten, left mouldering in prison. In order to ensure an audience, Gillars always announced the names and addresses of the prisoners she would interview well before the program.[4]

In Paris, on German-sponsored Radio Paris, there was a fifteen-minute program each evening that listed the names of French prisoners held in Germany, often including prisoners' messages to their families in France. This slot regularly backed up to a announcement warning listeners against believing the misinformation emanating from British radio about De Gaulle and his "untrustworthy followers."[5]

Across Southeast Asia, the families of the two hundred and fifty thousand Allied soldiers and civilians, missing from early 1942, were desperate for any sort of information. Their distress was aggravated by the Japanese government's refusal to provide lists of prisoners of war even though it was required under the conventions of the United Nations. The will to listen to Japanese radio among POW families was strong. Those that owned a set that could pick up shortwave tuned in seeking the "fleeting embrace" of a radio message.[6] Even if without a family member incarcerated in a Japanese camp, they listened for those who were. Mrs Adelaide Levy of Rose Bay in Sydney was typical. Every evening, notebook in hand, she sat by the radio, glued to Japanese shortwave ready to take down the names of any Australian prisoners mentioned so that she could pass them on. She saw herself as carrying out the "war effort in a private capacity" even though, in her words, it meant that she was "exposed to the filth that came from the Japanese announcers."[7] Obviously, regular listening was restricted to households with shortwave radios. But, those without moved heaven and earth to acquire a set, as in the case of three young Australian women who pooled their savings for a shared radio in the hope of hearing news about their fiancés.[8] The author's own grandmother tuned in nightly to Radio Tokyo in the hope of hearing some word of her son who, unbeknownst to her, had been sent as a prisoner to the Burma railway.

All the stations within the Japanese network—Tokyo, Batavia, Singapore and Saigon—offered regular segments of prisoner messages. Over Radio Tokyo, from mid-1943, there were scheduled programs that included time slots with information about individual prisoners and about POW life. The very first broadcast containing POW information was heard over Radio Batavia on December 19, 1941. It was directed to "Mrs F. Borden" whose son, a first lieutenant in the Australian forces, had been captured in Indonesia. The announcer stated that young Borden was now "safe with the Japanese army," had "received hospitable (sic) nursing" and wished to tell his mother "there is no need to worry."[9] Between December 16, 1942 and January 29, 1943, when statistics were collected, forty letters from Australian POWs were read over Radio Batavia. By May 1943, messages were sent daily. A year later, Radio Singapore was sending out a couple of batches every morning and evening. Civilian messages were regularly heard from Shanghai.

From mid-1943, the POWs at Bunka Camp produced programs focusing on prisoners of war. *Zero Hour*, first created in March 1943 by Cousens, Ince and Reyes, was joined in December 1943 by the *Hino Maru Hour* (Flag of the Rising Son), later renamed *Humanity Calls*. The contents offered music, Japanese news and short lists of POW names. *Three Missing Men*, written by Provoo, Ince, Dooley and an American, Edwin Kalbfleish, was a spoof based on life in the POW camp. There also was a segment *War on War* with what were claimed to be real POW reports about their terrible experiences as soldiers in battle. Ostensibly created as part of the Emperor's aims for peace, the Japanese managers at Broadcast House canned the program when the stories became too gruesome. From around August 1944 until the end of the year, a light-hearted program, *Jamboree*, played on Saturday nights. It consisted of group singing, jokes and improvisations and included a music hall skit "Aussie and Yank" in which announcers, with the appropriate accents, hammed up the stereotypes of each of the Allied nations. Briefly on-air in 1944, *Camp Reporter* linked up vignettes about the conditions of life in POW camps. It fell foul of the Japanese censors for deviating from the program's specifications, which were to show life under Nippon in a cheerful light. *Postman Calls*, another Bunka program, contained a regular skit with "Mickey, Tim and the Major" played by Parkyns, Dooley and Cousens. Towards the end of the war, *Postman Calls* in its entirety was devoted to messages from prisoners of war.

Among the Australian groups who listened regularly to Japanese programs, the AIF Women's Association, the Prisoners-of-War Relatives Association and the Red Cross maintained a roster and contacted families whose men folk were mentioned. Information from broadcasts was passed on as well in an informal manner. When "Oklahoma" Atkinson, an American civilian contractor being held in a camp near Shanghai, broadcast to his father in the States, his mate's mother heard the transmission and alerted the Atkinson family. Eighty-three other people, listening on that night, also contacted the Atkinsons.[10] Similarly, the wife of an Australian prisoner named on Radio Tokyo received sixty telephone calls, twenty-five letters and six people previously unknown to her appeared at her door to tell her that they had heard her husband's message.[11]

The American, Fred E. Hahn, held in a camp outside Tokyo, sent a message in November 1944 in his own voice to his mother and sister in New York.[12] Captured in Mindanao when the Philippines fell, Hahn after several moves had ended up with two hundred and fifty other prisoners crowded into a single barracks on the Japanese mainland. As it happened, Hahn's mother, on the East Coast of America, was out of range of the direct shortwave transmission, but two listeners on the West Coast sent her recordings.

The usual POW information was broadcast in a short personal message. Or the announcer might read out a list of names, addresses and army identification numbers.[13] Much less frequently, the voice of the POW himself was heard. (There is no evidence of women prisoners being involved.) The typical format was that, in an interruption to a news broadcast, a voice would announce that a POW spot was anticipated, at an unspecified later time. It ensured that those tuned in remained close to the set. Hahn's example from a POW in a camp outside Tokyo illustrates one sort of recording. The Japanese guards in his camp announced that ten prisoners could send family messages, the prisoners themselves drawing the broadcasters' names from a hat. The lucky ten were required to submit their messages to the Japanese censor. The content was to run for no more than three minutes and was checked, returned, rewritten and resubmitted for a final review. A few days after this process, Hahn and the others were taken under military guard by train to Radio Tokyo. Through a glass window into a studio in Broadcast House, they watched a woman announcer as she introduced them on-air. She spoke English with an American accent and Hahn identified her after the war as Iva Toguri. At designated breaks in the program, a Japanese interpreter indicated which prisoner was to step forward and read his message.

In another process, recording staff from NHK travelled around the prison camps collecting written messages and taping prisoners' voices on mobile recording units.[14] A great many of these messages contained stock phrases indicating that the Japanese had a hand in their framing. But some did not. Parkyns, Cousens and Dooley insisted at the end of the war that only "Buddy" Uno had rewritten POW messages for broadcast on-air, and that once he had been transferred to Manila, all messages over Radio Tokyo were genuine. Other evidence, however, suggests that many were concocted. The addressees and the content of the messages probably were lifted from prisoners' Red Cross letters or from censored mail posted to the prisoners from home.

John Parkes, a twenty-year-old Australian signalman, had a message read over air by an English announcer at the end of January 1944. Directed to his mother, who was living on a dairy farm outside Sydney, it said: "Dearest Mother, I am fit and uninjured. Don't worry. Keep cheerful and optimistic for the day must come when I shall be able to return home." Mrs Parkes did not hear the message, but someone in the Weather Bureau on the opposite side of the country, who had been listening to Japanese shortwave from Singapore, passed it on to the Australian Department of Defence. The official who wrote to Mrs Parkes cautioned her that the material was "part of an enemy propaganda program and should be accepted with reserve." Having had no word at all of her son since his enlistment, Mrs Parkes was overjoyed, though in fact John had not sent the message. Indeed the first he heard about it was when he returned home. At the time of the broadcast he was as scrawny as a scarecrow, bootless and clad in a G-string laboring under the terrible conditions on the Burma railway. He had sent a couple of Red Cross cards, one just before Christmas 1943, that contained the same sentiments and it was probably from these that the information was taken.[15]

In late 1944 Lena Strong, in Albuquerque, New Mexico, received a number of letters from American radio listeners who had heard a long message read to her over Radio Tokyo from her husband, Dale. Beginning with "Hi there, darling" and signing off with the assurance that she was "still her husband's sunshine" his one hundred and fifty words contained references to family members and their activities and his own plans for their future on his release. Dale Strong had not sent the message, but it was clearly based on information contained in the letters that Lena and the family had been sending from Albuquerque since his disappearance at the fall of Bataan.[16]

The continuity scripts that the announcers read in the POW broadcasts were often misleading. For example a message sent in *Postman Calls* from "An Australian machine gunner," Corporal D. W. Barrett, to his girlfriend in Perth stated simply "All my love. In best of health, Lance" (which was the soldier's nickname). The announcer in Tokyo added a long observation which was that "Lance is particularly fit" that he "trains daily by running a mile or two before breakfast" and that he had "reaped the benefit in Sports Day in both long-distance running and the tug-of-war." The announcer also added the extra information that "Lance is a section commander and is doing a very good job indeed." In another episode of the same program, after reading a short message from Len Schurs to his mother in Queensland that stated "Doing fine, Love to all, your son Len," the announcer added "when speaking of doing fine Len is miles in front of George Washington for the truth. His real condition is super good."[17]

For two brief periods, at Christmas 1942 and from August to December 1943, Radio Batavia broadcast messages from Australia, sent by Australian families to Australian prisoners in Asia. These had been transmitted to Indonesia from Melbourne over the Australian Broadcasting Commission's shortwave service. By December 29, 1943, three hundred messages had been sent from Australia. In Tokyo, they arrived between 8:15 and 9:15 in the morning and at Bunka Camp, when they were to be received, two POWs transcribed them in the Front Office as they came over the receiver. Each message was then typed on a "roneoed form" and given to the Japanese staff, in theory, for dispatch to the prisoner in whatever camp he might be. There is no evidence that any of these messages were ever delivered. The POW broadcasters in Bunka, however, made a point of acknowledging the messages they received on their next transmission over Radio Tokyo to Australia. In two instances, the Melbourne station rebroadcast the messages after Radio Tokyo announced that bad weather had interfered with the transmission.

The Australian government was unenthusiastic about these Australian family-to-POW exchanges. It was feared that the contact might provide an "avenue for Japanese propaganda" by encouraging "even more Australian citizens to tune-in to Radio Japan." The Australian Broadcasting Commission and the State Publicity Censor, the institutions that oversaw the recording of Axis broadcasts, rebuffed all requests for transcriptions, even when they came from the Red Cross or from leading community groups. These two wished to obtain copies of messages that had been broadcast in order to send them to the families who lacked radios. After much lobbying and letter writing from constituents, the cabinet asked the Prime Minister's Committee on Morale to examine the matter with a view to banning private citizens' access to foreign shortwave. After much huffing and puffing, and a great many meetings, the committee decided that it would be counter-productive to the morale of the thirty thousand Australian prisoners' families to prevent their tuning-in to Radio Tokyo. (Moreover, such a policy was unenforceable.) Instead, the official listening post in Melbourne was instructed to contact families quickly, when POW names were identified. This would ensure that other families, who might be tempted to tune-in, would know that they too would receive word without the need to listen themselves if a family member came over Japanese shortwave. The Australian Broadcasting Commission was ordered to tailor its programs so that they would offer information that would counter the propaganda emanating from Radio Tokyo.[18] In the United States, a similar service with the same instructions was provided by the Federal Communications Commission that maintained listening posts on the West Coast.

Prisoners knew the importance to the families at home of receiving a message and if given the opportunity to frame it in their own words, they tried to send a signal that would have a special meaning known only to close family members. The stories of the coded messages that were sent home by prisoners have passed into the folklore of the Pacific war. Two related anecdotes are common. In both, members of a family agree that if one is ever in trouble they will send a postcard in red ink. In the other version, the captive individual will attach the stamp upside-down as a signal of distress. Subsequently, one of the sons is taken into Japanese captivity and writes home in glowing terms about life under Nippon, but in a postscript adds that the only thing he lacks is a bottle of red ink or a postage stamp.[19]

The truth was that as delighted as the POW families were for any information at all, many POW messages sent in code were incomprehensible. Norman Dillon, nineteen years old and unmarried when he enlisted as a signalman in the Australian Eighth Division, had been transported to work in a Japanese steel works. When three Japanese civilians brought a recording machine to Dillon's camp, his senior officer sanctioned the broadcast, seeing no reason for him not to send word to his parents living in the Sydney seaside suburb of Bondi. Dillon sent his mother a long message on July 30, 1943 and it was rebroadcast the following day. She did not hear it, but was grateful and puzzled by the letters that arrived from listeners as far away as Wellington in New Zealand and Idaho in the U.S. All of them mentioned that her son had included his child in the greeting. Before the war, Norm and his older brother, Neil—in 1943 away fighting in the Middle East—had bought the latest model "Baby Austin." The car was their pride and joy and before the brothers left on overseas service they put it up on blocks for the duration. After reassuring his mother that he was well and had received some letters from home, Norm had added that he hoped "Baby Austin was giving no trouble."[20]

When Tim Dooley in Bangkok was given the opportunity to transmit a message in his own voice, it was that he was very happy, in good health and sent a special greeting to "Dr Broughton Hall," a reference to the name of the Sydney lunatic asylum. "Broughton Hall" was the punch line in a genre of 1940s jokes and probably a good number of Australians, at least those living in Sydney, would have twigged to the reference. In any event, the message has passed into POW folklore.[21] Others that came from Dooley were more abstruse. He sent word to his nine-year-old daughter that when he returned home he would "tell her a story about tigers, an elephant and cherry blossoms." From this she was supposed to deduce that her father had been in Burma, Thailand and Japan. And even more elliptically, he announced on-air that "the sun grows daily in strength and benefit" which was to signal to his Australian listeners that the Emperor's party that desired peace was in the ascendancy. Later, again, he instructed his family to "tell Teddy and Darcy to quit fooling with that garden, the earth is disturbed enough." This was code that they should read, though it seems highly unlikely that they could have, that the groundwork had been done and it was time for the allied invasion.[22]

Dooley made a number of commentaries or broadcast those penned by Cousens. Their object, as the two Australians saw it, was to help Allied commanders by alerting them to events in the Pacific war as seen from the Axis side. In many cases, however, the gist of what they wanted to say would have been almost impossible to discern.[23] After the saturation by American bombing raids over Tokyo in early 1945, Dooley broadcast "Quiet Night." It described the absolute peace of Tokyo in the evenings, presuming that the "monitors" on hearing it would immediately realize that the broadcast was announcing that the bombers were right on target. In March 1945, with the support of Domoto in Bunka and probably written by Cousens, Dooley produced five broadcasts that were to indicate that the Japanese had no "ambitions south of Manchuria" and in a "carefully guarded manner to our authorities" the Allies should drop the demand for unconditional surrender. He called the first broadcast "Magic," the "gist of which was the magic of words to warn that something important was to follow."

Cousens worked on a set of commentaries with an individual from Japanese Foreign Affairs who worked in the Bunka Front Office. Ostensibly, the talks were to give direction to the allies. Dooley read them on-air. Based on *Aesop's Fables*, it was assumed that any astute monitor who had been through the Australian education system would seize on the fact that these were familiar allegories and in this case related to the current state of international relations. For example, the story of the lion and the fox, in which the two animals fight over who owns a dead animal that they have found while a third animal "slinks in and steals away the carcass," was a warning. While the Allies differed over how to finish the war, the Soviet Union would invade and steal away the dead body of Japan.

In late 1944, Cousens and his Bunka group became convinced that leading newspapers in the United States, like the *Washington Post*, the *Baltimore Sun* and *The New York Herald Tribune*, were writing editorials in reply to Cousens' radio commentaries. In a rather convoluted explanation, Cousens reported that he also took confidence in the fact that the Allied governments never mentioned his coded messages about the alternative group of anti-militarist liberals within the Japanese elite. He took the silence as proof that they were listening. When American and Australian broadcasters over home shortwave transmissions castigated Radio Tokyo for broadcasting propagandist and unbelievable news, Cousens read this and the lack of comment on his "real messages" as proof that the Allied governments did not wish to blow his cover. Several POWs who followed Cousens' strategy for dealing with the Japanese were convinced that his ideas resonated with certain section of the Japanese elite, especially a very senior official who became a kind of mythical figure in Bunka conversations and was referred to as the man who "occupied a whole floor at the Imperial Hotel."[24] Members of Cousens' faction in Bunka believed that even the Emperor's April 1944 Rescript, on the correct handling of POWs, had in some manner or other been influenced by what had been said in Cousens' broadcasts.

For prisoners in very poor condition, living in captivity could produce a disoriented sense of reality that was totally encompassed by what they confronted in the pressing struggle to survive day to day. Ideas of escape traditionally have provided the central component in the prisoner of war mindset. Escape formats the prisoners' daily thoughts and gives substance to their dreams and fantasies. In the classic narratives of captivity, the prisoner outwits his guards by force of heroism and a superior morality and makes it safely home. Jean Renoir's film, *La Grande Illusion*, about French prisoners of war in World War One and Douglas Bader's *The Great Escape*, about British prisoners in World War Two, exemplify the genre. World War Two Allied prisoners in Asia, however, had little hope of such deliverance. Caucasians could not melt into their surroundings, rarely spoke the local languages and were often interned in remote and inhospitable terrain. Added to this was the appalling physical deterioration that was the lot of prisoners of war under Nippon. The months in captivity robbed previously fit men of their physical stamina and when there was little hope of achieving a real escape, fantasy was the only outlet from the sordidness of the surroundings.

Some of what seems odd behavior among the Tokyo broadcasters may be explained therefore by the effect of their terrible conditions. For example, at the end of 1942 and again in March 1943, Charles Cousens wrote to Tsuneishi, the Japanese commander in Bunka, requesting that the Imperial government parachute him into Australian territory so that he could negotiate a peace between the Australian and the Japanese governments. He considered himself the ideal person for the venture because he knew plenty of important people in Australia, and he guaranteed that he would return to Japan within a few weeks with the answer. Interrogated in Yokohama, he explained forlornly that it was the only means of escape that he could devise. Similarly, Mark Streeter also had come up with the idea, though he saw himself heading off to Washington "as a peace emissary" between Japan and the United States.[25] Most likely, these quite fantastical ideas were propelled by the combination of a powerful desire for escape and a large degree of displacement from the surrounding social reality.

In the postwar trial, Charles Cousens' defense rested on the claim that he had been sending disguised messages back to Australia that contained information helpful to the war effort. Specifically, the Australian broadcaster from Tokyo argued that he was attempting to indicate to the radio monitors in Australia and America that there was an anti-militarist group within Japan who should be encouraged. His plan was to take over the Japanese commentaries on shortwave in order to have a mouthpiece through which to articulate this position. Somewhat paradoxically, he figured that he needed to reassure the Japanese controlling shortwave broadcasting that his intentions were pro-Japan so that they would give him access to the information from overseas shortwave news and a free hand to write the commentaries that other English-speaking announcers would broadcast on-air. Even while accepting that this was the Australian POW broadcaster's objective, it cannot but sadly strike a reader, sixty years after these broadcasts took place, that it would not have been easy for listeners on the home front to discern the double-meanings that were being conveyed.

There are a great many examples in Cousens' commentaries in which it would have been difficult for the listener to deduce that the message was anti-Japanese. The first of a set of four broadcasts that he produced very soon after his arrival in Tokyo, as he tells us, was in order to "see what [he] could get away with." However, they fit easily within the genre of nature and foreign travel writing in Japan. Tracing the trip he had made from Burma to Tokyo, Cousens described the landscape, the roads, the lack of bridges, the absence of garrisons and how other Japanese ships were also traveling the route. He included details of the kindness he had received at the hands of two Japanese merchant sailors and mentioned that the ship carried a cargo of wolfram. Information about the last, a mineral vital in armament production, would have been of great interest if passed on to the War Office in London. The climax of the fourth broadcast was a lyrical description of the exultation that Cousens experienced when first viewing Mt. Fujiyama, the "high point of all Japanese scenic experience." Probably, few listeners who might have heard them would have registered these broadcasts as anti-Japanese. By contrast, Cousens assumed the Australian radio monitors would comb the talks for useful information such as the many destroyed bridges he noted on the way, or how long it took him to travel by train from Hiroshima to Tokyo.

A very early transmission from Tokyo, made on August 12, 1942, was the central piece of evidence on which the charge of treason was later laid in Sydney. The broadcast portrayed the Japanese as generous and courtly. It was written during the first disorienting days when Cousens was alone in Tokyo. Families of the Allied POWs in other parts of Asia, where they had been taken into captivity in the first months of 1942, were frantic about the fate of their men and, there is no doubt, that in this talk the broadcaster is attempting to allay their fears. The announcer employed such hyperbole and exaggeration to get his message across, however, that it would not be surprising to find that his sentiments were interpreted as pro-Japanese. Cousens began by explaining that he wished "to bring you a special message of cheer to the homes of those Allied soldiers now in the Japanese prison camps."[26] He emphasizes several times that he can be believed because "I myself am a prisoner," and therefore he is speaking from his own experience. The broadcast stated in part:

> *I have seen a number of Japanese centers a thousand miles apart and I can tell*
> *you that your men are being treated considerately by the Japanese. While there are*
> *some places where food is short the simple reason is the dislocation of farming and*
> *to such centers the Japanese have now been sending food ships and I have myself*
> *travelled on two such food ships. The regulations issued by the Japanese Authorities*
> *in the various prisoner of war areas are very strict so no deviation from them is*
> *tolerated. But the regulations are generally fair and reasonable, and where they*
> *entail due hardship, I have found the Japanese officers willing to listen to sensible*
> *suggestions. Games, concerts and various forms of entertainment are allowed as*
> *well as regular education classes. There is no interference whatever with religious*
> *worship. Health and hospital facilities are Japan's first concern. This is a statement*
> *of fact based on personal experience as I am, as I told you, a Prisoner of War myself.*
> *I have no doubt that this statement will prove unpopular in some quarters as stories*
> *of frightfulness seem to play a major part in modern total war, but be that as it*
> *may, I make this statement freely as a matter of common human duty. I have a*
> *secondary motive that is I have personally been shown such remarkable kindness*
> *by so many Japanese that I feel this is an opportunity to express my gratitude for*
> *that kindness. They have treated me, an enemy national, as a valued friend. In the*
> *interests of the world tomorrow I am glad to put these facts on record now. You*
> *may care to know some details. Where there are places where civilian prisoners are*
> *interned, regular concerts are held and there are no restrictions on the internees*
> *going for walks unescorted in the surrounding countryside. In a nearby POW camp*
> *they occupy the palatial barracks put by the British Authorities. Ration scales when*
> *I was there was light but whenever men were called upon to perform heavy work*
> *the ration was increased. Finally I finish with the hope that I will be able to return*
> *home to you and take part in building that new world which we all want so much.*
> *Goodbye and God bless you.*

It is worth underlining the particular circumstances in which this broadcast was made. These were the early disorienting days of defeat. The Australian journalist Rohan Rivett, whose *Behind Bamboo* is generally lauded as a true and moving account of Australians as prisoners of war, described as the "main preoccupation" of most of the soldiers when first interned in Java was the "anxiety that would be weighing on the families." Every captured Allied soldier in Asia was aware that no one at home had any idea what had happened to the men of the Malaya Command. In Rivett's camp, in the first weeks after the Allied surrender and in the hope of getting word back to the relatives, more than a hundred soldiers wrote letters that were broadcast over Radio Batavia.[27]

Cousens later gave other talks that would be less likely to be interpreted as pro-Japanese. For example on February 4, 1944, in "War Without Purpose" he applauded Australia's prewar Prime Minister Robert Menzies' notion that Australian interests after the war would be best served by a prosperous Japan. The theme in many of the Australian's commentaries that Australia's rightful place was with its Asian neighbors, in Japanese terms as within an Asia Co-Prosperity Zone, was considered pro-Japanese, but today is commonplace.[28]

Grace Cousens and her young son were living with her parents in the Blue Mountains outside Sydney when her husband's first broadcast came over the air. Since their radio was without shortwave, the first she heard was when reporters arrived at her door. That night, at a friend's place, she listened to Radio Tokyo. According to her description of the event, when she heard her husband's voice she had a "ghastly feeling" and was "stunned then horrified and chilled to the very marrow." The voice was instantly recognizable though the tone shocked her— "flat, lonely and sad" and far removed from the ebullient vitality of the voice so familiar on 2GB. For her, it was "unthinkable" that her husband had "deserted his men to become some despicable Lord Haw Haw." She "doubted that even the threat of death could have made him a pliant enemy tool," unless the Japanese were in some way "threatening his men." Later, she admitted, it was "sweet agony" to listen to her husband over the air. She knew that he was often sending her a message by the music he played on the *Zero Hour* program, and by the references he made to events and places, such as the name of his first sailing boat or a holiday house on the Hawkesbury River, that only she would recognize.[29]

The Bunka broadcasters, and their Japanese overseers, imagined that the POW families at home would provide a channel of communication to their Allied governments. Family members, as careful listeners, would use the information in the broadcasts to pressure their governments to end the war. The files of government correspondence in reply to questions from anxious POW families, however, reveal that officials were more often hostile than helpful. For many senior government figures, prisoners of war were much like defeated chessmen off the board and out of the game.

CHAPTER 10

Iva Toguri in Wartime Japan

Zero Hour, created in mid-1943, was a central piece in the Japanese Army's planned expansion of psychological warfare. The objective of the program was to make the Allied soldiers homesick. By reminding them of everything that they were missing in Pacific combat, far from home, military morale would drop and the soldiers become "too discouraged to continue to fight the Japanese people."[1] This rather convoluted objective was never achieved. Far from making the listeners miserable, *Zero Hour* became genuinely popular, probably the only program anywhere on Axis radio to achieve such a feat.[2] Charles Cousens, Norman Reyes and Wallace Ince demonstrated professional flair in putting together a hip program that relied on the racy sound of the latest American music. It was an inspired choice, as well, to use Iva Toguri as the disc jockey, a sassy-sounding female with a distinctive voice and an on-air patter that was peppered with American slang.

The manager of the program, George Mitsushio, came up with the idea to take on a female announcer to increase the sex appeal for male listeners. Unusually perhaps, Cousens picked the twenty-seven-year-old Toguri, a Japanese American who was employed as a typist in the Business Section across the hall from the *Zero Hour* staff. Cousens had noticed Toguri and her "gin-fog" voice and that she spoke in a distinctive "Yankee and mannish manner." Ince and Cousens knew, too, from surreptitious contact that she was an American national who longed to return home to California.

Japanese employees at the radio station were supposed to have only minimum contact with foreign prisoners, no more than was necessary to carry out their radio tasks. The policy, however, was never rigidly enforced. Though there were *kempei* in the building, prisoners themselves were not under guard. The bustle of a busy radio station created an atmosphere that was entirely different from the pervasive and looming violence at Bunka Camp. Radio supervisors at Broadcast House were not given to face slapping or the more brutal methods commonly used in POW camps to ensure orders were carried out. And there were plenty of opportunities for discreet communication between Japanese and POW broadcasters. This was especially so with Cousens and Ince, the two highly skilled professionals who were supposed to raise the broadcasting standards of the Japanese staff. Initially assigned to a "prisoner's room" away from the main thoroughfare, the two were soon moved up to the third floor to share a room with several Japanese on the radio staff, later including Iva Toguri.

She had noticed the prisoners on her first day at Broadcast House and had been struck by their "shabbiness" and the general wretchedness of their situation. Ince in particular, whose digestion could not accommodate Japanese food, was a "walking bag of bones." Several days later, on the stairs, she had slipped them a small packet of food and subsequently handed over medicine and tobacco that she scoured from the black markets around Tokyo. On hearing that a prisoner in Bunka was desperately ill, Toguri produced a woolen blanket that she had brought from the United States and Ince smuggled it back to camp wrapped around his body under a raincoat. Even more important to the prisoners' morale, Toguri passed them information about the war's progress that she gleaned from her fiancé Filipe D'Aquino who was a typesetter at the Domei news agency.[3] In mid-1944, when Cousens was hospitalized, Toguri brought him food and medicine, as indeed did several other Japanese Americans from Radio Tokyo. In the last year of the war, when food shortages were dire and the Bunka prisoners were starving, Toguri regularly brought Cousens and Ince rations which they hastily consumed on the spot or hid under their clothes to take back to camp.

The program *Zero Hour* took its title from the term that designates the anticipatory moment immediately before battle. It also powerfully evoked Japanese patriotism—the pride of the Nippon air force was the zero and the symbol recalled the red circle of the rising sun at the centre of the Japanese flag. *Zero Hour* began on March 1, 1943 as a twenty-minute slot with Norman Reyes as the single, English-speaking disc jockey. Three months later, it occupied an hourly slot every evening at 6 P.M. Tokyo time, just after the GI dinner break. By then it used a brace of English-speaking broadcasters, and when Iva Toguri joined in November 1943, it ran for an hour and a quarter. By the end of 1943, the program's support staff, renamed the Front Line Section, occupied a large part of the third floor at Broadcast House.

Each afternoon, before the program went to air, Cousens took Toguri through the script. Usually he read it first, asking her to note what he had done with his voice in different sections and encouraging her to copy his pauses and changes of tempo. These, he said, were the keys to successful broadcasting because it was the way to hold the attention of an audience. He insisted that she should make herself smile when introducing the program, as the physical action of changing the muscles in the face would "lift" her voice into an appealing register. He also explained to her the rather crackpot contemporary theory of the "radio wipe" whereby it was believed that an announcer could expunge from a listener's mind the information they had just heard. Much-discussed in the 1930s, in the new world of commercial radio it was imparted to neophyte announcers to guard against their accidentally doing away with a piece of paid advertisement. According to Cousens, it had been observed in the radio world that if a piece of copy was run too close to the preceding announcement, the listener would forget the first message in favor of the second. This was because it had been "proved scientifically" that the human brain cannot cope with two pieces of information at the same time. Therefore, as Cousens testified in Toguri's defense, whenever a segment of her program was scheduled to follow the Japanese news, he would write into the script that she should repeat "thank you, thank you, five times and quickly" in order to "wipe clean" the listeners' recollection of the preceding Japanese news.[4]

After the war, she and Cousens both emphasized that the aim of the POW broadcasters and the expatriate American civilian had always been to entertain the soldier-listeners who tuned to *Zero Hour* and, by this method, subvert the Japanese military objective.

Japanese Americans in Japan and in the United States

Iva Toguri was among the fifty thousand young, second-generation, foreign-born Japanese in Japan when Pearl Harbor was bombed. Her experiences in Tokyo during the war, and indeed her treason conviction in the United States after the war, can only be understood within the context of the habits and the history of the Japanese community in North America. These were the crucial factors that influenced the choices made by Toguri, and indeed by the other Japanese Americans like her, stranded in Japan for the duration of the war.

Within the United States, since the passage of the Alien Act of 1798, American naturalization had been restricted to white immigrants. The Gentleman's Agreement with Japan in1907 limited the numbers of Japanese immigrants to the United States, and the Immigration and Naturalization Acts in 1924 further reduced immigration and proscribed citizenship for the Issei, that is, Japanese residents of the USA who had been born in Japan.[5] They had settled mainly in Hawaii or on the West Coast of the United States, predominantly in California, but also in Washington, Oregon and parts of Utah. A great many of them were farmers and rural worker, who had been pushed into emigration by the pressure on Japanese farmland from a growing population and expanded industrialization. By dint of hard work and great frugality, a few Issei who had begun life in the United States as farm workers managed to buy land. Alien law restricted the length of leases permitted to non-American farmers and prohibited outright alien land ownership. In some cases, however, Japanese-born farmers were able to get around the ownership restrictions by a process of guardianship whereby the legal title to the land was held in the names of their American-born offspring.

The second generation, like Iva Toguri, the Nisei, children of the Japanese-born, were American citizens by birthright. They were unlike their parents in that they had grown up in the United States, were imbued with American values through the school system, spoke English as natives, and often had little or no Japanese.[6] As American citizens, they could vote when they achieved their majority and in general their expectations were much like those of their Anglo peers—they wished to obtain a college degree and a good job. Many commentators have pointed out the social experiences and cultural formation of the two generations, the Issei and the Nisei, were quite distinct. The exigencies of emigrant marriage under restrictive entry laws, with the consequent plethora of single men, created a demographic skew in which late marriage and the birth of offspring created an age disparity between the older and the younger generations. Communication was often hampered by the parents' lack of English and the children's poor Japanese. What the generations, Issei or Nisei, shared was that they had all experienced profound social and economic discrimination. The older generation, even individuals who had achieved considerable financial success, remained in agriculture as truck farmers, fruit and vegetable growers, florists, nurserymen and gardeners or in the small businesses that serviced these occupations.[7] Few of the next generation escaped this narrow occupational ghetto or could ever hope to achieve high occupational status. Despite having completed an American education and, in many cases, acquiring university degrees, most Nisei were unable to find work appropriate to their skills and education within the mainstream Anglo American community.[8] As a consequence, many continued to work in the sorts of businesses that had been dominated by their parents' generation or, if they were employed outside the agricultural sector, it was as maids, gardeners, housekeepers, cleaners and building attendants.[9]

The Issei generation, probably in great part as a consequence of their social and political exclusion in America, retained close ties with Japan. Within the Japanese diasporic community it was customary to register a child's birth in the municipal record of the parent's home region in Japan as well as in the civil records of the host country. In Japan, it ensured dual citizenship and, in theory, at least in peacetime, meant that the Nisei could function in both places. Along the West Coast of the United States there was an extensive and active network of prefectural societies that kept close links to the region of origin at home. As well, within the Buddhist and Christian churches, which served the Californian Japanese American community, there were strong links between Japanese Americans and the home institutions across the Pacific. For Issei and Nisei, too, there were the ties that bound them to family and relatives in Japan, sustained, as far as finances permitted, by regular trips to visit relatives and participate in family celebrations.

Local cultural organizations from the 1920s strongly promoted pro-Japanese sentiments. The nationalistic push overseas was supported from the home government in Japan. Enormous crowds of Japanese Americans turned out to welcome the junior members of the Imperial family when they toured California. Equally enthusiastic were the public gatherings to greet various Japanese naval vessels that made official visits along the California seaboard. However, nothing approached the exuberance, bordering on hysteria, with which Japanese Americans of all ages greeted Nippon athletes at the Los Angeles Olympic Games in 1932. When these young performers arrived from Japan, a flotilla of large boats packed with well-wishers accompanied their steamer into the harbor at San Pedro and several thousand cheering admirers crowded onto the pier. Japanese American fans bought up the seats wholesale at the Olympic swimming pool and the athletic track whenever Japan athletes competed. The sight of the Rising Sun ascending the flagpole, each time Japan achieved a victory, evoked frenzied applause.[10]

The Sino-Japanese War in 1937 produced another great outpouring of patriotic sentiment among Japanese Americans on the West Coast. Funds were raised and comfort packages sent to soldiers at the front. As well, young Nisei groups made contact with American youth and church groups, giving the official explanation for Japan's invasion of Manchuria in order to counter any local Anglo sympathy for the plight of the Chinese.[11]

From the earliest days of Japanese emigration it was common for Japanese families to send their children back to Japan for extended visits, during which they would learn the language and be exposed to the culture. Japanese is a very difficult language and commonly these American-educated Nisei spoke it poorly, with heavy foreign accents. Much like colonial upper class families of yore, however, the Californians usually faced a real financial struggle. Issei families sent their offspring, when secondary education was completed, to be finished with an immersion in Japanese culture in contact with Japanese relatives.

From 1926 there were organized study tours to Japan for young Nisei, sponsored by Japanese language newspapers in California. With an astute combination of subscription marketing linked with a cultural project, the newspaper *Nichibei Shimbun* in Los Angeles and later the *Shin Sekai* in San Francisco sponsored annual trips by groups of Nisei youth to Japan. An important, reciprocal objective for the founder of the tours was to break down the common belief in Japan that the Issei and their offspring were "uneducated and uncouth" and the "dregs of Japanese society."[12]

The Nipponese perception of overseas Japanese as less cultured than those at home had a long provenance and several consequences. In 1939, a study carried out by a Tokyo school which specialized in teaching foreigners of Japanese descent found that many Nisei in Japan felt like "misfits" and found life in Japanese society extremely difficult.[13] Many of these foreigners had left California in despair at anti-Japanese racism, only to find that in what was supposedly their other homeland they confronted a pervasive xenophobia directed at them as outsiders.[14] Among Nisei visitors surveyed, a great many were critical of the Japanese school system, the customs, the food and the "mode of living." Respondents noted that the language problems they faced in Japan were as daunting as those that their parents had confronted in America. In the survey, Americans of Japanese descent described themselves as "Japanese in features, American in ideas." Hardly surprisingly, the survey informants frequently expressed a strong desire to return to the United States.[15]

Nippon hostility towards the foreign-educated of Japanese descent was perhaps most marked in Japan towards young Nisei women. At the end of September 1941, Japanese women's organizations were amalgamated into a single group dedicated to what they believed to be their role, to stay at home and devote themselves to the "proper upbringing of Japanese children." At the same time the head of the Japanese Women's University railed against the bad example that foreign women set in Japan, which had influenced the Nippon female intelligentsia to prefer a life outside of the home.

In 1940, the fifty thousand Nisei then in Japan came mainly from the United States and Hawaii.[16] In all the larger Japanese cities there were special schools dedicated to the education of young Japanese from abroad. They provided intensive language teaching for foreigners and served as crammers for those students whose parents wished them to prepare for Japanese university entrance. There were also courses for foreigners in well-known universities such as Waseda. Women's schools, for example the Nippon and Tokyo Joshi Dais, were reserved to foreign women, and, as well, there were coeducational colleges and boarding houses to provide for the cohorts of young Nisei students sent abroad for an exposure to genuine Japanese culture. In these institutions, students were taught not merely Japanese speech, history and geography, but also the niceties of Nippon manners and aesthetics, in order to add some finesse to what, in Japanese eyes, was the galumphing behavior and rowdy demeanor of the western-educated young.

Mary Kimoto Tomita, a Californian Nisei, has left an engaging record of her time as a young American-educated woman during a cultural tour to Japan.[17] Although she and Iva Toguri never met, Mary's Tokyo record provides a fine foil for Toguri. The Tomitas, small farmers outside Modesto in central California, worked daylight to dark growing vegetables. When Mary was twenty-one years of age she was sent to spend half a year in Tokyo. The plan was that she would get to know her Japanese relatives and learn the language. By the beginning of December 1941, she had finished her Japanese sojourn and was on her way home. The day of Pearl Harbor, Mary was on the high seas for California and as soon as the news came through that war had been declared, the Japanese steamer turned back to Okinawa. Mary was stranded in Japan for the rest of the war. Between mid-1939 and January 1947, she wrote regularly to her friend Miye in California and her chatty letters provide extraordinary insight into wartime Japan from the point of view of a young woman, despite Issei parents and her Japanese looks, who remained very much an American girl.

From the beginning, Mary was dazzled by the city of Tokyo with its seven million inhabitants. For her, there could not have been a greater contrast between the pace and glitz of the capital and the life she had known at home on the farm. In the Ginza, Tokyo's glamorous Fifth Avenue, there were elegant shops with beautiful clothes and exquisite objects on display. Whole streets were occupied by nothing but bookstores, where it was possible to find titles in Japanese or foreign language translations on every imaginable subject. Tokyo nightlife took Mary's breath away, especially in the months before the dampening effect of war had set in. Brightly lit thoroughfares teemed every night with shoppers and merrymakers. Theatres offered performances of traditional Kabuki or western plays in translation. And there were any number of concerts from which to choose. Students could obtain cheap tickets to hear classical Nippon or European composers. Having grown up in a household where cash was scarce and leisure rare, Mary was entranced by the Asian habit of eating out. In downtown Tokyo or even in the smallest neighborhood, stalls and restaurants served an unimaginable array of delicious dishes to thronging diners at all hours.

Away from home, Mary enjoyed more freedom than she had ever known. In California, farm chores absorbed the time outside school hours and leisure consisted of Sundays spent at the Holiness Church, a branch of a Japanese evangelical Protestantism favored by Issei families in the Modesto district. In Tokyo, Mary rented a series of rooms in boarding houses that specialized in providing accommodation for young overseas students. Living on American funds, she had plenty of money and relished her independence, staying out late at night with a crowd of Nisei friends and foreign and local students. The host Japanese families frequently were at odds with their unruly American boarders, who were ostensibly in Japan to study, but were also high-spirited and up to pranks and adventures. Mary was chided frequently by her Japanese elders for what they considered were her wild ways. The mother of the Nagata family, with whom she first boarded, asked her to leave because she disapproved of Mary's freewheeling style. A friendship had blossomed between the young American and the son of the house and the two often sat up talking into the early hours. The last straw, perhaps, for Mrs Nagata was when Mary was seen engrossed in conversation, sitting on the son's bed. As Mary later wrote to her friend in California, such behavior was unthinkable for a young woman brought up in Japan. They were what Mary scathingly described as "demure Japanese maidens" whose delicately restrained manners were light years away from Mary's own exuberant ways. By comparison with those raised in Japanese surroundings, Mary claimed that she was glad that she was who she was: "Browned and tough. Boss of the world. Slave to no master."[18]

A constant theme in Mary's letters was the difficulty of learning Japanese and the endless problems she encountered as she struggled with the language. For example, with her "strange accent," she was sometimes mistaken for a Korean. The *New York Times* correspondent, appointed to Tokyo in early 1941, found the same disconnect between the language abilities of locals and the Nisei visitors. When seeking to hire a bilingual secretary, he found that Japanese educated in Christian mission schools could speak English, but that their efforts at translation were atrocious, whereas the American-born Japanese spoke "perfect English," but knew next to no Japanese.[19] In Mary's case, even when her language had improved so that she could read signs and was beginning to understand the newspaper, she never mastered the polite form in which cultivated Japanese women spoke. The problems of imperfect Japanese were magnified for Nisei stranded in Japan during World War Two. Cut off from funds from home, the only hope these Japanese Americans had of earning an income was in organizations such as overseas monitoring services for shortwave radio where English was needed. There was a growing demand for people who could fill these jobs, but such employment was not always easy to find.

In the course of almost five years in Tokyo, most of them during wartime, Mary became more and more sympathetic to the Japanese people and the Japanese government's attitude to the Pacific war. She changed in other ways as well. At the start of her sojourn she looked down on Japanese plumbing, found the intricacy of local manners stifling, and derided the "passivity of Orientals." By the latter years of the war she had become much more critical of the United States. She berated the American leaders and admired the Emperor and the valorous young Japanese soldiers devoted to their nation. None of this is surprising. Mary was living with Japanese people, friends and relatives, most of whom treated her kindly. As the war progressed Mary suffered, as did they—the wearying hunger from food shortages and the horror of Allied bombings that flattened Tokyo and the other large cities in Japan.

Throughout her time away from the United States, Mary always thought of herself as a "Californian girl" and "full of pep," to use her own favorite expression. Her references to herself and her life were all anchored in American popular culture. She talked in her letters about Blondie and Dagwood comics. She loved Betty Boop and Myrna Loy and she held Scarlett O'Hara above anyone else as the model for an independent young woman. What she missed most was the *Readers Digest*. On the rare occasions that she received a bundle from home, or someone in Tokyo passed on a copy, her joy knew no bounds. On August 15, 1945, when the Emperor announced the defeat, Mary, like everyone around her, was shocked. Very quickly, however, when the American Occupation forces took over, she was able to find well-paid work with them using her English and her American passport. In very short time, she had happily brought to the fore the American side of her identity.

Mary Kimoto Tomita's experiences shed an interesting light on those of Iva Toguri in wartime Japan. Both young women were products of a Californian education and shared a perception of themselves as independent and energetic American girls. Similarly, they had been caught in Japan for the duration of the war. The notable difference between them was that, when the conflict ended, Mary returned the United States and simply took up the pieces of her previous life.

Iva Toguri in California and Japan

Iva Toguri was a "genuine Yankee Doodle Dandee," meaning that she was born on Independence Day, the 4th of July.[20] She was the second child of Jun and Fumi Toguri and their first American-born. The parents were from the Yamanashi Prefecture in Tokyo and Jun, who worked for a Japanese export company for many years, made regular trips to the West Coast of the United States, immigrating to California, via Canada, in 1899. Fumi followed him in 1913, bringing their three-year-old son Fred Koichiro. In Los Angeles three years later, Iva was born and in 1920 and 1925 her sisters June and Inez arrived. As was common among her parents' generation, her father registered his daughters' births in the municipal register of their Japanese prefecture. In 1932, perhaps at Iva's own request (certainly by this age she was a self-assured young student) her birth registration in Japan was withdrawn. In all these ways, the trajectory of her life before the war replicated that of many young Californian women with Japanese-born parents.

The family spent the first decade of Iva's life in various towns in Southern California, following Jun the breadwinner. She went to primary schools in Calexico and San Diego and in 1928 the family moved back to Los Angeles to live in a freestanding wooden house at 11630 Bandera Avenue in Watts. When Iva's brother had almost completed a law degree at UCLA, he left university and started a grocery business with his father. Early in 1935 they leased a store on Wilmington Avenue, a block away from the house, where they sold Japanese variety goods and groceries as well as fruit and vegetables. Fushi Toguri, Iva's mother, who was a diabetic, suffered a stroke in 1937 and henceforth was bedridden. Much like many Nisei and their Isei parents, Iva's mother spoke little English and her daughters' Japanese was poor, the two generations communicating in a mixture of both. In 1937, Jun bought the store on Wilmington Avenue, and a year later he acquired a block of land opposite for a nursery. The property was placed under guardianship in Iva's name, as she was the oldest Toguri child to hold American citizenship. When Iva went to Japan, the power of attorney was passed on to the next eldest sister June.

Iva was very bright and enjoyed school. Her particular interests lay in the sciences and biology. From McKinley Junior High, where she graduated with honors and made the class graduation speech, she moved to Compton High School and then graduated to Compton Junior College. In January 1950, by which time she was in a federal prison, the President of Compton College sent Toguri's school record to her parole board in West Virginia with her results from a standard battery of tests conducted in the Californian school system. They indicated that Iva had a very high IQ with outstanding verbal and reasoning skills. The principal added, probably with no racism intended, that Iva Toguri, "like most of the Japanese students we had here before the war, was one of the outstanding students" who had the "usual characteristics of industry and talent of the Japanese people."[21] At the start of 1934, Iva began a science degree at UCLA. After suspending for several semesters with appendicitis, she graduated in June 1941 a Bachelor of Science with major in Zoology, and began graduate work in that field.

Zoology was Iva's passion. She became an active member of Lamba Sigma, the Life Sciences Club, which catered for students interested in biological science who went on weekend field trips and expeditions to carry out observations and collect specimens. In 1949, when the Justice Department was preparing the case against "Tokyo Rose," FBI agents assiduously tracked down and interviewed a great many of Toguri's Lamba Sigma contemporaries, as well as her teachers at UCLA. Almost without exception, they recalled a "boisterous girl" who invariably was the "life of the party." According to these descriptions, Iva Toguri was very "Americanized," even, as one informant described her, the "All-American girl."[22] Her physics teacher recalled that she was a "good mixer" and "not an introverted type like many Japanese" and "had always associated with Caucasians."[23] Betty Hashii, who had known Iva for many years, recalled that she used a lot of American slang and never expressed any interest in things Japanese. On campus she avoided the Nippon Society and was not part of the sporty crowd of Nisei in the "Japanese Students for the Bruins" who turned out to cheer the UCLA team at all their games.[24] Elsewhere, though, the FBI investigators found an informant who recalled that, like many people at the time, Iva Toguri had been skeptical of the stories in the press that the Japanese troops had committed atrocities at the time of their invasion of China.[25] A single UCLA acquaintance was hostile in general to Japanese Americans and to Iva Toguri in particular even though the two had "chummed around" together in college. Dorothy Webley seemed to resent that the young Nisei woman had "plenty of money to spend" and drove a car. In their political discussions, she recalled that Iva had been "strongly isolationist" and anti-Roosevelt because he favored a European war.[26] Given that this take on politics was shared by many Republican Party members at the time, it is probably not surprising, as FBI records showed, that in 1940 when Iva had first registered to vote she did so as a Republican and voted in the 1940 elections, presumably for the same party.[27]

The Toguris, evidently, were not short of money. It seems too that they allowed the older children a good deal of latitude. Iva, sometimes accompanied by her brother, took to driving to UCLA in a late model four-door Chrysler, picking up her friends on the way. She recalled that her father provided the petrol and when her classmates gave her money for gas she could use it for her own expenses. In the recollections she provided in Tokyo before her arrest, Iva described herself as a "typical Californian teenager." She had been a Girl Scout, played the piano, mooned over the latest Hollywood movie stars and, like thousands of other young American women, had a crush on Jimmy Stewart. The generation that came of age in the late thirties swooned to the songs of Deanna Durban and felt their heart strings tighten with Myrna Loy and Greta Garbo's on-screen love affairs. The Toguri sisters loved to jitterbug and on Friday nights at home they would roll up the rug and dance to radio music. A bobbysoxer in pleated skirt, saddle shoes and cold-waved hair, Iva saw herself as squarely in the mainstream.[28]

When the FBI agents began collecting testimony for the Justice Department's prosecution of Toguri as a traitor in 1949, they were at pains to collect as much information as possible about her family in Los Angeles. The Anglo neighbors were forthcoming. Their descriptions provide an interesting, if dispiriting, sidelight on Japanese American relations through the prism of perceptions of a single Japanese American family in a small east L.A. neighborhood. The Toguri family was clearly successful. They had built up a thriving business; their children were hardworking and helpful and doing well at school and university. The internment of the Toguris permitted the neighbors to express an antagonism that may have been just below the surface all along.

Like many middle-class girls, the Toguri sisters learned the piano. The local teacher, Mrs Mildren Thoburn, who claimed to have been "in and out of their house over the years," was quizzed at length by the FBI.[29] She recalled that the children were "polite" and that, of the three, Iva was the "most outgoing, aggressive and ambitious." She noted that the Toguris always claimed to be Christians, but they "never seemed to go to church." When pressed by the FBI investigator though, she could not recall ever seeing a shrine in their house. She also remembered that when war was declared, Mr Toguri was "very disappointed," and had blamed the "military element" in Japan. Another neighbor was sure that the Toguris had a "small temple" placed in front of the shop with "rice cakes." The neighbors at the back claimed that they had "never trusted the Toguris" and had "always suspected that the whole family was disloyal." The evidence was that Jun Toguri had planted a row of cypresses to "screen off their backyard." And, on another piece of land the Toguris owned near the nursery, they had "put up a radio tower with the obvious purpose of listening to shortwave broadcasts from Japan." The FBI agents, picking up immediately on the whiff of treason, carried out an elaborate investigation only to find that the radio tower had been erected by Edison Power on the easement they owned over a strip of the Toguri's land. The same neighbor reported that she had taken great umbrage in the shop when she had heard Mr Toguri say that "boys in Japan were more respectful and better brought up than boys in this country." She had also been very suspicious about all of the luggage that had been loaded up when Iva left for Japan. Her doubts were confirmed, though the evidence suggests loyalty to the home-city rather than the reverse, when she had heard on the Watts grapevine that Iva was homesick and "to keep her happy" her father had been sending her the Los Angeles newspapers.

Neighborhood relationships were altered forever by the roundup of the West Coast Japanese community. In Wilmington Avenue, the neighbor who took over the Toguris' shop greatly benefited when the Japanese residents were cleared out of the area. Viola Young (in the words of the FBI, "should be noted is a Negress") had known the Toguris for years. Their children played together and she was a regular customer in the market. When the notice of their internment arrived, Mr Toguri asked Mrs Young to look after the shop and the Toguris' personal belongings that they were forced to leave behind. She had felt very sorry for them and when Mr Toguri telephoned from the relocation camp in Tulane, she had driven up there to bring them warm clothes from home and supplies from the shop. By the end of the war, however, Mrs Young had changed her tune. By then, as the FBI agent noted, she was the "proprietor of the well-stocked store" and "had no further use for the Toguris or any of the other Japanese families who formerly lived in the area." She now remembered that Mr Toguri had often said "how nice things were in Japan" and that "all along" she had suspected that "he had been a sharp duck."[30]

In the spring of 1941, Iva abandoned her university studies. Her mother's sister in Tokyo was very ill, and after more than thirty years, wished to see her sister. As it was impossible for the invalid Fumi to travel, it was decided that Iva should go in her stead. It was planned that she would stay in Tokyo for a year, visit her relatives and study Japanese. Three months before departure, Iva began Saturday morning lessons to improve her spoken Japanese. As the day drew near, friends from the Sigma Club threw a farewell party. Clair Steggall, who later obtained a doctorate at UCLA, recalled that Iva had told her at the gathering that she was going to Tokyo because her father desired it. While she was there, she hoped to get into medical school. It seemed that among Iva's mother's Tokyo family there were several doctors who might be able to smooth the way for her, whereas in California it would be nearly impossible for a female and one of Japanese descent to be admitted to a medical degree.[31] Betty Hashii, who helped Iva sew some new clothes for the trip, remembered that her friend had not seemed keen to go to Japan, but had said that it was her father's wish. Before she left, Iva said goodbye to the neighbors in Wilmington Avenue. Later, when the FBI interrogated them, several recalled the mountain of luggage that the Toguris had sent to the relatives in Japan.

On July 1, 1941, Iva sailed for Okinawa on the *Arabia Maru*. She took twenty-seven pieces of luggage that included presents and food, clothes, medicine unobtainable in Japan, and a sewing machine for a cousin. She did not have an American passport, but carried the requisite documentation of an Identity Document from the US Customs and Immigration Service and her Californian birth certificate.[32] Traveling with her, also without passport, was another young Nisei woman from Watts, Chieko Ito, making the trip back to Japan to meet the relatives and learn the language.

Toguri in Japan

In Tokyo, Iva settled down with the family of her mother's sister, Shizu Hattori. Her uncle, Hajime Hattori, was a tailor with a substantial business employing thirty cutters and seamstresses. Iva claimed, later, that though the family was very kind, she was homesick and in the beginning suffered a good deal of culture shock. She was taken aback to see so many Japanese faces everywhere in the city and noted that before going to Tokyo she had never stepped inside a "proper" Japanese home. Japanese customs were alien, even peculiar, from the mundane convention that shoes were left at the door and one washed with soap and water before entering the bath, to the more fundamental matters of eating, sitting on the floor with legs tucked neatly underneath. Japanese food tasted strange to a palate raised on an American diet. Her cousins had to explain many conventions that struck the American as arcane such as that Japanese people always bowed in the direction of the Emperor's palace whenever they were in that neighborhood. Very early on, Iva discovered how inconvenient life was without a car when she, her uncle and a cousin hauled home by commuter train the vast pile of her American luggage. Most difficult of all was the fact that Iva's Japanese was poor. She could neither read nor write; in her words she was "perplexed by the language." And she faced the strain of many young western women in Japan as they confronted the relatives' expectations that the American visitor would lead the restricted life of a well-brought-up Japanese girl.

On September 8, 1941, during her first week in Tokyo, she had registered as an American citizen at the United States Embassy filling in an application for a passport, which she was told would have to be sent to Washington for processing. She enrolled in a language school run by missionaries and began to look for a job. In November 1941, still unhappy and worried that US-Japanese relations were deteriorating, Iva asked her father's permission to come home. In turn, he urged her to remain and take advantage of the opportunities to learn the Japanese language. A week before Pearl Harbor, however, Jun telegraphed Iva that she should seek a passage home on the first available boat. A steamer was soon to leave for the West Coast of the U.S.A., but without a passport, Iva was not able to purchase a ticket. And, of course, after December 7, all regular traffic between North America and Japan ceased.

Switzerland was the protecting power for Allied countries in wartime Japan and Swiss consular staff arranged the passages for Allied citizens out of Japan and oversaw the property they left behind. On March 30, 1942, Iva registered at the Swiss Legation as an American citizen who wished to be repatriated to the United States. At this time she was told that it was highly unlikely that she could be exchanged because she was without a passport. However, on September 2, she was called to the Swiss Legation and informed that there was another exchange planned and a possibility that she could be evacuated to the United States. The arrangement would shift foreigners from Japan to a neutral country from where they could obtain a passage home. The transport out of Japan was gratis, but the passage from the neutral power to the United States would cost about four hundred and fifty dollars, which funds Iva no longer had. Toguri explained to R. Straeule, the Swiss consular representative, that she no longer wished to leave. She did not have the fare and did not know where her family had been located. Also, she was afraid that, without a passport, she would be refused entry to the United States. The Swiss official asked Toguri to make a statement in writing that she no longer wished to be repatriated but would remain in Japan, which she did.[33]

Later, at her trial, it was suggested that Toguri's relinquishing the possibility of repatriation was evidence of her belief in the victory of the Japanese and her desire to participate in it.[34] The situation of the Toguri family in California, however, was the determining factor. The Japanese media made a good deal out of the mistreatment of Japanese in American internment.[35] Iva's family had been rounded up in Los Angeles in February 1942 and, along with the other one hundred and fifty thousand Japanese Americans, relocated to the American interior. The Toguris ended up in Arizona at the Gila River Relocation Centre and in May of their first year in detention, Iva's mother died.[36] Chiyeko Ito, Iva's traveling companion from Los Angeles, affirmed that both she and Iva had heard about the evacuation of their Japanese families in California and knew that they too faced internment if they returned home. And in any event, all normal travel was cut off. Toguri shared a future with several thousand other foreign-born Americans of Nipponese descent also stranded in Japan for the duration of the war.

As soon as war was declared, the *kempetei* began to visit Toguri urging her to take up Japanese citizenship. They came at all hours of the day and night and although, in later testimony, she stated that they had never physically threatened her, it was an unenviable position to be a national of a country with which Japan was at war. The constant attention from the police made Toguri's aunt and uncle uneasy. They were embarrassed in front of their neighbors, so much so that in early in 1942, Iva moved into a boarding house to live on her own. She continued to refuse all requests to register as "a Japanese" even though it was difficult to buy supplies without a Japanese identity card. At the same time she combed Tokyo for work, also not an easy task for a foreigner without good Japanese.

Despite the difficulties, Iva's behavior in wartime Tokyo bordered on bravado. As she described it, she reveled in an American-ness that set her apart from her surroundings.[37] Chiyeko Ito and a Nisei from New Jersey at Ito's language school were her closest confidants. The three clung to their identity and were determined never to relinquish the citizenship of their birth. When together, their conversation revolved around how differently they felt themselves to be from the Japanese around them—"these people" or "the Japs" as Iva called them. The three bolstered their courage by reassuring each other that America would win the war. And they exulted, secretly, over their success in avoiding the patriotic initiatives of the Japanese government, such as buying small war bonds or Iva's habit of getting off the trolley before the Imperial Palace to avoid paying obeisance to the Emperor.

In mid-1942, her language skills landed her a job in the English monitoring service of the Domei News Agency. Later she helped Ito to find a position there. Both joined the team of the foreign-born English speakers used to transcribe and type overseas programs picked up by the Japanese listening posts.[38]

At Domei, Iva met her future husband. Filipe D'Aquino, at twenty-one years of age, was five years her junior. A handsome Yokohama-born Portuguese of Japanese descent, he had been educated in Catholic schools and spoke fluent English. Thirty years later, he could clearly recall the impression that Iva had made when he had first seen her in the corridor. She was "outspoken, rather noisy and often in scrapes." With her "happy-go-lucky demeanor" she had struck him as "not at all like a Japanese."[39] The two became close friends and very soon discovered that they also shared the hope that the United States would defeat Japan. Despite being surrounded by patriotic Japanese and North American Nisei all anxious to demonstrate their pro-Nippon fervor, Toguri quite unabashedly disagreed with coworkers when they claimed that Japan was winning the war. This in turn produced acrimonious exchanges and arguments, in one of which D'Aquino punched a coworker who had insulted Iva.[40] Later, in December 1943, Toguri left Domei for a more congenial job at the Danish Legation and, from August 1943, she supplemented her income with a second job late in the afternoon typing at Radio Tokyo.

In joining the English language section of the Japanese overseas broadcasting service, Iva became part of a radio venture that war had transformed. In order to service Japan's expanding shortwave transmissions, Radio Tokyo and the other news agencies required more and more staff that were fluent in English. In this unfamiliar milieu, Iva Toguri made her way as best she could and, as a result of her reaching out to the prisoners of war at Broadcast House, she became the female voice associated with the station's most successful program and along the way her future became inextricably bound up with the legend of Tokyo Rose.

CHAPTER 11

Listening to Radio Tokyo at the Pacific Front

Iva Toguri had been reluctant when first invited to join the program broadcasting to soldiers in the Pacific because she knew nothing about radio. Charles Cousens' assurances that he would write the scripts, provide voice coaching and instruct her on the principles of disc jockeying eventually won her over. Evidently he was a gifted teacher. In a very short time, Toguri became an effective broadcaster with a distinct on-air personality. It was Cousens who suggested that she take the radio name of "Ann," from the notation on the script for "Announcer." In a typical introduction to her segment, Toguri would refer to herself as "Orphan Ann" or "Orphan Annie" and greet her soldier-listeners as "Boneheads" and "My own orphans of the Pacific." The latter expression, which was much bandied-about at her trial, was a reference to the Japanese government's claim that Australia in misguidedly following the British Empire had been abandoned as the orphan of the Pacific.

Without a doubt, the core to *Zero Hour*'s appeal was American music. American and Australian soldiers, whether packed like sardines on naval warships or bivouacked under canvas throughout the islands, were drawn by the music. Swing, pop, "hot" and "cold" jazz, the foot-tapping rhythms of the big bands and the languorous notes of romantic ballads and the "sweet" semi-classics teased the ear. The Boston Pops playing Gershwin's "Strike Up the Band" was the program's signature tune, and arrangements from Benny Goodman's Band were standard fare. The romantic voices of Deanna Durban and Nelson Eddy received much airtime, as did Rudy Vallee and Paul Robeson, the latter often singing Negro spirituals, particularly "Old Man River." Among the light classics, Tchaikovsky's *Nutcracker* and the *Dance of the Sugar Plum Fairy* were perennial favorites. From time to time, even music from Gilbert and Sullivan was heard, a risky choice in a country where *The Mikado* was banned outright. As well, a regular segment showcased very contemporary pieces including the latest Gershwin, Louis Armstrong and newest sound from East Coast big bands. The platters that were spun were selected with great care from Radio Tokyo's extensive library of some twenty thousand albums.

The staff on *Zero Hour*, arriving at work after lunch, spent the afternoons preparing the scripts for that evening's broadcast. There were daily production meetings to discuss the material for presentation and planning meetings to brainstorm ideas for scripts that would constitute future broadcasts. The general routine, reflecting the predominance of the American-educated, was that the staff, with the exception of Cousnes, typed their own material. He had never been expected to type at Radio 2GB in Sydney and therefore wrote his material in longhand. The finished scripts, often completed very close to the hour they went to air, were handed over to the program censor to check, after which they were typed on a stencil by one of the young American-born typist. Carbon copies were then distributed to the Japanese officials who oversaw shortwave broadcasts and to individuals in Broadcast House.

Iva Toguri usually began her segment with the lighthearted greeting of "How's tricks" or with "Hullo friends, I mean enemies in the Pacific" and kept up a lively patter. It linked the musical pieces with plays on words in American slang. There were, also, many joking references to that core purveyor of American culture, the corner drugstore, with mouthwatering descriptions of the talismanic delicacies to be had there, the sundae and the banana split washed down with a brimming ice cream soda. The highly stylized banter evoked the carefree lives of the prewar American bobbysoxer—Bill and Betty Co-ed, on a Saturday night date, sitting in the car, under a full moon, listening the to the latest dance music on the radio.

The teasing tone elicited amusement rather than nostalgia. "Ann" saluted her listeners as the "honorable enemy" and urged them to "stop fighting the mosquitoes and start listening to the music." On a Monday, she might say, "Here I am, wash day for some, rifle cleaning for others or just another day to play." Or she joked that she had "some sweet musical propaganda for my dear little enemy orphans wandering in the Pacific." Sometimes she mimicked a Japanese accent, which Cousens explained was based on a well-known Californian radio comedy, "Frank and Archie," rebroadcast in Australia. Frank was the Japanese servant and spoke in a pigeon accent always asking if "you-no-likee."[1]

American Employees at Radio Tokyo

The Japan Broadcasting Corporation employed a stable of some forty English-speaking foreign language announcers. Connected to Japan in various ways, all could pass as native speakers. For example a son of Japanese diplomat educated abroad spoke perfect idiomatic English. Margaret Kato, with an English mother, was raised in London. Probably not surprising, given their shared English origins and accent, Kato became Cousens' preferred script reader and in the first months while he was alone in Tokyo he would often return to the station when she was on night shift. Warned by the *kempetai* that she had become too friendly with an enemy POW, Kato left Radio Tokyo in September 1943 for work at the German Embassy.

Most of the Japanese Americans possessed the typical, Nisei-bifurcated identity, having family ties and residential stints in both the United States and Japan. *Zero Hour*'s manager, George Mitsushio, was typical. Born in San Francisco and a graduate from a Sacramento high school, he had traveled to Japan several times with his parents. Having spent a year at the University of California, Berkeley and two at Columbia University, he dropped out, becoming a court interpreter (English and Japanese) in Los Angeles. Afterwards he wrote in English for *Rafu Shimpo,* the Los Angeles Japanese daily. In 1940 he went to Japan and in early 1943 became a Japanese citizen, shortly afterwards marrying a Japanese girl. After the war Mitsushio returned twice to San Francisco to appear for the prosecution in Toguri's trial, providing damming testimony that he had heard Toguri making treasonous broadcasts. Years later, after Iva Toguri's pardon was underway, Mitsushio admitted that he had perjured himself because an FBI agent threatened to have him picked up by the Occupation government and sent to the United States where his Japanese nationality would be discounted and he would be charged with treason.[2]

Seizo "Dave" Huga, a regular broadcaster on *Zero Hour,* had been born in Japan but moved to the United States, in 1936 graduating from the University of Dayton in Ohio. After completing a year in graduate school at Cornell, Huga returned to Japan in January 1940 and was drafted into the Japanese army. In January 1943, he was transferred to Radio Tokyo to boost the English-speaking staff. Nil Motomu, a Nisei from Honolulu, had completed a degree at the University of Southern California and stranded in Japan by the war ended up in the English section. He was kind to Cousens, arranging for a heater in the POW room at Broadcast House where the prisoners were quarantined in the early days and visiting Cousens when he was hospitalized in mid-1944. According to Foumy Saisho, in testimony at Cousens' trial, Motomu brought the Australian to his house for drinks and a meal. Ken Moriyama studied journalism at George Washington University in Washington, DC, but had never been able to find work on an American newspaper. In the mid-1930s, he had gone to Tokyo and been hired by the Domei News Service. He worked on *Zero Hour* for several months and was then transferred to Manila where he oversaw an equivalent music show directed at Allied soldiers and also with a female announcer. Kenichi Oki, the production supervisor, completed a degree at New York University where had been a star footballer, but after graduation could never find a suitable job. Finally he went to Japan and found work on an Okinawa newspaper. "Chuck" Yoshii with a teaching job in English language at a Tokyo university and a Japanese wife, filled in on *Zero Hour.* A graduate of the University of Oregon and a part-time broadcaster in Portland, he had joined the Japanese Broadcasting Corporation in June 1935.

The dozen women who were involved with *Zero Hour* were almost all second-generation Japanese American. Sato Masuko, for example, was born in California, graduated from Downey Union High School and Woodbury College. In December 1940, with her five sisters, she had come to Japan to visit relatives. Ruth Hayakawa, born in California, broadcast from time to time. Foumy Saisho, a censor of English language programs at Radio Tokyo, had completed undergraduate and post graduate studies in the United States. Her family had court rank and, unlike the other female staff, Saisho was outspoken and rather domineering which led her colleagues to suspect she was *kempetai*. The Australian Attorney General used Saisho to testify for the prosecution in the Cousens treason trial that took place in Sydney after the war. June Suyama, a Canadian Nisei, and Betty Oki, an American whose brother, Kenchiki Oki, oversaw production, regularly stood in on the airwaves when Toguri was absent. Catherine Muraoka, Mary Higuchi and Mieko Furuya, who later married Kenchiki Oki, did likewise.[3] Mary Ishii, who had been educated in England and Japan, and whose brother was also an English language broadcaster, had started as a secretary in the overseas department at Radio Tokyo and from late 1944 went on to present a program of light classics every Sunday evening in the *Zero Hour* slot. Ruth Sumiko Hayakawa had been born in Japan, but held permanent residency in California, where her father ran a nursery. She had attended Abraham Lincoln High and City College in Los Angeles. In early 1941, she was sent to Japan to live with her grandparents and attend Keisen Girls School in Tokyo.

There were several other overseas programs using female announcers. The *Women's Magazine of the Air*, transmitted late in the afternoon, several days a week, began in early November 1943 and continued until the end of the war. The program, *War As I See It*, was supposed to reflect a women's point of view. Katherine Fujiwara, Yuneko Matsunaga, Ruth Hayakawa, Mieko Furuya and June Suyama were at various times involved. Written by Japanese journalists and translated into English, these programs pulled no punches in propounding Japanese propaganda. For example in an episode of *War As I See It*, dedicated to the Australian soldier, the female announcer stated, "You Aussies are fighting a war in New Guinea while the Americans are back in your country running around with your wives." On the *Women's Magazine,* female announcers often urged "mothers and families at home" to call a "halt to the war" as they were the only ones capable of ending "the carnage." The *German Hour,* which began early 1942 and continued throughout the war and with a principal male announcer provided by the German Embassy, included half an hour in English presented by female announcers. It came on-air immediately after *Zero Hour*. Regularly, the female announcers taunted their listeners that "boys back home are making the good money and can well afford to take your sweethearts out and show them a good time." Or, "your girls and wives are betraying you" and "4Fs working in a war plants are making big bucks while stupid soldiers like you fight in filthy foxholes."[4]

There were non-Nipponese women regularly on-air as well. They included the elderly Frances "Ma" Topping, an American missionary long-resident in Japan, the Swiss Dr Lily Abegg, and the British women Diana Powers and Frances Hopkins. Regional stations around the Pacific, like Bangkok, Batavia, Nanking, Singapore and Saigon, also employed female announcers. Manila Radio enjoyed the services of Myrtle Liston, sometimes called "Manila Myrtle." An American Filipina *mestiza* who had learned the announcer's trade in Shanghai before the war, Liston was the centerpiece of a program whose popular music was strung together with a bantering commentary very much in the mode of *Zero Hour*. Liston's speciality, however, was sexual innuendo. Those who saw her broadcast claimed that her tendency to tipple before the program only increased the sharpness of her repartee. Her monologues, which became more stridently risqué as the hour and the drink wore on, frequently took as a subject the contrast between the soldiers' horrible current predicament—"trapped in mosquito-infested foxholes" like "suffering jungle rats"—and the happy times they had known before the war.[5]

Most of the English-speaking female announcers in Tokyo were Nisei for whom Pearl Harbor had turned them into "strandees." Foreign women in wartime Tokyo faced real hardship. For those who found work in the overseas section of Radio Tokyo, it was a haven. The English-speaking department functioned in that language and provided a safe and relatively liberal environment for a working woman, and the pay was reasonable and regular. The American-born announcers socialized within their Nisei group and during the course of the war there were several marriages within the group. These conditions were in marked contrast with the experience of young Nisei women employed in other Japanese industries.[6]

At Broadcast House, Iva Toguri held herself aloof from the Nisei crowd, rarely socializing after her shift.[7] Because she worked two jobs, Iva arrived at Radio Tokyo later than the other broadcasters on *Zero Hour*. It was also her practice to leave early, usually before the end of the program, in order to get home at a decent hour. When she moved in with Filipe's mother on the edge of Tokyo, it was a two-hour trolley ride from Broadcast House. She was present, however, at an evening party to celebrate the marriage of Kenchi Oki and Mieka Furuya. And she attended when summoned by Major Tsuneishi to a special dinner in a restaurant where he congratulated the broadcasters for the success of *Zero Hour*, when it began to attract comment in the American news media.

The top military brass in Japan were delighted in late April 1944 when a Radio Tokyo monitor picked up a news item from *Time* magazine which mentioned that a female broadcaster on Japanese shortwave was attracting the attention of American soldiers in the South Pacific. The GIs called her "Tokyo Rose" and *Time* on April 10, 1944 listed some of their comments about the racy style of the program. Within the overseas section at Broadcast House there was discussion about who this Tokyo Rose might be as it was not a name that had ever been used at the station. Cousens testified in San Francisco in 1949 that he and Mutsushio had concluded that it had to have been a female broadcaster "down south," presumably Saigon or Batavia. It seems more likely, however, that the broadcaster with the risqué banter was Myrtle Liston in Manila.

By mid-1944, *Zero Hour* had reached the height of its popularity. From then it lost ground. In July, Cousens was hospitalized for three months and Ince, greatly weakened by his having been beaten by the Bunka guards, involved himself only with programs put together in camp. Without a scriptwriter, Toguri, on Cousens' advice, recycled previous scripts, inserting different music into the same structure and sequences of dialogue. Early in 1945 in preparation for her marriage, she was away from the radio station for an extended period. The new program managers had none of the flair of Cousens and Ince and were never able to achieve the previous pizzazz. In late 1944, for example, the new announcers had attempted to produce a *Zero Hour* using music of a pirated soundtrack from *Gone With the Wind*. Though the movie had been a blockbuster around the world, the Radio Tokyo program was a flop.[8] And of course it did not help the smooth running of the station that, throughout much of 1945, Tokyo was under constant bombardment, disrupting transport and public services and wearing down the nerves of those living through the nightly pounding.

Listening to Tokyo Rose in the Pacific

When FBI agents were collecting testimony for Toguri's prosecution in 1949, they went to great lengths to find informants who could recall the voice of "Tokyo Rose." The United States law of treason required two separate witnesses to the act, and because the U.S. Attorney General would claim that Toguri's treason had taken place over the airwaves, the identification of her voice was vital. Informants who knew her before the war recalled her voice and manner quite clearly. The information from the soldiers on location in the Pacific, however, was contradictory. Though it was clear that a great many soldiers and sailors listened to radio at every opportunity, and were adept at fine-tuning the dial to pick up music, it was difficult to identify the voice of a specific announcer.

Almost all of Toguri's associates from university days recalled that her voice had a very distinctive quality.[9] They noted, too, that Iva spoke very fast and used a great deal of American slang. Her biology lecturer remembered that her voice was "deep and mannish," pitched extra low. Another UCLA associate stated that characteristically she "blurted out her words."[10] Raymond B. Cowles, a university teacher, said her voice was loud and she "joked a lot with her fellow students." Another biology department member who had visited her home described her tone as "similar to some Negro and Hawaiian voices."[11]

The agents of the FBI were assiduous in tracking down returned veterans who might have heard Tokyo Rose while they were on station in the Pacific. Those who claimed that they had gave a variety of descriptions. She sounded: "like Dinah Shaw"; "similar to Lauren Bacall"; like "Mae West with a Boston dialect"; "like brown sugar with a touch of soy"; a voice of "silken voiced roses"; and a "sugary voice that purred." Someone else noted that she spoke in a broken accent "like a Mexican or a Spaniard with an accent on the end of every word." Another was sure she was an American because she "pronounced the 'and' and the 'if' like an American" in contrast to the difficulty that Japanese speakers have with conjunctions.[12] John Legget on the *USS Elden* recalled her voice as "native American with a dash of soy sauce."[13] Another informant described her as "an excellent singer who sang the most up-to-date popular American songs."[14] Another swore that she "always played the 'Lone Ranger' before and after the program"; and, from another, that her broadcasts were always accompanied by "screeching Japanese opera."[15] Thirty years later, a Pacific war veteran recalled that Tokyo Rose had a voice that "resonated with a clang like an iron bell."[16]

Not all soldiers were so sure. Colonel Carl Shoemaker, with a postwar position in the police department in Portland, had been stationed in Brisbane and New Guinea and in both places "night after night" had listened to Radio Tokyo.[17] He recalled that there were female announcers, but he doubted after three years that he could identify any one in particular. Dr Horace N. Miller, in the University Of Oregon Dental School, also declined the FBI on the same grounds that too much time had elapsed. Another Portland resident had served in the Pacific on the battleship *South Dakota*, between July and August 1945, and had heard Tokyo Rose every morning. The female announcer, however, must have been on another program because *Zero Hour* always aired in the early evening. Another Oregonian, attached to the 20th Construction group of the Seabees on Woodlark Island, between July 15 and 27, 1943, could clearly recall having heard Tokyo Rose "almost daily," though this obviously could not have been Iva Toguri because she had not begun on-air by that date. Similarly, Henry E. Wagner was adamant that he had heard Tokyo Rose broadcasting when he was at Guadalcanal prior to November 1943 and he had continued to listen to her again in New Zealand from December 1943 to February 1944.[18] He was sure that the female voice was the same on all of these occasions. There is no reason to doubt that this may have been so, and even that it was one of the stable of females from Radio Tokyo, but it was not Iva Toguri as she was not on-air before November 1943. A sergeant in an American Radio Squadron stationed near Calcutta from September 1944 to March 1946 had regularly listened to Radio Tokyo and, though he revealed that there would often be "five different female voices" on the same program, he offered to pick out the one whom he had most often heard because he assumed that would have to be "Tokyo Rose." As well, in Oregon, an informant contacted the FBI to offer information that Tokyo Rose was part of the world Jewish conspiracy.

An army journalist stationed during the war at Milne Bay, New Guinea and Manila had listened carefully to Radio Tokyo in order to pick up information that he could use in a unit newsletter he published.[19] *Zero Hour* was his regular fare because the news bulletins often contained domestic items from the States. He reported that the female announcer on the show had never referred to herself as "Tokyo Rose." Rather she introduced herself as "Orphan Annie." Though he was a committed listener to Japanese shortwave and was one of the group of first journalists to enter Japan after the surrender, and had been present at the joint press interview of Toguri in Yokohama in September 1945, he could not hear her voice clearly enough to tell if it was the same female announcer previously on *Zero Hour*.

Several soldiers remembered an individual in their unit in the Pacific who has been a "radio nut." Every evening without fail he twiddled the dial of a set he possessed in order to pick up on shortwave his favorite woman broadcaster. When the FBI managed finally to track down this individual, it turned out to be Axis radio beamed from Berlin to which, nightly, he had become addicted. And the American female broadcaster was "Axis Sally" the on-air name for Mildred Gillis.[20]

As the previous examples suggest, there was an enthusiastic audience for shortwave radio in wartime. A "Bluejacket" on a battleship in the South Pacific recalled that they had listened to Radio Tokyo constantly, but it was hard to hear the voices sometimes as the volume was controlled from a central place on the ship. He also recalled that once U.S. Forces Radio from San Francisco came on-stream the sailors listened less to Tokyo because they preferred United States radio and its more current dance music programs.

There was also the predictable variation in reporting what it was that "Tokyo Rose," if indeed it was she, had said to the troops. Some recalled that it was "Americans should lay down their arms and be welcomed by the Japanese." Another sailor heard her telling Australian servicemen that American forces were "loafing in Australia" and they would "find increases in their families when they returned to Australia and, though they would know the identity of the mother, they would never know who the father was." And at another time, a female broadcaster had said that the Americans in Australia were an "occupation force and were stepping out with the wives and sweethearts of Australian soldiers."[21]

While in New Guinea, and later on New Britain, W. H. Thompson listened to the radio and heard a woman who called herself "Eva, Orphan Ann and Tokyo Rose" and addressed the soldiers "knuckleheads, boneheads and orphans, and the forgotten men of the Pacific." She would ask them to "remember yourself with your best girl at the Californian drive-in" and reminded them they could be there if they "quit this fruitless fight." At another time he recalled that she had called them "bloody butchers of the Guadalcanal" and had anticipated the arrival of the 1st Marine Division at Cape Gloucester on New Britain. Located in the same region, another soldier remembered that while the soldiers fought in the "steaming jungles," Tokyo Rose talked to them about "juicy steaks, cool water and ice cream sodas." On Saipan, Jules I Suttar Jnr listened regularly to Tokyo Rose and heard her say "who do you think your wives and daughters are out with tonight, maybe a four-F." Some soldiers were alarmed because they claimed she knew about troop movements. But others said they liked the American dance music and got a "big kick" out of the broadcasts. Many people thought of *Zero Hour* as joke. In fact in the *Stars and Stripes*, the newspaper of the American troops, awarded Tokyo Rose a medal for her contribution to keeping up the soldiers' morale.[22]

A submariner from New York, John Haren, serving for three years from October 1941, recalled very clearly hearing Tokyo Rose and that her words had been very demoralizing to the members of his crew.[23] He had been on the *USS Stingray,* when he had first heard the woman whom he was told was "Tokyo Rose." As far as he could recall, she had referred to herself by this name and had been introduced as "Rose" at various other times. He knew the date when he had first seen her, January 4, 1942, because on that day *Stingray* had sunk its first ship and that evening Tokyo Rose had berated the U.S. Navy claiming that it had broken the Geneva Accords. After this he listened to her about twice a week. In February 1942 while the *Stingray* was off Java, the ship had run out of food and at this time Tokyo Rose had had talked about "meatless Tuesdays" in the U.S.A. The fighting men would never see meat again, but would have to eat "slop" and Australian goat meat. This had made the crew very upset as did her references to the coalminers going on strike for more wages when soldiers were dying for their country in the Pacific. Haren recalled that she had asked the sailors, "Do you think that people like that are worth fighting for?" And many of the submariners had agreed that indeed they were not. Men had expressed the wish to go home and deal with the unpatriotic strikers themselves. He could recall also very clearly an incident at Christmas Day 1943 when the crew sat down together to Christmas dinner and the voice of Tokyo Rose had come over the radio. She had played Bing Crosby singing "White Christmas" which had made all the men stop eating and listen. She asked them were they having a good Christmas and reminded them that the wives were at home "warm in bed with the war workers." He recalled that the sailors had been very gloomy and the cook had "got mad because supper got cold and was messed up." He felt that the men took her messages seriously and the morale of the entire crew had been hurt. While some of the detail of Sergeant Haren's narrative seems odd, such as having Radio Tokyo tuned in during Christmas dinner on an American naval ship, and the unlikelihood of a tight connection between Radio Tokyo topics and the minutiae of daily life on the *Stingray*, there seems no reason to doubt the substance of the recollections. The dates of the events described, however, mean that the "Tokyo Rose," whom he recognized, could not have been Iva Toguri.

There were a great many incidents that had become part of the fund of stories that soldiers retold from the Pacific and in them listening to the radio, and Tokyo Rose the putative female announcer often played a part. Frank Farrell, a frontline soldier stationed in Cape Sudest, New Guinea, recalled a particularly pernicious incident in which Tokyo Rose had "undermined the manhood" of American troops.[24] While he had not himself heard the broadcast in question, secondhand reports being common, other members of the First Marine Division had talked about it a great deal. Tokyo Rose had stated that "while 4F's and other combat dodgers back home were having a good time with the wives and sweethearts of men in the First Marine Division, the front line troops were slowly medicating themselves into a state of sexual impotency caused by daily doses of Atabrine." The chemical substitute for quinine, Atabrine was taken under military orders every day in order to ward off malaria in an area in which the disease was rife. After the broadcast, the incidence of malaria increased as men stopped taking their dose until the field commander ordered that the capsules were taken daily on parade.

Marshall Hoot was a Chief Boatswain in the Fifth Fleet in the Gilbert Islands late in December 1943 and was assigned to the crew of a patrol boat rescue unit.[25] Waiting for a call to action, Hoot and his mates listened to *Zero Hour* coming over Radio Tokyo, at other times they listened after they had finished their evening meal. He recalled that the women in the show used to "heckle" the listeners about being away from home and that their best girls and wives were "stepping out on them." He and his mates recalled being out in the boat one evening and hearing the female announcer congratulate the new Commander Perry who had just arrived, but warning him that he would soon be sorry. Several nights later "Charlie and his washing machine" came over and the squadron took a direct hit and several American pilots were killed. Later Hoot's boat crew deduced that it must have been this to which Tokyo Rose had been referring.

Another Californian, Ted E. Sherdeman, had been sent to northern Australia as part of the Radio Adviser to the U.S. Information and Education office which was overseeing the creation of broadcasting programs for the U.S. military.[26] He listened carefully to *Zero Hour* because it was such a successful program. He thought the mix of news and music and light banter was successful. The female broadcaster who often introduced herself as "Ann Your Friendly Enemy with your favorite program the *Zero Hour*" set a bright tone. She would invite her listeners to "come and relax, light up a cigarette and listen to Bing Crosby." She often asked them teasingly about whether they would like to be "in the nice cool corner drugstore sipping a chocolate soda with their best girl." At other times she would talk in detail about eating banana splits and ice cream sundaes. Sherdeman, perhaps subject to a successful "radio wipe," could recall little of the news broadcasts except that the editorials were often derogatory about President Roosevelt.

The FBI appeared to have overcome the uncertainty of who it was that the GIs heard when an agent assigned to collect evidence against Toguri tracked down several soldiers who came from the Toguris' Los Angeles neighborhood. Gilbert Velasquez had enlisted in the army at the end of 1942 and had known the Toguris for many years, living about a block away from the Wilmington Avenue market.[27] He saw them every few days, when his mother shopped in their store, and he had gone to school with Iva's younger sister Inez. Even when his family moved to Downey, Gilbert often came back to the old Watts neighborhood to see friends and drop in at the Toguris' market. He recalled that all the Toguris were very friendly though he never saw the mother, an invalid who kept to her bed. In September 1944, while stationed in New Guinea, Velasquez listened every night to Radio Tokyo. The first time Velasquez had heard Iva Toguri's voice he had recognized it immediately and, with great excitement, had told the GIs in his bunk unit that the voice coming over the radio belonged to a girl from his L.A. neighborhood. Not only did his comrades flatly refuse to believe him, they had teased him mercilessly for imagining that a poor Chicano from Watts would know the broadcaster on Japanese shortwave. So humiliated had he been by their taunts that he had stopped talking about her, though he was convinced that the voice belonged to Iva Toguri.

Transferred to Hollandia in Dutch New Guinea, Velasquez was out of range of Radio Tokyo, but at the end of October 1944, when he was located to Leyte Island in the Philippines, he was able to listen nightly to *Zero Hour*. Toguri's light "chit-chat" prior to playing records, Velasquez recalled, touched on familiar things at home that any GI from Southern California would recognize. The announcer referred to herself as "Orphan Ann" or "Orphan Annie," never "Tokyo Rose," as Velasquez clearly remembered. He also noted that she did not broadcast on the weekends and the female announcers on these days sounded nothing like the young woman from the Wilmington market. Velasquez recalled that she said often that the soldiers would be better off at home stateside and, once, that the "Japanese were kicking hell out of us at Palo." He was sure he remembered that comment, because he had been at Palo, himself, and knew that it was the Japanese who had been defeated.

Other neighbors from Wilmington and Bandera Avenue were systematically unearthed, but had been in combat in Europe, or were like Harold Lima. He had lived in the same house in east L.A. all his life, knew Iva Toguri well and while stationed in the Pacific listened regularly to the music on Radio Tokyo, but had never been struck by the female voices on air.[28]

The problem, with a lack of clarity in what people heard, seemed to have been solved when the FBI came up with an expert witness in El Paso, Texas.[29] A "Special Employee" of the FBI, a radio operator and a corporal with the U.S. Marines, David Gilmore could recall precisely the time of day and the dates, between July and October 1944, when he had listened to *Zero Hour* while in the Marianna Islands. Gilmore remembered the female radio announcer who had called herself "Orphan Annie" because she had played records like "Deep in the Heart of Texas" and "Stardust." When asked to identify three cuts of the phonograph, Gilmore unhesitatingly indicated that Tokyo Rose was the voice on cut one and an "entirely different person" was speaking in cuts two and three. As the FBI notation indicated, however, two and three comprised the voices of Iva Toguri. Presumably, the impossibility of identifying and tagging voices over the air, despite the extraordinary effort and the resources the FBI sank into collecting the testimonies, was the reason that the evidence was not used in court.

Japanese Surrender

In the last days of the war, as the city of Tokyo lay in ruins, staff at Broadcast House, on the orders of Japanese high command, shredded scripts and documents. Iva Toguri, who welcomed the end of the war, stayed at home. It seems not to have occurred to her that her involvement with *Zero Hour* might place her under a cloud with the occupying forces. In all cases, she was forthcoming when interviewed by the press and the United States Counter Intelligence Corps. Similarly, she seems to have been consistently open in the interrogations she underwent while in detention, off and on, between 1945 and 1948.[30] Even in April 1947, after two considerable periods in prison, when she was interviewed by the

FBI Special Agent, Fred Tillman, sent by J. Edgar Hoover to collect information for her treason prosecution, she spoke unguardedly about her war years in Japan. When Tillman asked whether she regretted her work on Japanese shortwave, she replied that she regretted nothing because it had given her the opportunity to assist allied POWs.

A swarm of journalists came with the occupation forces, representing newspapers that were avid for stories about the enigmatic enemy that for the last four years had filled American news. Two reporters in the Hearst media stable led the hunt in Tokyo for the woman whom they considered, "after Tojo, was the most known member of the enemy."[31] Harry T. Brundidge, a correspondent for *Cosmopolitan,* and Clark Lee, attached to the International News Service, sought out Broadcast House where they interviewed staff members who told them that there were a number of women broadcasters on NHK, but none was called "Tokyo Rose." The Americans were persistent. Eventually Kenchiki Oki, still employed at Radio Tokyo, took them to the down-at-heel rooming house where Filipe D'Aquino and Iva Toguri lived. The couple repeated the information: there were several female announcers and none was the famed "Tokyo Rose." The journalists offered Iva Toguri a contract for two thousand American dollars if she would give them an "exclusive" on the life and radio experiences of "Tokyo Rose." It was a very large amount of money in penurious postwar Tokyo and, probably not surprisingly, Toguri signed up though she and her husband denied under oath that she had ever claimed to be "Tokyo Rose," but only that she could give the detail about broadcasting on *Zero Hour.*[32] The Americans whisked her and Filipe away to the Imperial Hotel in Yokohama where they interrogated her about her life and her shortwave broadcasts. While Lee asked the questions, Brundidge typed the story straight onto his typewriter. A few days later, Dale Kramer, a correspondent from *Yank,* the magazine of the American army, separately tracked down Iva Toguri and convinced her to speak again about broadcasting over Radio Tokyo. This meant an end to the Hearst monopoly, but as it turned out, and to Brundidge's chagrin, the *Cosmopolitan* editor had already reneged on the contract, refusing to pay a "potential traitor" for a story. On September 5, 1945, with Filipe just out of the camera's eye-shot, Iva fronted a huge media circus at the Bund Hotel in Yokohama. While a hundred journalists shouted questions and the photographic lightbulbs popped, she told her story about how she came to be in Tokyo and her experiences broadcasting on *Zero Hour.* After the press gathering, the *Yank* correspondent turned Toguri over to the Counter Intelligence Corps. The couple were interrogated and held overnight and then let go. Almost two months later, U.S. military police picked her up again, though without a warrant for arrest, and held her incommunicado for seven months in the section of Sugamo Prison designated for Japanese war criminals. Like many held by the occupation forces, Toguri suffered the humiliation of detention. In her case, though, she was a captive whose notoriety had spread especially among GIs who had listened to Japanese shortwave. Consequently, she was constantly harassed by souvenir-seeking Americans. Perhaps the most troubling part of the imprisonment was that Toguri was refused visitors, even her husband. Nor was she allowed to write letters to her family or seek legal counsel. In April 1946, after seven months in Sugamo, she was told that the Counter Intelligence Corps had carried out a legal enquiry and there was no charge against her.[33]

Soon after rejoining her husband, Toguri became pregnant, the birth expected in January 1947. As an American Nisei with Issei parents who had been interned as aliens, Toguri was more aware than most of the importance of securing her child's American nationality by ensuring the birth took place in the United States. And, not surprisingly, the new mother longed for the support of family. Therefore, the pregnant Toguri applied to the U.S. consulate in Tokyo for a passport. The baby was born in early 1947, but tragically survived less than a day, probably as a result of maternal deprivation from the years of war and the months in Sugamo Prison.

Word of the passport application, however, had reached the American press and set off a hue and cry within anti-Japanese community groups in the United States. The Native Sons of the Golden West and the veterans' organization, the American Legion, ran a letter-writing campaign to "keep Tokyo Rose out of the States." Several journalists, including Brundidge and Lee, fanned the xenophobia to promote their own careers. The result was a media maelstrom. The dye was conclusively caste, however, when Walter Winchell, a ranting right-wing populist whose press and radio columns drew a huge following, took up the cry against Tokyo Rose with the mawkish claim that he was responding to the request from a Gold Star mother of a Pacific veteran killed in the war. In Winchell's words, the "Jap Tokyo Rose was a prosecutable traitor."[34]

There was a coincidence of interests between Winchell and his readers. With the 1948 elections approaching Winchell attacked what he described as the progressive liberalism within the Justice Department where he accused left-leaning lawyers of turning a blind eye to "Jap traitors." His political views resonated strongly with the sentiments of many of his followers who were caught up in fierce hatred for all things Japanese. Through the loud expression of anti-Japanese rancor, these Anglo Americans were able to pass over the suffering that internment had brought to the Japanese American community and as importantly allowed them to evade the thorny question of whether Nisei property that had been seized in the 1942 roundups would be returned to the rightful owners now that the war was over. Confronted with the high blast of Winchell's publicity, the U.S. Attorney General, Tom Clark, recommended the rearrest of Iva Toguri. Taken from her home in August 1947, again without warning, she was re-incarcerated in Sugamo Prison. In that racially segregated institution, she was held, as before, in the section restricted to Japanese nationals. Her husband was permitted a single twenty-minute visit per month.

After a year, the Department of Justice officials in Washington determined that in order to demonstrably answer their critics, Toguri should be tried in San Francisco. With no warning to her or her husband, she was hustled onto a U.S. military vessel, *General Frank Hodges*, that was bringing home GIs from Japan.

The ship docked in San Francisco on September 25, 1948 to a wharf filled with cheering families. As the exuberant soldiers hung over the railings waiting to disembark and a military band on the wharf played "California Here I Come," Iva Toguri, flanked by two FBI agents and appearing nervous and frightened was the first passenger to come down the gangplank.[35] This humiliating treatment by overbearing FBI agents, and with a Department of Justice determined to use Iva Toguri's prosecution for their own political ends, presaged the tenor of her trial.

CHAPTER 12

Trying an Australian Traitor: Charles Cousens

In Sydney on October 4, 1946 and an hour before the doors opened, a large crowd jostled for places outside the central court. They had come to hear the magistrate hand down his judgment in the committal hearing of Charles Cousens, the Australian prisoner of war charged with treason for having assisted the Japanese as a broadcaster. The trial had created enormous interest not least because it was the first case of treason in Australia for almost a century.[1] The legal issues were complex. Embedded in the differences between the laws of the Australian Commonwealth and the states, they produced sharp differences between counsel in court and contradictory commentary in the press.

The defendant had been a well-known announcer on Sydney radio before the war and the hearing of his case took place in a period of high public emotion. The months preceding the trial coincided with the demobilization of returning soldiers. Troop ships brought home servicemen from Europe and North Africa as well as the fourteen thousand emaciated survivors from Japanese captivity. The joy of reunion for some families was matched by the sadness of others as they confronted the painful fact that their loved one was among the eight thousand prisoners who had perished.[2] As the weeks passed, the overwhelming relief at the end of the war began to abate, replaced by a nagging uncertainty about the nation's future. At the same time, many families struggled in private with the strain of picking up the threads of lives cruelly disrupted by the war.

The prosecution as a traitor of an Australian prisoner of war raised strong and often contradictory feelings among civilians and soldiers. Community hostility to Japan and Japanese people was intense. The horror of Japanese wartime behavior was elaborated in great detail almost daily in the Australian press in reports on the work of the allied legal commissions collecting evidence for the Japanese war crimes prosecutions that had begun in January 1946. Hostility to Japan and Japanese people flared into intense indignation when it was discovered that the Australian government was bringing two Japanese witnesses to speak against Cousens at the trial.

Australian Attitudes to Japan

The daily papers followed the courtroom polemics as defence and prosecution argued the rights and wrongs of their cases. Australian responses to the Cousens trial can be judged from letters to the newspapers and also from the flurry of mail that constituents sent to Australian politicians, particularly the Minister of the Army Frank Forde. Some correspondents argued that it was unacceptable for an Australian soldier, even under the harshest conditions of captivity, to broadcast for Nippon. At their most forthright—and they were a minority—these writers wanted the Australian government and the Australian army to throw the book at Cousens and the rest of the suspected collaborators. But even the most adamant among them was aghast that any Australian, let alone a returning soldier, could be convicted on the testimony of a "Jap," to employ the expression invariably used. Those who argued that, whatever the rights or wrongs of the case, it was time to put the war behind them and plan for a peacetime future, also felt it was an unconscionable error to bring Japanese witnesses to testify in Australia.

A good number of those who wrote to Forde pointed out that all prisoners of war had been forced to work for the enemy, and therefore if one was prosecuted all the others were guilty as well. A thoughtful letter sent to the Minster from the secretary of the Women's Union of New South Wales reiterated the point that Cousens' prosecution could lead to the trials of prisoners who merely worked as "road builders, camp doctors and workers," and that even those who had done no more than "exchange their personal possessions for food" might be considered as having "traded with the enemy." The same correspondent noted bitterly too that after years of the government's having "by every means at its disposal" tried to convince Australians "to hold the Japanese in utter contempt, to distrust their broadcasting and to be horrified at their atrocities," it was now suggested that they could be credible witnesses.[3]

The Returned Servicemen and Women from Sydney's Hornsby branch informed the minister that although they would not wish to comment on Major Cousens' guilt or innocence, they wanted "simply to protest against enemies being brought to this country to testify against His Majesty's Forces." Echoing the same idea, another writer noted that the "Japs have queer ideas about honor and will manufacture the evidence." For an ex-serviceman it was "damn disgusting to bring these sword-happy barbarians" into the law courts. Another woman correspondent noted that the "craftiness and treachery of the Japanese" would make for a "travesty of justice" and do no more than give "an opportunity for Japs to vent their sadistic spite on Australians." An ex-prisoner warned that "only those who had put in time with the Nips could know that they are notoriously unreliable and would not and could not tell the truth." A Sydney civilian who claimed to have listened often to Charles Cousens' broadcasts and had found them "ordinary and innocuous" declared that it was "a well-nigh unbelievable scandal and an insult to Australians" to use the Japanese as witnesses at an Australian trial.

Most commonly, ex-prisoners and returned veterans took the opportunity of the Cousens case to complain that prisoners of war and returned servicemen were not receiving from the government what was their due. For example, former servicemen from Tenterfield in the New England area of New South Wales used the Cousens case to write to their local member of Parliament to express their deep bitterness about the treatment of returned soldiers in their area. They protested that civilians were filling government jobs, and that the statutory provisions of the Returned Soldiers Preference Act were being overlooked. In a similar vein, another ex-POW in his letter to the minister began with the Cousens case, but moved quickly on to express outrage at the fact that the government was claiming that POWs were "liberally treated," when in fact they were not being paid the extra subsistence money to which they were entitled. The writer was furious that he could not raise the money to buy a set of tools that he needed in order to find work, while thousands of tools were being held back in government stores. Another disgruntled POW asked the minister querulously why it was that Cousens was "getting all the publicity" when there were other ex-prisoners who had been far more harshly treated while in captivity. At this time a number in the army top brass saw POWs as "quitters" and the Australian Defense Department and the Returned Servicemen's League officially opposed any form of special compensation for prisoners that was not also given to rank-and-file soldiers who had not been taken prisoner.[4]

After Cousens had been brought home under military arrest, the Australian foreign correspondent in Japan, Denis Warner, wrote a series of intemperate articles in the *Melbourne Herald* claiming that Kennoske Sato was to have been the Japanese Administrator of Australia if Japan had occupied the country. According to Warner, Sato had indicated that there were a number of leading Australians who were prepared to cooperate willingly with the Japanese.[5] This may or may not have been the case and Warner gave no indication of the names. The report hit a raw nerve, though, and three Australian officers wrote to the press that Sato had interrogated them and that subsequently they had been tortured dreadfully in a POW camp outside Tokyo. The incident probably did damage to Cousens' case as it was almost impossible not to think of him in relation to the charge that Warner had made even though there was no evidence that he had been part of a prewar grouping, if such a group existed, and certainly he was not named.

When Charles Cousens began broadcasting from Tokyo in 1942, the Australian Security Service combed past records for evidence that he had been a secret Japanese agent before the war. Much of the information they accumulated is of little value and can be disregarded—such as the elaborately collected, but banal, observations of the baker's delivery boy or the anonymous statements and unsigned letters which reveal malice and mischief-making—but it was thought that his involvement with the Japanese journalist Sato could be a sign of earlier pro-Japanese sentiments.[6]

While he was a POW in Tokyo, Cousens bumped into Kennoske Sato with whom he had worked in Australia in 1935 producing a book on the trade links between the two countries. According to Sato, as he described it during his 1945 post-war interrogation, the two had recognized each other on the street, but given Cousens' reduced circumstances and the Japanese's wish not to embarrass an old acquaintance, Sato had delicately avoided asking any questions.[7] Cousens gave a similar version of this brief Tokyo encounter. Fuomiko Saisho, the Japanese witness brought to Sydney in 1946, testified however that she had seen Sato and Cousens in a Tokyo restaurant during the first months of the Australian's captivity. In a sworn statement to the Advanced Headquarters of the Australian Military Forces in Tokyo, the Japanese naval commander, Baron M. Takasaki, also recalled a conversation he had had in the lobby of the Dai Itchi Hotel where he and Cousens were staying. It had taken place after Sato had introduced Cousens to Takasaki. Cousens had said that he "was under army control," living in the hotel and going each day to Broadcast House. Takasaki recalled that at the time he had thought it "rather strange" that an Australian prisoner of war should be living in the hotel.[8] The Australian political historian, Drew Cottle, in his 2002 book, *The Brisbane Line,* uses some of this information to back his claim that there was a pro-Japanese conspiracy in Australia before and during the war. The evidence he offers, however, is not entirely convincing.

It is hardly likely that Charles Cousens was part of a prewar pro-Japanese conspiracy. The strongest evidence to the contrary is his keenness to enlist with the Australian army as soon as war was declared. It is likely, however, that Cousens shared the general sentiments of a group of Australians between the wars who were interested in Japan and believed that more trade between the two nations would benefit Australian producers. From Tokyo, Cousens made several short-wave broadcasts that argued that Australia was located within what the Japanese referred to as the Greater East Asia Co-Prosperity Zone and that therefore Australia's economic future lay with Asian nations in this area.[9]

Contacts between Australian pastoralists and Japanese wool buyers, for example, had long been mutually productive and often based on a warm mutual regard. The fine-wool growers, the Whites of Belltrees Station in the Hunter Valley in New South Wales, enjoyed a long and cordial association before the war with the Japanese wool buyers who imported their wool, the family employing as a jackeroo the son of the Japanese firm that bought Belltrees fleeces.[10] Indeed in Sydney until 1940, a strong network of personal and business relationships flourished between Australians and Japanese immigrants and visitors.[11]

Throughout the 1930s the Melbourne academic and linguist Peter Russo had been dedicated to promoting cultural contact between Australia and Japan.[12] Russo lived in Japan for almost a decade, functioning as a go-between interpreting Australia to Japan and vice versa. In 1931, he had travelled to Tokyo on a University of Melbourne scholarship to study the language and had remained there, becoming a lecturer in modern languages at Hitotsubashi University and an adviser to the Japanese government. He was actively involved with the Japanese National

Society, which promoted Japan's international cultural relations abroad. In August 1935, Russo accompanied a Japanese diplomatic mission to Australia and New Zealand, which was the impetus for the 1935 volume to promote Japanese Australian trade, with which Cousens was associated. Russo was instrumental in having Japanese language lessons broadcast over the Australian Broadcasting Commission, though they were abandoned in late 1939 when enrollments fell precipitously from seventy-eight to eight.[13] As war loomed Russo came to feel a chill wind of anti-western attitudes. Perhaps because his mentors in the Japanese diplomatic service were opposed to the military faction, the Japanese security police put him under surveillance and repeatedly searched his rooms. In April 1941, at the urging of his Japanese friends, Russo returned to Australia, but until the attack on Pearl Harbour he continued to defend Japanese foreign policy.

Once war in the Pacific was declared, the pre-war connections with Japan were abruptly severed. In the postwar decades when it has been government policy to underline Australia's place in the Asian region in order to trade and engage with its Asian neighbors, none of the ideas that Cousens propounded seem outlandish. In wartime, however, talk of Asian co-prosperity was seen as a cover for Japan's real objective, which was to assume the imperial role previously the prerogative of the European colonial powers. And by then Japan had demonstrated that there would be no restraint on the violence wrought on the occupied populations that constituted the new Japanese empire in Asia.

The Sydney Trial

The Minister of the Army had stopped Cousens' pay in November 1945 when he was arrested in Japan as a suspected renegade. As the weeks dragged into months, the Sydney newspapers that had followed the charges began to make adverse comments about "legal nitter-natter" and bureaucratic "shuttlecocking" and that Cousens should be brought to court quickly or else released. Behind the scenes, there was a flurry of activity as the Australian Attorney General and members of the Australian Military Board engaged in intense discussion about how and where to prosecute the ex-POW and what substantive evidence could be marshaled against him. There were very few broadcasts in which Cousens' voice had been identified, and until late in the war, listening post monitors had been left to make transcriptions as they themselves saw fit. In the end, a civil trial was favored. In a military court, a breach of the Army Act had to have taken place within three years of the charge which would mean that the early 1942 and 1943 broadcasts, for some of which there were transcripts, would have been inadmissible. The Director of Legal Services for the Australian Military Forces indicated that he preferred a civil trial because the usual penalty for a violation of the Army Act was "cashierment" whereas civil treason was a capital offense.[14]

The case raised complex legal questions. Section 24 of the Commonwealth of Australia Crimes Act defined treason as an offense committed within Australia's borders or within the territories under the Commonwealth of Australia's control. Because Cousens' actions had taken place in Japan, prosecution under Australian federal law would normally be precluded. Therefore, if the case was to proceed, charges would have to be brought within the jurisdiction of the states' legal systems where British common law prevailed and the British Treason Act proscribed any action, within the realm or abroad, that aided the King's enemies. Four leading practitioners at the Sydney Bar—W. R. Dovey KC, R. Windeyer KC, Garfield Barwick KC and Rex Chambers—who provided the federal government with an opinion were unequivocal that the evidence against Cousens was sufficient to indict him as a traitor and that he would have to be prosecuted through the state of New South Wales courts. However, when the Commonwealth Crown Solicitor asked the New South Wales Attorney General to file an indictment for treason on the Commonwealth's behalf, he declined to do so. The New South Wales law officers saw the Commonwealth's involvement as potentially compromising the legal and administrative autonomy of the state.[15] After further consultations with senior counsel and a full meeting of the Australian cabinet, the Australian Attorney General undertook the much-less-common step in instituting a preliminary hearing by having a Commonwealth officer lay a charge under the New South Wales Justices Act.

On July 23, 1946, Cousens was arrested by police warrant and appeared that day at the Central Court in Sydney to answer an Information that had been laid by A. W. Blackett, in his capacity as a Commonwealth intelligence officer. Charged under the Treason Act of 1351, Cousens was accused of having traitorously contrived to aid and assist the enemies of the King and his Allies.[16] Refused bail, he was remanded to appear on August 6, 1946. On the same day, Bradley KC and J. W. Smyth, Cousens' defense counsel, appealed to the Full Court of the New South Wales Supreme Court for bail and for an Order Nisi for a Common Law Prohibition on the grounds that a charge of treason committed in Japan could not be brought within the New South Wales legal jurisdiction. Cousens was granted bail on a five hundred pound surety put up by his father-in-law. In the second matter, however, the defense was unsuccessful and their application was discharged with costs.[17]

The preliminary hearing, before Mr Farrington SM, began on August 20, 1946 and ran for seven and a half weeks, occupying twenty-four full sitting days. The sworn statements for the forty witnesses for the prosecution alone amounted to more than seven hundred pages and the transcript of courtroom proceedings ran to over a thousand. The daily papers were agog at the cost—Cousens' defense reportedly came to more than eight thousand pounds and the Commonwealth, with three overseas witnesses in Sydney for several months, spent more than a million pounds.[18] These were staggering amounts in these penurious times when food and petrol rationing was still in force and items of new household equipment, let alone cars, were unobtainable. People still remade threadbare clothes, and on the street it was not uncommon to see army greatcoats and other bits and pieces of military clothing worn with civilian dress.

Charles Cousens, tall and good-looking, wore his military uniform to court each day. Mrs Grace Cousens, handsome and well-dressed, attended all the hearings with her husband. An equally fashionable sister, reportedly married to one of England's leading barristers, traveled from London to support the family. The tabloid press carried striking photographs of the family grouping with descriptions of the women's outfits as though they were in town for a day at the races. The trial must have been a tremendous ordeal for Mrs Cousens, but in public at least, she remained poised and in interviews invariably optimistic about the clearing of her husband's name.

Four overseas witnesses added to the spectacle. George Guysi, brought to Sydney for the prosecution, was the American intelligence officer attached to SCAP in Japan and had questioned Cousens in Yokohama at the end of the war. As the transcript of that interrogation shows, Guysi was extremely skeptical about Cousens' claim that his involvement with Radio Tokyo had helped rather than hindered the Allied war effort.[19] The ex-intelligence officer however was only willing to come to Sydney for the trial on condition that his new wife accompany him. The Commonwealth agreed to pay both fares. The couple drew admiring attention—he in GI uniform and she in post-rationing full-skirted dresses and with hair styled in the latest cold-wave. For the two weeks they spent in Sydney, the young Americans were photographed in a number of love-struck poses at scenic spots around the city.

The defense flew in their own American GI, Lieutenant George H. "Bucky" Henshaw, also young and photogenic in a spruce air force uniform. He had been a prisoner in Tokyo with Charles Cousens and had made many broadcasts over Japanese shortwave. Unlike the man in the dock, however, at the end of the war Henshaw had been promoted three grades to a lieutenant colonel and invited to assist American intelligence in Tokyo identifying Japanese war criminals. While in captivity, he had kept a secret diary, which the defense claimed would exonerate Cousens as it documented at firsthand the violence that Bunka broadcasters had suffered under the Japanese.

It was the arrival of the two Japanese witnesses that galvanized the Australian press and the Sydney onlookers. The RAAF flew Foumiko Saisho and Hiroshi Niino into Sydney in the middle of July, and the Australian security service was at pains to keep them out of the public eye. By contrast with the easy celebrity granted to the American visitors, the Japanese were assigned a plainclothes police escort and each day a Commonwealth car brought them to court. Their arrivals and departures caused such pandemonium that they were driven directly into the courthouse via the underground entrance for the prison vans. And to avoid the excitement that even a glimpse of them caused in the corridors, the two entered the courtroom directly from the cells below. At lunchtimes their driver whisked them off to a secluded place where they could avoid the gaze of the curious public. So persistent were journalists in tracking the two witnesses that, it was said, the officers of the security service had to use "G-man tactics" to shake off the press cars that invariably tailed the Japanese at high speed through the Sydney suburbs.[20]

After much searching, the security service had located a Japanese family in Randwick, the Iwatas, with whom the Tokyo Japanese could stay. Having gone through the humiliation of internment in Australia, however, the family was very reluctant to take on Japanese boarders.[21] Before she would agree, Mrs Margaret Iwata obtained a letter of assurance from the Australian government stating that the family's involvement with the Tokyo pair would not prejudice any future relations with the Australian government. Despite their agreement, the Randwick Japanese greatly resented having foreign Japanese foisted upon them, and at every opportunity made it clear to the visitors that their presence was extremely unwelcome. Foumiko Saisho eventually convinced the prosecution's legal team to allow her to live in a hotel in the city. She had found it too difficult to bear the Randwick family's constantly chiding her about the war, and their endlessly reminding her about the disapprobation that the militarist Japanese government had brought upon Japanese living abroad.

Foumy, as she was called, had been a script supervisor at Radio Tokyo.[22] This meant that she checked what the Allied prisoners of war wrote, in order to ensure that the broadcasts aired included no information that was out of step with Japanese government policy. She testified that she had never had need to censor any of Cousens' material. Thirty-two years of age, "small and energetic," Foumy spoke with only very slightly Japanese-accented English. Born in Japan, Saisho had taken a bachelor's and a master's degree in arts at the University of Michigan. Subsequently she had spent a year in Honolulu, and in Tokyo until war was declared, she had worked at the Canadian legation. When the foreign diplomats pulled out, she had found a job in Japanese broadcasting. Ever since the war had ended she had been working as a journalist on *Nippon Times*, the English-language Tokyo daily. With the Allied Occupation of Japan, Saisho had acted as interpreter for an Australian journalist, Massey Stanley, who by the time she came to Sydney was a roundsman for the *Daily Telegraph*. The two remained very friendly and were often seen on outings together during the weekends. Before she left Australia, on January 8, 1947, Saisho wrote a long piece for her Tokyo paper about her impressions of Australia. Reprinted in the *Telegraph*, it consisted mostly of her attempts to explain the national Australian obsession with horseracing and cricket and the continuing commitment to the White Australia Policy.[23]

The other Tokyo witness, Hiroshi Niino, thirty-seven years old, was described by the *Daily Telegraph* as "diminutive even for a Japanese."[24] He had been born and educated in Honolulu, and moved to Japan at the age of twenty. During the war he was a senior announcer in the English section at Radio Tokyo and, when hostilities ceased, he had stayed on as an employee. It is not clear why the prosecution chose Niino. He had not played a central role in the POW programs, although he was able to testify that Cousens had provided the training that had greatly improved the Japanese broadcaster's on-air technique. Probably it was assumed that Niino would have had a good knowledge of the structure and the workings of Japanese broadcasting. Also, the prosecution was pressed to find witnesses who could be in Australia by the time the arraignment was filed in the magistrate's court. The Australian officers working with SCAP in Tokyo had been helpful, tracking down likely figures for the prosecution, and they probably came up with Niino. In the event, he turned out to be somewhat of a handful and the testimony he gave was a very mixed bag.

In Sydney, adapting to the local custom, Niino began to drink at the Regent Hotel in Daceyville, often returning home to Randwick well under the weather. According to his landlady, when in this frame of mind he was "boastful" about Japanese military prowess and endlessly talked about why it was that "Asia should be run by Asiatics" and that the "Philippines belonged to Filipinos not the United States." Perhaps not surprisingly, he frequently got into fights with the returned soldiers from the nearby Returned Soldiers Settlement in Matraville, who also drank at the Regent. An anonymous letter-writer to Commonwealth Security reported that Niino had had an altercation with some Australian returned soldiers who had challenged him to tell them what had happened to the Australians in Bougainville. The correspondent, probably his landlady, ended with what was presumably meant to be the clinching argument against Niino which was that he was "still a loyal Japanese subject and disregarded all democratic principles."[25] To be fair, Niino had come to Australia on the understanding that he would be away from Tokyo for only one month. The legal arguments around the case, however, had dragged out his visit into half of a year, during which he became more and more anxious about the penurious state of the family he had left behind. As he complained to the Commonwealth Attorney General, his wife was "living on the generosity of his colleagues at Radio Tokyo." Eventually the Commonwealth government sent a packet of money to Tokyo for Mrs Niino via the diplomatic bag to the Australian ambassador. Rather curiously, and presumably to the prosecution's chagrin, when the Cousens arraignment was over, Niino telegrammed a message of congratulations, which stated "Good Luck to The Voice," using Cousens' nickname among English-speaking Japanese at Broadcast House.

Prosecution and Defense hired leading Sydney silks. The Commonwealth Solicitor General took Garfield Barwick KC and W. R. Dovey KC with Rex Chambers as junior counsel. Cousens' lawyers were in no-less-exalted bracket. T. J. McFadyen of the city law firm of McFadyen and McFadyen brought in three leading Sydney barristers—Mr Bradley KC, J. B. Shand KC and J. W. Smyth as junior. Shand was famous for his overbearing and abrasive courtroom manner to which, for Cousens' defense, he gave robust play, especially when cross-examining the prosecution's Japanese witnesses.

The Crown's prosecution worked on two main fronts. The pro-Japanese content of Cousens' broadcasts, some fifty transcripts of which were available, were fore-grounded, as was Cousens' involvement in coaching Japanese broadcasters to improve the on-air delivery.[26] Cousens' defense rested on the claim that he had been sending disguised messages back to Australia that contained information helpful to the war effort. Specifically, the Australian broadcaster argued that he was attempting to indicate to the radio monitors in Australia and America that there was an anti-militarist group within Japan who should be encouraged. His plan was to take over the Japanese commentaries on shortwave in order to have a mouthpiece through which to articulate this position. Defense also hammered the claim that whether Cousens' strategy was successful or not, it had been carried out under the extreme duress of captivity.

The prosecution headed off all lines of argument that offered evidence of Japanese mistreatment of prisoners of war. To this end, counsel for the Crown succeeded in having excised the parts of Cousens' own sworn testimony that included reference to Japanese brutality. Similarly discredited by the prosecution were the testimonies by Cousens' fellow POWs. Henshaw in the dock and the others in sworn statements were unanimous that the violence of the Japanese guards towards prisoners was unremitting. Any attempt by Cousens to openly resist Japanese orders would have resulted in his immediate execution.

In rebuttal, Barwick and Dovey offered evidence from the two Japanese witnesses that the Japanese managers at Radio Tokyo were never violent towards POW broadcasters. In the words of Saisho, Radio Tokyo's policy was "to make comfortable the prisoners of war in order that they would cooperate with the Japanese staff and be more fitted to do their work properly."[27] Dovey KC taunted Cousens with the suggestion that in Tokyo he was in "fine condition" and in "full bloom of health" and had experienced an "easy war" in comparison with the "boys in Burma."[28] Shand and Bradley kept coming back to the fact that the prosecution's case rested on the word of "Jap" witnesses against the testimony of Australian and American soldiers who had suffered unimaginable brutality in Japan. In Shand's summation, "It would be as absurd to convict Charles Cousens of treason as it would be to convict the men who helped build the Siam Railway."[29]

Farrington SM handed down judgment on October 4, 1946. It was that on the evidence presented there was a *prima facie* case for the prosecution of Charles Cousens on the charge of treason. This meant, of course, not that the defendant was guilty, which under law could only be decided after the case had been heard before a jury, but that on the evidence presented at the preliminary hearing it would be "not unreasonable for a properly instructed jury in the Supreme Court of New South Wales to find that Charles Cousens had given aid and comfort to the King's enemies." In the normal course of events, the next step would have been for the case to proceed to a higher jurisdiction, in this case the Supreme Court of New South Wales, with the state attorney general presenting the indictment. In the event, however, the New South Wales Attorney (though of the same Labor Party as the Commonwealth government) again declined to proceed, influenced by the advice from officers in his legal department who were anxious most of all to avoid any muddying of the division between state and federal legal administrations.[30] The outcome was that, to the chagrin of the Commonwealth law officials, the treason charge against Cousens lapsed.

The finding of a no-bill had immediate consequences for the prosecution of the second treason case that the Commonwealth was preparing against the civilian Tokyo broadcaster, John Joseph Holland. Born in Western Australia and having had a colorful career on the east coast, including a stint in Emu Plains prison farm for having passed bad checks, Holland had left Australia sometime in 1937 in pursuit of various business schemes in Southeast Asia. By January 1941 he was employed as a journalist on a German shortwave station in Shanghai where under the name of 'David Lester,' he made regular pro-Axis broadcasts. Shanghai was home to a small community of expatriate Australians who formed the pro-Japanese Independent Australia League and the Australian Breakaway Movement that advocated Australia severing all ties with Britain in favor of full cooperation with Japan.

Holland joined the English-speaking staff at Broadcast House in October 1942, but unlike the prisoners drafted into broadcasting, Holland came to Tokyo by his own choice and as a free man. Guaranteed a salary of six hundred yen a month and comfortable hotel accommodation, he was free to come and go as he liked. All his talks on-air advocated the need for Australia to recognize that her interests lay with a victorious Japan. According to Cousens, in interrogations at the end of the war, he and the other Australian POWs gave Holland a wide berth because they feared his closeness to the Japanese could cause them trouble. Their caution was warranted in that Holland had told Japanese staff at Broadcast House that he was an Australian Nazi. He fell out with the managers in the English section when they refused his request to transfer to the Tokyo newspaper, *Nippon Times*. Their differences became acrimonious to the extent that in April 1943 he was arrested by the *kempetai* and sent to a prison camp in northern Japan for having attempted to "destroy the morale of the Japanese people." Two days after Japan formally surrendered, the Red Cross freed Holland, but a couple of weeks later he was re-arrested by U.S. Military Intelligence as a suspected collaborator and shipped for interrogation to Yokohama where he remained until June 1946.

Much like Cousens, Holland had been brought back to Australia under guard. As a civilian, however, once on home ground he could not be kept in custody without a formal charge having been laid against him. While the law officers mulled over legal procedures, he was free to travel within Australia. During a visit to Perth, ostensibly to see his parents, Holland obtained a merchant seaman's ticket and found a berth as crew on a merchant ship that left Fremantle on September 7, 1946.

In relation to the charge to be brought against Holland, again the advice from Dovey KC, Windeyer KC and Barwick KC was unanimous that a "clear case of high treason can be established." And in their opinion, the New South Wales criminal court was the proper venue for the prosecution. Given the outcome of Cousens' case, however, Australian Solicitor-General K. H. Bailey was more cautious. In his assessment it would be "quite useless to go to the trouble and expense of extraditing Holland" if the New South Wales Attorney General persisted in his obstructive attitude and again chose not to file an indictment. Therefore, Bailey approached British Director of Public Prosecutions (DPP) Theobald Mathew to raise the treason charge against Holland within the English courts where it would be "unembarrassed by the previous jurisdictional questions." Seeing no "jurisdictional difficulty," the DPP in London acceded to the Australian request.

The DPP swore a warrant and arrested Holland in England on February 18, 1947, remanding him in custody. Holland appeared at Old Bailey Sessions on March 18 before the Lord Chief Justice Goddard charged with having violated UK Defense Regulation 24, by actions likely to assist the enemy. It carried the penalty of penal servitude for life. The ten counts that Holland confronted comprised ten broadcasts he had made over Radio Tokyo between November 1942 and March 1943. The Crown set out the case against him and Holland entered a formal plea of guilty. His counsel then made a speech in mitigation which emphasized that Holland knew he had committed a very serious crime and had come to repent his actions and in Japan had refused to continue broadcasting. As a consequence, he had been placed in a prisoner of war camp where for two years he had suffered great hardship.

The Lord Chief Justice found Holland to have "done a dastardly act against his own country." When Australia was at war and while his countrymen had "fought manfully" against the nation's enemies, Holland had lent himself to the Germans and to the Japanese. In mitigation, however, the bench stated that it was "bound to take notice" of the fact that the defendant had spent time in a prisoner of war camp where it was common knowledge that "British subjects imprisoned by the Japanese were subject to what only can be called terrible torture." In the judge's estimation, the accused, having been sent to a Japanese prison camp, had already suffered what "no sentence in a British court could equal" the "torture of hell" that he endured during his two years in Japanese captivity. In light of these factors, the Lord Chief Justice took the "wholly exceptional course" and bound Holland over on bond of good behavior for a period of five years.

The Holland verdict was a great disappointment to the British DPP and the Commonwealth Solicitor General. Bailey in Canberra explained that in Australia the result had left a "kind of uneasy feeling" and in "service circles people were frankly disconcerted" because the outcome suggested that the British courts looked on the Pacific war as less important than the war in Europe and therefore were not disposed to treat collaboration with the Japanese with the same severity as when dealing with the Germans. Mathews in London, too, found the result a "surprise," and given that the Lord Chief Justice had "no reputation for leniency," the DPP read the sentence as an indication that the "judges feel that the time has come to write 'Finis' to this type of prosecution."

For Charles Cousens, despite the no-bill, it was not the end of the matter. In December 1946 the Commonwealth Crown Solicitor called a conference in Canberra with legal counsel, senior law officers from the Attorney General's Department and senior military staff to reconsider the whole Cousens matter. There was unanimous agreement that a "strong case existed" against Cousens and the group shared the "grave concern" at the failure of the New South Wales Crown Law authorities to proceed with the case. A new court-martial was considered but rejected because it would "have an appearance of persecution" and risk drawing adverse publicity.[31] Therefore the Military Board of Australia asked Cousens to show cause why he should not lose his commission. And on January 22, 1947, in a closed tribunal, the Military Board of Australia stripped Cousens of his commission.[32]

Apart from the humiliation that included the loss of service medals, the decision carried egregious penalty. Cousens had been an Australian volunteer soldier who had spent the full span of the war years in service overseas. Yet, he was denied all accrued recreation leave and the so-called "war gratuity" which was the loading paid to Australian soldiers on overseas service and the extra allowance made to their families for the hardships that had been suffered during the absence of the breadwinner. He was also excluded from a reestablishment payment made to POWs and returned soldiers to assist in their reinsertion into civilian life. And he was expressly precluded from war service loans for housing or business. In what could be seen as a final, gratuitously mean-spirited gesture, Cousens was required to return to Victoria Barracks all military clothing, excluding used underwear. (Demobilized soldiers normally retained their boots and other clothing.) In civilian clothes, he stood out at the Sydney Showground among his fellow returned soldiers and ex-prisoners of war on the day he signed his demobilization papers.

CHAPTER 13

Iva Toguri and the Trial of Tokyo Rose

The charge against Iva Toguri stated that although owing her country allegiance, she did "knowingly, willfully, unlawfully, feloniously, intentionally, traitorously and treasonably adhere to the enemies of the United States." Eight instances were then specified in which "overt acts" of treason had taken place, all related to broadcasts that Toguri had made over Japanese shortwave. With a glaring absence of legal specificity, each charge carried a rider that the precise date on which the alleged incident had taken place was unknown. Toguri was denied bail. Despite the protestations of her counsel that even the leader of the defeated Confederates after the civil war had been bailed, Toguri was incarcerated during the months of preparation and the twelve weeks in court in a small cell in the San Francisco County jail. The trial began on July 5 and after more than a million words of testimony and depositions, the jury handed down the judgment on September 29, 1949.[1]

There are several notable issues relating to the legal consequences of Iva Toguri's war years in Japan. The first was the unrelenting determination with which the United States government prosecuted her. This was especially remarkable when this official persistence is compared with the government's abandonment of the prosecution of comparable cases. Whether Toguri was or was not pro-Japanese during the war, and whether she intended to entertain Allied troops or turn them against their own side, the timing of her arrest after the war was unusual. And equally singular was the manner in which the San Francisco trial took place.

Although several thousand Japanese Americans spent the war years in Japan, only a handful were arrested and just two, including Iva Toguri, served a prison sentence. Most Japanese Americans who had remained in Japan claimed voluntary repatriation after the war, that is they invoked the legal loophole that they had given up their American citizenship and therefore could not be tried as traitors. And subsequently, they applied to the United States Embassy in Tokyo for new American passports, or simply returned to the States on their prewar documents.

Toguri's arrest and trial took place at a time when a great many other wartime prosecutions in Japan were being dropped.[2] The cold war reconfigured international relations and transformed previous alliances and enmities. The trend was exemplified in the trials in Tokyo of the major war criminals. Further prosecutions were dropped, but exactly at that time Iva Toguri was rearrested. Between May 1946 and the end of 1948, "Japan's Nuremberg," the International Military Tribunal for the Far East, was sitting in judgment on what was to have been the first of a series of trials of Class A war criminals. These were the Japanese leaders accused of the most serious crimes. After the first group of twenty-five had been tried, further prosecutions were abandoned. All of the Class A war criminals that came before the tribunal were found guilty. Seven were executed, but none of the remainder who were found guilty ever completed their sentences. The hundreds who had been charged and were waiting prosecution in Sugamo Prison were quietly let go at the end of December 1948, even though among them were several long-standing leaders of the Japanese extreme Right and the senior Japanese officials from the puppet state of Manchuko who had overseen the enslavement of thousands of Chinese laborers.[3] It was apparent, then, that by the end of 1948 the strong feelings of revenge against the Japanese had ebbed before the new international focus to retain Japan within the U.S. sphere of influence.

Iva Toguri was treated unconscionably during her arrests in Japan and in a manner that caused her great distress. While she was in U.S. military custody her husband, Filipe D'Aquino, was not permitted to see her. Nor was he allowed to accompany her when his wife was transported for trial to the United States. Indeed, the U.S. Customs and the U.S. Immigration Service obstructed in every way his travel to San Francisco in order to speak in Iva's defense. Eventually, in order to obtain an entry visa to the United States, D'Aquino was forced to sign a declaration stating that he would leave the United States as soon as the trial was over and never again attempt to reenter U.S. territory.[4] The effect of the ban was that after 1949 husband and wife never saw each other again.

The other notable feature of Toguri's trial in California was the absence of any community voices raised on her behalf. Her father attended court each day and her youngest sister, who lived in Los Angeles, came to the early sessions, but there was no one else. In San Francisco, except for her lawyers, Iva Toguri was on her own. Members of the Japanese American community and their organizations studiously ignored both Toguri and her trial.[5]

There is no doubt that the immediate postwar years were difficult for Japanese Americans. Mass evacuation and internment dealt a heavy blow to self-confidence and material well-being. At the end of 1949, many Americans of Japanese descent were attempting to reestablish themselves after the traumatic experience of having been forcibly removed from the West Coast in early 1942 and interned in camps in the American interior. By September 1948, the last twenty-five internees had been released.[6] Well into the 1950s, however, displaced Japanese Americans were still struggling to make a new life, often in a different part of the country and having lost both property and savings. Toguri's own family is a good example— forced out of their neighborhood in Los Angeles, they rebuilt their later lives in Chicago. Even more dispiriting for many Japanese Americans was the knowledge that a good number of their fellow Americans continued to regard them as traitors who had collaborated with the enemy.

From the end of the war, a number of Nisei community organizations worked to raise the consciousness of Anglo Americans to the hardships that Americans of Japanese descent had endured between 1942 and 1945. The most influential, the Japanese American Citizens' League (JACL), sought at every opportunity to demonstrate that their members were patriotic Americans. The JACL executive took the decision very early in the war to actively cooperate with government directives, including those from the War Relocation Authority, the instrumentality that administered internment. They undertook this step in order to counter any perception that Japanese Americans were less than loyal. Probably, the JACL's most successful public relations initiative, associated with the effective lobbying by the organization's activist Mark Masaoka, was to demand that Japanese Americans be permitted to enlist. From the time of Pearl Harbor they were excluded from the American armed forces. When a combat unit was formed, entirely composed of Japanese Americans, but led by Caucasian officers, Masaoka was the first to volunteer. The "Fighting 442nd" served with great distinction in France and Italy, winning more medals than did any other American combat unit in World War Two.

In July 1948, as a result of effective postwar lobbying by the JACL, and in part probably in recognition of the contribution of the 442nd , the U.S. Congress passed the Japanese American Evacuation Claims Act which gave Japanese American citizens the right to apply for some restitution for losses incurred in evacuation and internment.[7] The battle for the rights of the "renunciants" and for monetary compensation was not easily won and the personal cost of the salvage was high. But at least it suggested that there was some movement towards normalizing the idea that a great injustice had been carried out against Americans of Japanese descent. Paradoxically, however, measures that won some sympathy for Japanese Americans further isolated Iva Toguri.

Community leaders who led the push for redress carefully framed their cause as an issue falling within the purlieu of national domestic politics. The rights of Japanese Americans were presented as matters of American justice for Americans of Japanese descent. Conversely, care was taken to quarantine the demand for redress from any association with wartime Japan or the subsequent occupation of Japan by the United States. In the JACL-inspired version of the past, the Second World War had simply been the catalyst that released deep-seated and misconceived fears within the United States towards its own Japanese American citizens. The consequence of framing the past in this way was that the injustices could be redressed by the simple act of the federal government's paying reparations to Japanese American citizens.

The treason trial of "Tokyo Rose," and the parallel trial of Tomoya "Meatball" Kawakita, sat awkwardly within this carefully crafted landscape. It is worth outlining Kamakita's story because he was also found guilty of treason though his circumstances in wartime Japan were in strong contrast with Toguri's. A Californian Nisei, Kawakita's life had followed the familiar trajectory. In 1939 he had gone to Japan to study the language and Japanese culture and had remained in Japan during the war, giving up his American citizenship and joining the Japanese army. Because of his English language skills, he was placed in charge of English-speaking POWs in a nickel mine where it was alleged, he brutally mistreated them. At the end of the war, Kawakita simply returned unmolested to Los Angeles and took up his previous life as an American citizen. A couple of years later, an ex-POW recognized Kawakita in a department store in Los Angeles, followed him, noted his car registration and reported him to the FBI. As a consequence, in 1948, he was tried and found guilty of the capital crime of treason. In 1953, President Eisenhower commuted his sentence to life. Two days before his own death, in 1963, President John Kennedy granted Kamakita a pardon on the condition that he left the United States to live in Japan. The presidential file includes several previously unsuccessful petitions from Kawakita's family, but gives no reason for the final pardon.[8]

The columnist Larry Tajira, writing in the JACL's newspaper *Pacific Citizen*, at the time of the trials, admonished Toguri and Kawakita, whether they were guilty of the charges or not, for "play[ing] fast and loose with the well-being of Americans of Japanese ancestry."[9] The two cases were "individual affairs" that did not reflect on the loyalty of the whole Japanese American population, a matter that had been settled once and for all by the deaths of the six hundred Nisei GIs who had served with valor in Europe in World War Two. Tajira reminded readers that at the very time in which the Imperial Valley-born Kawakita was placed on trial, another young Nisei—also born in the Imperial Valley—was being laid to rest in Arlington National Cemetery, having earned his "American hero's burial" on the battlefields of France. As for "Tokyo Rose," in Tajira's opinion she was the architect of her own "comic opera," having "renounced any claim to American nationality by participating in war activity." He also accused her of a "peculiar form of megalomania" and had actually "enjoyed her year of notoriety." Even when she had been placed in Sugamo Prison "along with Japan's other war criminals," Toguri had drawn attention to herself by "demanding special privileges and writing poetry on her birthday."

A similar editorial on July 17, 1948 reassured *Pacific Citizen* readers that "despite a few Kawakitas and Tokyo Roses," Americans of Japanese ancestry as a result of wartime loyalty have "won a secure and permanent place among the people of America."[10] Echoing the sentiment, a columnist from Manhattan, Roku Sugahara, revealing not much understanding of what had happened in Japan to stranded Japanese Americans, observed that "Tokyo Rose's case seems quite clear-cut." She "could have abstained from the war effort in Japan as did thousands of other Nisei." That she did not would "react on every Nisei in this country" as there will be stories and reports that can only bring the Nisei "notoriety."[11]

Toguri's guilty verdict, and for that matter Kawakita's, complicated the notion that the distrust of Japanese Americans during the war had simply been misplaced. A great many Americans probably shared the sentiments of the American Legion, and the returned soldiers in the Veterans of the Golden West, who lobbied their congressmen for Toguri's prosecution. And presumably many Anglo denizens of Los Angeles stood behind the resolution passed by the City Council on December 8, 1947, which vigorously opposed her return to the United States. In their official words, although Iva Toguri had been born in Los Angeles and despite the "easy forgiveness and the broadminded generosity of the American people" she should be refused entry.[12] It seemed that for many Anglo Americans, Iva Toguri represented the "typical bad Jap." Or in the much-quoted, blunt racism of the Military Commander of the U.S. Western Division, General De Witt: "A Jap is a Jap is a Jap."

It was in this mordant light that many Anglos and Japanese Americans viewed the trial of "Tokyo Rose." It seemed to be of no interest to either group that Toguri herself was California-born and had remained steadfastly committed to her American nationality throughout her years in Tokyo; or that these things had made her a victim of injustice. The sentiment of distrust was not easily dispelled, even after many years. In the early 1970s, within Japanese America, a small committee led by Dr Clifford Uyeda and notably backed by a group of U.S. veterans in Oregon began to agitate for a presidential pardon for Iva Toguri.[13] In April 1975, Uyeda managed to have a motion placed on the agenda of the annual JACL congress to the effect that Iva Toguri had gone through hardship.[14] Almost a year later, on October 1, 1976, the *Pacific Citizen* noted that although several Anglo American veterans' groups favored it, not a single Nisei veterans group was on record as supporting an exoneration.

Even then, though, when the *Pacific Citizen* ran an historical feature on her case, the editor received a number of critical letters. As one correspondent complained, it was more important to highlight the positive achievements of Japanese Americans in the war, like the Congressional Medal of Honor given to a 442nd member, than to drag out again the dirty washing around the case of "Tokyo Rose." It seemed that the figure of Tokyo Rose disrupted the fragile relationship with Anglo Americans that many Japanese Americans after the war were attempting to build. And reminders of the trial also reopened the divisions within the Nisei community.

In popular understanding, the name of Tokyo Rose was synonymous with Japanese wartime propaganda. Her trial exposed matters that many believed were better passed over. There was the thorny question of whether Japanese Americans could be relied upon as loyal Americans and what the links were between the Japanese diaspora in the United States and the postwar discredited government of Imperial Japan. Underlying all, there was the troubling question of how to comprehend Japanese brutality towards Allied prisoners of war and where to fit these perceptions into the historical matrix of World War Two.[15] In the trial, Toguri's defense lawyers contended that as an American in Japan, she had had no choice but to do as she was told and therefore could not be held responsible for her part in the programs at Radio Tokyo. Toguri's defense called for statements from the Bunka ex-POWs—Charles Cousens, Kenneth Parkyns, Norman Reyes and Wallace Ince—who testified that the Japanese had been brutal masters who had forced the prisoners to broadcast under pain of death and had suffered starvation, neglect and terrible violence. The prosecution, in turn, repeated the argument that Iva Toguri had enjoyed her work and had not been coerced into carrying it out. The long list of prosecution witnesses included many American-born Japanese who had spent the war in Japan and had been happy enough to abandon their American citizenship and work for the Japanese government. The evidence offered by both prosecution and defense, therefore, problematised any simple picture of Japanese Americans and the relationships between the United States and Japan. While Toguri's defense harped on the violence of the Japanese state and Japanese savagery towards POWs, the prosecution paraded a line of ex-Japanese Americans who in wartime had freely chosen the Emperor and Nippon in preference to Uncle Sam.

It is understandable why those in the Japanese American community who led the movement for redress would be at pains to keep separate Japanese racism in the Pacific war from the new discourse they were creating which highlighted their own suffering as victims of racism in America. In Japan, after the war, it was possible to counter the evidence of Japanese violence towards Allied prisoners of war by highlighting the horror and devastation that the atom bomb had caused. In a balance sheet of horrors, the Japanese in Hiroshima and Nagasaki were war victims as pitiable as were Allied POWs.[16] This strategy, however, was not available to Japanese, born within the United States, where to criticize Hiroshima would place them outside the pale of the patriotic national story in which dropping the bomb brought the war to a swift end and saved the lives of American soldiers. In much the same way, Iva Toguri symbolized different things in different places. In Tokyo, where in effect she was at the mercy of the U.S. military and had suffered personal privation—the loss of a baby, intrusions on privacy and the refusal to allow her husband at her side—she shared the sorts of indignities which many Japanese experienced under the American occupation. Once back in California, however, Toguri symbolized something quite different. Despite Allied POWs testifying to her kindness, and the fact that in Tokyo she was known to have expressed anti-Japanese sentiments, many Anglo Americans still reeling from the war saw Toguri only as "Tokyo Rose," one more "bad Jap." Many Japanese Americans, too, shrank before the detail provided by both defense and prosecution to simply hope that the Tokyo Rose case would end quickly and with as little publicity as possible.

The Treason Trial

The size of the legal teams was far from evenly matched. The prosecution was led by two assistant attorneys general, Frank J. Hennessy Jr. and Tom de Wolfe, the latter fresh from the successful treason prosecutions on the East Coast of the Americans who had broadcast from Nazi Germany. Wolfe was also preparing for the impending treason prosecution of John Provoo, one of the Bunka broadcasters whose nefarious actions in the Philippines had brought him disapprobation. With the Toguri trial, Wolfe was able to kill two birds with one stone. The Japanese witnesses transported to San Francisco for the Toguri case were sent on to Washington to appear for the US government prosecutors in the next trial. The prosecution in San Francisco also had backup legal research provided by two more Justice Department attorneys, Mr Hagan and James W. Knapp, who assisted with the prosecution's cross-examination. As well, three Special FBI agents—John Eldon Dunn, Harry Kimbell and Frederick Tillman—were attached to the case, the last having worked as J. Edgar Hoover's Special Envoy in Asia collecting testimonies. In addition, the prosecution had access to all the information gleaned through the network of FBI agents across the country that had mobilized when the FBI director publicly called for individuals to come forward who may have heard Tokyo Rose broadcast. A team of agents tracked down the Toguris' neighbors and acquaintances while other agents rounded up ex-servicemen stationed in the Pacific who might provide recollections about women broadcasters over Japanese shortwave.

In an almost risible contrast with the serried ranks of the prosecution, the defense team consisted of Wayne Collins, Theodore Tamba and George Olfhausen, all of whom had waived their fees. They were an unusual threesome. Collins, a World War One veteran and a founder of the American Civil Liberties Union in Northern California, had defended a great many of the Japanese who were interned in 1941 and after the war provided robust defense for those wishing to reinstitute their citizenship.[17] Tamba, a Swiss American and conservative Republican, had become convinced of Toguri's innocence. Olfhausen, a liberal scholar and polylingual, later settled in communist Yugoslavia.[18]

The prosecution brought twenty witnesses from overseas, including eight Japanese nationals, flown in on Pan American and accommodated comfortably in San Francisco during the preparations and the trial. All were paid generous per diem allowances.[19] For a number of them—for example Kenchiki Itchi, Erni Matsuda and George Mitsushio—it was an opportunity to revisit the land of their birth. The defense, by the bench's decision, was not permitted to bring alien witnesses to the United States. And, in any event, there were no funds for it. The government had refused a defense counsel's request for finance to bring any witnesses, despite Mildred Gillars having successfully made the same demand to bring defense witnesses from Germany in her very recent treason trial. The United States Justice Department, however, provided funds for Theodore Tamba to spend some weeks in Tokyo in order to collect depositions from potential witnesses. It was Iva's father, Jun Toguri, who paid the cost of a Japanese interpreter to accompany the non-Japanese-speaking Tamba to Tokyo.

Charles Cousens and Kenneth Parkyns flew in from Sydney. According to Cousens, it was a "debt owed Iva Toguri for her helping the POWs during the war."[20] He would have been unaware that J. Edgar Hoover had already requested all the transcripts and documents from his own Sydney treason trial.[21] Jun Toguri paid the Australians' fares, but they faced a serious hitch with the U.S. Immigration Service. Before they would permit the two to land, U.S. Immigration required them to post a substantial bond. To no avail, Collins complained at the "flagrant discourtesy to the two Australians and the arbitrary discrimination against Mrs D'Aquino who is penniless." He also deemed it disgraceful "to deny the right to enter this country to former Australian soldiers who have been our close Allies throughout the war" while "alien enemies of the United States" are permitted "free entry" to the country.[22] The bond was paid by Jun Toguri.

In court, the gist of the prosecution's line, much as it had been with Cousens in Australia, was that Iva Toguri was Tokyo Rose and that she had never been coerced into broadcasting. And equally false was her claim to have conspired to sabotage the military aims of the Japanese government. Rather, it was that she enjoyed her "glamorous job," which brought cash and kudos, while she basked in her notoriety as "Tokyo Rose."

The defense worked across a broad front. The first approach was to demonstrate that the United States government had not considered Iva Toguri to be an American citizen. The occupying forces had incarcerated her in the Japanese section of Sugamo Prison and had issued her with the "B rations" that were accorded to non-American nationals. The Portuguese government, via a letter from the Consul, provided evidence that Mrs D'Aquino was considered by that state to be Portuguese ever since the registration of her marriage to a citizen of Portugal. The prosecution challenged these lines of defense. In cross-examination and by obfuscation, it argued that marriage did not negate U.S. citizenship and that the "treasonous acts" were alleged had taken place before the marriage. All the defense efforts to demonstrate that Iva Toguri had taken the job at Radio Tokyo because she had been under extreme wartime duress evoked a barrage of interruptions and objections, as did the proposition that once she had begun as a shortwave announcer she was under the orders of the Japanese military. Evidence of the hardship of her life, such as the death of the baby, was successfully challenged as "incompetent, irrelevant and immaterial." As the court record makes clear, the presiding Judge Roche agreed with almost all the prosecution challenges, ordering the testimony struck from the record even when the evidence referred to documented cases of violence towards POWs.

The same prosecution tack extended to all efforts by Collins and Tamba to introduce evidence of the brutalities that Allied soldiers had suffered in Japanese captivity, and that Toguri had attempted to ameliorate their vile conditions.[23] Each reference brought an objection. Knapp, in cross-examining Cousens on August 16, 1949, scoffed at the suggestion that Toguri's providing supplies to prisoners of war was a courageous act and a lifesaver to the men in captivity who faced starvation. In the prosecutor's words, "people are always sending food to prisoners of war, even in our own country" and therefore the evidence was immaterial and struck out.

However much the prosecution might stonewall on the testimony of the ex-prisoners of war, the statements of the POW witnesses for Toguri riveted onlookers and the press. Cousens, called as the first witness for the defense, recounted the tortures he had been through as a prisoner of the Japanese. With a broad brush he explained the Australian Anzac legend whereby Australian soldiers were imbued with a feeling of mateship towards each other and demonstrated great dignity under terrible hardship. Cousens broke down when describing an incident he saw on the dock in Singapore when the Japanese had beaten a prisoner to death for stealing a can of onions. Unequivocally, he claimed that he was the author of all of Toguri's radio scripts on *Zero Hour*.[24]

Wallace Ince was a striking figure in court wearing the smart uniform of a United States major with a great row of service medals glinting on his chest. He too wept during the cross-examination when he described the beating he had received from Japanese guards in Bunka Camp. Norman Reyes was tripped up in the witness box. The young Filipino, who had been a disc jockey on Radio Tokyo, made a strong statement about Iva Toguri's kindness to the POWs, but he became flustered when the prosecution reminded him of a less charitable testimony made previously to an agent of the FBI. In it he had been suspicious that Toguri was pro-Japanese. Led by Collins for the defense, Reyes explained that before the trial the FBI investigator, Fred Tillman, had pressured him to cooperate because to do otherwise could jeopardize the U.S. government-sponsored studentship that he held at Vanderbilt University. Reyes claimed that the FBI agent had told him that his behavior in court could have serious consequences for his residency in the United States. The other Australian witness, Kenneth Parkyns, who underwent a similar abrasive cross-examination, announced on his return to Sydney that the "insulting and slanderous attitude" that the U.S. prosecution adopted towards himself and Cousens was disgraceful and had implied that they and "all the other POWs were Japanese collaborators."[25]

Both Toguri and Cousens when cross-examined denied that "Ann" had ever broadcast war information that would assist a Japanese victory. Cousens, in his clear announcer's manner, denied he had ever written the material and Toguri, in a voice that often dropped to a whisper, denied that "Ann" had ever broadcast information damaging to the United States. Similarly she steadfastly rejected any suggestion that she had discussed the sinking of American ships, the movement of Allied troops, Allied defeats in battle or the Japanese acquisition of territory. In addition, under oath both separately denied that "Ann" ever made salacious remarks about the wayward behavior of soldiers' wives and girlfriends at home: Neither that they were in bed with "Four F's"—American males who were able to evade the draft—nor that absent soldier's pay was not sufficient to keep a beautiful wife faithful; or that soldiers should abandon the "stinking mosquito infested islands" and go home. Cousens swore that he had never written nor had "Ann" ever broadcast the "smutty jokes" that listeners claimed to have heard a female announcer relate over Radio Tokyo.[26]

Several weeks into the trial, Hiromi Yagi, one of the prosecution witness brought from Japan, admitted to the defense attorneys that he had been bribed. An FBI agent had paid him in Tokyo to give evidence that he had heard Iva Toguri broadcasting in a treasonous manner. He now greatly regretted his action and wished to set the record straight and therefore was willing to spill the beans during defense cross-examination. Toguri's lawyers planned to call him to the stand, but when the time came, he had already been sent back to Japan.[27] At the same time, the agent who Yagi claimed had paid the bribe was struck from the prosecution's list of witnesses which prevented his being cross-examined by the defense.

At the center of proceedings, Iva Toguri appeared composed throughout the trial. Journalists described her demeanor as "calm and silent," even "stony-faced and unemotional."[28] Each day, she sat quietly beside her counsel at the bar table. With eyes lowered, her gaze remained fixed on the desk in front. In the witness box throughout Wolfe's abrasive and often insulting cross-examination, Toguri maintained her stoic demeanor. Even when he sneeringly referred to her as "our little heroine here who was broadcasting propaganda for the Japanese while the flower of young America were going to war and risking their lives," she sat with face impassive. At other times he likened her to "a female Benedict Arnold," the American general who went over to the colonialists in the War of Independence. And he called her an "arch-traitoress" and a "female Nipponese turncoat" of whom the evidence has shown is a "betrayer of her native land, and of our government in its time of need." In his final words of summing up, Wolfe derided Toguri's claim of loyalty that "she was one of our little soldiers, our Little Nell, working behind enemy lines." It was an "odious comparison" to speak of herself, beside "our young men and women risking their lives fighting a government which paid her, the woman they knew as 'Tokyo Rose.'"

A telltale sign of her great emotional distress, however, was that she grew thinner and notably thinner as the weeks wore on. She came to court every day in the same plaid suit, her threadbare wardrobe depleted by wartime shortages and the brusque departure from Tokyo taken without warning or preparation. It was rumored in the court corridors that she had lost an alarming thirty pounds. Certainly by the day of the judgment her clothes hung as loosely as on a scarecrow. There were only two instances in which emotion broke through her carefully managed guard. She wept quietly while listening to Charles Cousens' description of the barbarous treatment meted out to him. And tears fell, but noiselessly, when Judge Roche handed down the sentence: Conviction as a traitor, with ten years in prison and a ten thousand dollar fine.

The jury, equal numbers of men and women, but segregated by race with Orientals and blacks in one room and whites in another, had been closeted for almost three days. Having announced that they were at an impasse and unanimous verdict was impossible, Judge Roche refused to dismiss them, sending them back to try and again. The delay suggested that there was unease among several of the jurors, an impression that the jury foreman affirmed some years later.[29] After several hours, the jury men and women again returned, this time to announce that Iva Toguri was guilty of a single charge which was Overt Act no 6. This was that she had spoken positively to her listeners about the loss of American ships at the time of the Battle of the Gulf of Leyte in October 1944. The case against her was based on evidence presented by George Mitsushio and Kenkichi Oki who purported to have seen Toguri deliver broadcasts at Radio Tokyo. Oki was discredited in cross-examination, but Mitsushio's testimony held up. (Mitsushio confessed some years later that he had been coerced by the FBI to concoct the testimony.)[30] What is curious about the choice of this incident as the clinching piece of evidence for treasonable intent is that the battle of the Gulf of Leyte had been an American victory.

To no avail, Collins made an impassioned final defense, paying tribute to his client's "courage" and her "steadfast loyalty to her native country." He told the *New York Times* on October 6, after the sentencing, that "there had been a terrible miscarriage of justice." On November 15, carrying one small piece of hand luggage, Iva Toguri D'Aquino boarded a train in San Francisco with a wardress of the U.S. Prison Service. The four-day trip took them across the country to West Virginia where Toguri entered the Alderson Women's Prison.

Several things are striking, in reading the testimony and transcripts of Iva Toguri's trial, almost sixty years after the event. Whatever the charge might have been, there are elements in the trial that are reprehensible: The dishonesty of some of the witnesses, which has subsequently been proven; the bribes that we now know were paid for several testimonies; the behavior of some of the FBI agents and the main prosecution figures who were maneuvered into perjury. These things constitute corruption in any law-abiding society and therefore are a stain on American justice. However, this is not what is most striking about the case, at least for this reader. What stands out most starkly is the mismatch between the very mode of the trial itself and the events it was required to assess. The presumption of the law is that truth can be established within the legal parameters that underpin the rules of evidence and adversarial cross-examination within the courtroom. But Iva Toguri's circumstances depended on a whole raft of factors, some within her control, some without and some a function of historical contingency. The court tested these in a uniform manner against a uniform set of criteria which moved the possibility of the replication of the event in the courtroom further and further away from the actuality of its happening.

A transparent example, and one that was highly relevant to the outcome of the case, is apparent in the cross-examination of Wallace Ince. He was being questioned about a message that he had broadcast from Manila. The truth or otherwise of Ince's witness testimony in this incident mattered because if he could be considered reliable here, it could be assumed that he would also be truthful in his description of the duress under which Iva Toguri functioned at Radio Tokyo. An American enlisted in the military and living in the Phillipines, Ince was separated from his wife and two children when Corregidor fell. They were interned somewhere in Manila, and Ince was incarcerated in Bilbadil Prison. There is no question that the conditions in Bilbadil were atrocious and that the Japanese guards treated with unremitting brutality the unfortunate prisoners held there. After a month in Bilbadil, much as with Changi, a Japanese mobile radio unit turned up and offered some prisoners the chance to make a broadcast home. Ince leapt at the opportunity. He chose to send his message to his grandmother in the Midwest of the United States because he figured that she would be best placed to get word to all of the family that he was still alive. The message he sent was: "All fine. The food is good."

A few months later, when he had been transported to broadcast in Tokyo, Ince made his first radio broadcast. In this too he was careful to use his own name because he hoped that someone he knew would hear it and get word to his wife that he had been transported to Japan. During the Toguri trial, Ince was grilled in the witness box about the Manila message. The prosecution successfully argued that it proved that he had not been mistreated because he had not been badly fed. In fact, the prosecuting lawyer claimed that by his own word he had had an easy time of it as a POW. Ince's efforts to explain that though it was true that he had sent this message and his signature at the bottom of the message page attested to it, it was patently a lie. The court cross-examination permitted Ince only to answer yes or no—he had written the message, had signed the paper and had delivered the words about his own wellbeing on air. As his answer to all of these was in the affirmative, what he had said was true.

The Sentence Never Ends

After serving seven years in the Federal Women's Reformatory in Alderson, West Virginia, Toguri was awarded parole. Her records show her to have been a model prisoner, working as a skilled technician in the prison dental service and never having caused an iota of trouble. Ever since the news broke that Tokyo Rose was leaving prison, the press had gathered, commandeering every available bed and the town's only public phone. Toguri was released very early on the frosty morning of January 28, 1956. Her father, Jun Toguri, her elder brother, Fred Koichiro, and the younger sister, Inez, had made the long drive from Chicago to collect her. In the morning, by the glare of television's bright spotlights, journalists jostled for positions close to the prison gate. The Toguri family waited quietly in the car. As Iva D'Aquino Toguri emerged to the pop of flashbulbs, it was hard to believe that this small, unprepossessing figure with bird-like features and graying hair was the famed "Tokyo Rose," the "seductive-voiced siren" as she was described at the trial, supposed to have taunted Allied soldiers over the Japanese airwaves or seduced them with her "honey-voiced chit-chat." Outside the prison entrance, as Toguri climbed into the family car, a reporter shouted a question about her plans for the future. She replied that she wanted no more than to be reunited with her father, to get back on her feet and put the whole episode behind her.[31] As they drove off, there seemed no reason that this would not be the case.

Within two months Toguri was back in court. Even before she had been re-leased, the U.S. Immigration and Naturalization Service had begun the process of her deportation. She was served notice that she had thirty days in which to leave the United States voluntarily or face forced expatriation. There were several grounds.[32] The first and most easily answered, because Toguri had traveled to California under U.S. military guard, was that at the end of 1949 she had entered the United States without visa or passport. The other potentially much more se-rious charge was that as a convicted traitor she had lost her core rights of citizen-ship. The Immigration Department argued that a citizen found guilty of treason was automatically stripped of American nationality. Without it, Iva Toguri was an "undesirable alien" who was no longer entitled to reside legally in the United States. Several newspapers reported that Japan was the destination that the U.S. government had in mind. Elsewhere it was suggested that, as she had married a Portuguese citizen in Tokyo in 1945, Portugal was the place to send her.[33] Sud-denly, it was as though the intervening decade had never taken place. Despite the fact that she had fulfilled the penal sentence and been a model prisoner, the ghost of Tokyo Rose had been resurrected. In what must have seemed like a rerun of a bad dream, in February 1956 Iva Toguri left her brother's shop in Chicago and returned to San Francisco to live with the Collins family while Wayne Collins fought the deportation.

Before the Federal Court in San Francisco, Collins successfully argued that the order for Toguri's deportation was illegal.[34] Firstly, there were inconsistencies in the case. According to the 1952 McCarran Acts, aliens who violated American laws could be deported. Toguri's sentence, however, predated the promulgation of the act that rendered the Immigration Service contrary to the fundamental principle in American legal justice of the proscription of retrospectivity in the application of the law. Equally telling, as was pointed out, Toguri was not an alien, having been born in Southern California. As her counsel robustly argued, it was not possible simultaneously to have found an individual guilty of treason, which by definition is an act by a citizen against that citizen's nation, and at the same time deport that person on the grounds that she was an alien. After a series of court hearings that dragged on until July 1958, the Immigration Service dropped the charge.[35] The legal outcome was that Iva Toguri was a stateless person of American birth. Having been born within the United States and never having abjured her American citizenship, she was not a national of another country and therefore could not be expatriated. However, having been convicted for treason, she had been stripped of her American nationality.

The awkward legal conclusion was not the end of the matter. Nor was the prosecution finished with Iva Toguri. She was arraigned before the federal court for the non-payment of the full amount of her fine of ten thousand dollars. Her request for a court appearance, in which to explain that she had been in prison since the verdict and that her prison earnings were not sufficient to clear the debt, was denied. In 1968 the Justice Department re-summoned her and sequestered an insurance policy towards the fine. In March 1971, she was summoned again for the additional amount. The matter of the outstanding portion of the fine dragged on and on with summonses and negotiations, and despite Toguri's explanation that she did not have the money to pay in full because she was able to earn very little. The matter was not settled until 1972 when Jun Toguri, at his death, left instructions that what was outstanding in his daughter's fine was to be paid from his estate before any remainder was distributed among his children

Epilogue

As is convention and the law, English traitors are buried in unmarked graves in un-consecrated ground. In Amery's case it was within Wandsworth Prison. Several days after the execution, his mother tried unsuccessfully to speak about her son's last hours with the prison chaplain, H. T. Smith, who had accompanied John at the end of his life. Two years later, the Amery's parish priest from St. Peter's in Eaton Square interceded on Mrs Amery's behalf again to ask the chaplain whether he would be willing to meet with the still-grieving mother. By then, Smith was the Senior Chaplain at Wormwood Scrubs and one might expect that offering consolation to distressed prisoners' families would be a familiar part of his pastoral responsibilities. But it was not so. Smith recorded his reluctance in a letter to the prison governor explaining that he would "hate the job," but if instructed to do so would speak to the distressed woman. The Prison Commission firmly declined Mrs Amery's request.[1]

Perhaps in displacement of her own inconsolable sorrow, Mrs Amery pined to visit her son's last resting place, in her words, "to stand or kneel by his earthly remains" and "leave some flowers." Six months after the execution and then again at regular intervals, she petitioned the home secretary for permission to visit Wandsworth Prison to "put [her] hand on [her] darling son's grave," assuring Chuter Ede that she would "not take the time of anyone who had to accompany me" and above all would "make no fuss." All her requests were refused. The prison governor opined, "given her persistence, this poor lady will not be content with one visit and if she is allowed a visit she will apply as she has done before to visit again and again." In one of his last communication with her, the home secretary apologized for "appearing hard-hearted," but reiterated that it was not possible because "there must be a very large number of parents of persons who have been executed who would like to pay visits to their children's graves."[2] Her forlorn reply was to ask whether even if "we all went, would there be so many sorrowing parents?" Florence Amery died in February 1975. Twenty years later, and just before his own death in September 1996, Julian Amery (by then Baron Amery of Lustleigh) arranged to have his brother's remains disinterred from Wandsworth Prison and cremated. The ashes were scattered in France, over the Dordogne.[3]

John Amery was dazzled by the New Order that Hitler and Mussolini promised. In the 1930s his sentiments were the staple of the European radical Right to which he had been exposed at close quarters in Nationalist Spain. And, at least until 1940, there were many in Britain who thought as he did. In Occupied Europe, during the heyday of German ascendancy, Amery was swimming in the strongest current of the mainstream in railing against the evils of Bolshevism and Jewry. Without a doubt he was misguided and a fabulist and was too easily bought. His execution, however, makes no sense. His actions were not unlike the rest of the cohort of British broadcasters in Germany and his broadcasts no less irrelevant than were all of theirs. Certainly, in pleading guilty, John solved the Amery family's embarrassment. And he saved his brother from the prosecution's interrogation in the public court about Julian's dealings in Madrid with disreputable Falangists and fascist exiles who had faked the documents that were supposed to prove John's Spanish identity. The guilty plea, however, was a bad legal decision and a very curious one. The grounds for the pardon, upon which the plea was predicated, were extremely uncertain while the mitigation of McNaghten Rules could never be applied after the fact. Lickford's considerable experience and his conscientiousness as defense counsel for a raft of the so-called "ordinary" traitors, as well as for William Joyce, makes the choice of the defense strategy even more curious. However, what is clear in light of the pattern of sentencing in the other treason trials is that had Amery's trial taken place even six months later it is unlikely that he would have received a capital sentence. By then, the impulse to punish suspected traitors had ebbed.

The same factor of chronology was at play in Cousens' case. It is clearly so in light of the Holland verdict whereby a few months later Holland, who had joined the Japanese short wave by choice and had pleaded guilty to treason, received a short good behavior bond. And none of the other Australians involved with Japanese overseas broadcasting was ever prosecuted. From all accounts, Cousens was an outstanding radio broadcaster, never so energized and sharp as when he was behind the microphone. And clearly the exercise of his profession brought him great satisfaction. At the time that he was drafted to Tokyo, Cousens imagined that he could make a difference to the conditions of Allied POWs. To state this, though, is to say no more than that like everyone else he had no crystal ball and no way of knowing what lay ahead in the remaining years of the war in the Pacific. Equally, this does not mean that Cousens was a willing collaborator or favored Japanese victory. He was after all a prisoner of war, and his first-ever shortwave broadcast had been made in Changi at the direction of his superior military officers. Once in Japanese territory, even if his broadcasting skills marked him out for better treatment than other radio staff, as a prisoner in captivity he had no capacity to resist the Japanese.

After the trial, Cousens returned to his prewar job as an announcer on commercial radio. Later, briefly, though not with great success, he read the news in Sydney on the new medium of television. Charles Cousens died in Sydney at the age of sixty on May 9, 1964.

For Iva Toguri, after having had her plight studiously ignored for decades by Japanese Americans, the JACL, in 1974, formally apologized to her for their previous lack of support. Dr Clifford Uyeda, a Californian who had become the energetic chairman of the "Free Iva Toguri Committee" had managed to shift public opinion within the community. With the groundswell that began for Toguri's pardon, all sorts of forgotten wartime figures emerged. George S. Guysi, who had been a chief interrogator for the U.S. Counter Intelligence Corps in Tokyo, interviewing all the Bunka prisoners and testifying in Sydney against Cousens, wrote to the *Wall Street Journal* on February 23, 1976 that he had always found it "inconceivable" that Mrs D'Aquino had been tried for treason. He claimed that all along he had been sure that there were others of "far more questionable conduct" and with "far less mitigating circumstances" who had gone free.

By the mid seventies, opposition to the Vietnam War had placed the question of patriotism back on the agenda and there were regenerated arguments about how the government should deal with dissenting Americans. When set against the nuanced moral landscape of the Vietnam War, Iva Toguri's example appeared straightforward. Certainly, she had been caught on the wrong side when war was declared and had always declared that her dearest wish was to live as a citizen in the land of her birth. This was quite unlike the sentiments being expressed by disaffected Americans in the sixties and seventies. The new crop of "American traitors"—to use the sobriquet often given them by their conservative detractors—those opposed to the Vietnam War delighted in flaunting their disrespect for the United States government and relished being out of step with the values of their parents and grandparents. Many veterans of the Second World War, who were disturbed by the anti-Vietnam movement, looked back with nostalgia to World War Two and recalled Tokyo Rose with warmth. According to the *New York Times*, she appealed to the retro sentiments because "much like reveille, general quarters, dirt, boredom and Spam," Tokyo Rose was an artifact of a simpler ideological era.[4] And one should add also, because she was a figure who had been conjured up in the GI imagination, she was easily reinserted into a new and re-imagined landscape.

Three decades after the war in the Pacific, the radio programs and the music of the forties evoked a less complicated time.[5] A retired brigadier general, writing to the *Los Angeles Times* on September 3, 1972, encapsulated the sentiment: Tokyo Rose was part of the "good old days when Patriotism was still in flower and treason meant something." For him, what she had done was nothing when compared to "our late-blooming Americans beauties," that is, Jane Fonda and Ramsay Clark (though the letter writer may have forgotten that it was Clark's father as U.S. Attorney General who had prosecuted Iva Toguri). Another veteran opined that Tokyo Rose may have been a traitor, but she had provided "good, clean radio entertainment for the troops" and therefore should not ever be put in the same category as the "cowardly traitors" who were abandoning the United States to avoid being drafted to Vietnam.[6]

In achieving Toguri's pardon, the role of the Japanese American Senator S. I. Hayakawa was critical. His hard-line with student demonstrators while he was president of the San Francisco State University had made him the darling of American conservatives. Subsequently, he became the Republican senator for California and the high-profile face of the Japanese American community. Hayakawa backed the pardon and personally lobbied Gerald Ford, who was then the American president. On Ford's last day in office, January 19, 1977, he granted Iva Toguri a full presidential pardon. She died in Chicago in October 2006 at the age of ninety.

Notes

Introduction

1. As István Deák emphasizes, the numbers caught up in collaboration, resistance and retribution in World War Two outstripped all previous periods, *Politics of Retribution in Europe*, 3.

2. There was symmetry in the perceptions of Right and Left. The foreign volunteers, who made up the International Brigade supporting the Spanish Republic, also saw the civil war as the curtain raiser to World War Two.

3. Jan T. Gross in discussing the evolution of social behavior that constituted collaboration with the Nazi occupiers emphasized the discrepancy between the initial engagement with the occupier and the contribution that this involvement made to the reprehensible outcome of that occupation. See, "Themes for a Social History," in *Politics of Retribution*, 28–31. POWs in the Pacific, despite the memory literature that highlights the prisoners' stoicism and mateship, were in great measure flummoxed by the Malaya defeat and when first taken into custody had few indicators of what years of captivity held for them.

4. The term comes from Gross, p. 28, who argues that for a social history of war experience and collaboration because it can encompass endogenous processes, in "Themes for a Social History."

5. For the legal overview see: Law Commission of England and Wales, *Codification of the Criminal Law: Treason, Sedition and Allied Offences*; Australian Law Commission, *Review of Sedition Laws*; Steinhaus "Treason: A Brief History with Some Modern Applications"; Simon, "Evolution of Treason"; and Hurst, *Law of Treason in the United States*.

6. Simpson, "Detention without Trial in the Second World War: Comparing the British and American Experiences"; and his *In the Highest Degree Odious: Detention Without Trial in Wartime Britain*; and Stammers, *Civil Liberties in Britain During the Second World War*.

7. The list constantly under revision was distributed to military intelligence and consular staff abroad, in WO 204/2556/18232 PRO.

8. Director of Public Prosecution (DPP), London to Australian Solicitor-General, Canberra, February 7, 1947, Attorney-General's Department, Commonwealth of Australia, W31409 NAA.

9. The numbers were provided by the Home Secretary, James Chuter Ede in April 1946 in response to a parliamentary question, *Times* (London) April 12, 1946.

10. For details of Schürch's trial see *Times* (London) September 13, 1945; September 18, 1945; January 3, 1946; and January 5, 1946.

11. Murphy, *Letting the Side Down*, 226. Closer to the mark is Doherty's comment that it is "hard to understand the shocking inconsistencies in the penalties meted out," in *Nazi Wireless Propaganda*, 183.

12. The German spies George Johnston Armstrong in July 1941 and Duncan Scott Ford in November 1942 were hanged in Wandsworth Prison and Oswald Job on March 11, 1944 in Pentonville Prison.

13. His pro-Nazi radio talks revealed a "maniacal anti-Semitism," Doherty, *Nazi Wireless Propaganda*, 185; and see HO 144/22823 PRO.

14. A Sandhurst graduate, Baillie-Stewart had been convicted in 1933 under the Official Secrets Act and had left Britain permanently; see his *Officer in the Tower*.

15. The broadcasts, vintage Wodehouse, traced the bumbling adventures of himself and enraged British listeners while his North American fans pestered the German and the British government with enquiries about his safety; see McCrum, *Wodehouse*.

16. Reynolds, "Treason: Defunct or Dormant."

17. Keene, "Treason and the Trial of Traitors in Twentieth Century Australia."

18. Ruddy, "Permissible Dissent or Treason?" 158; and Hurst, *Law of Treason in the United State*, especially "Treason Cases and Doctrine 1945–1970," 236–59.

19. Loane, "Treason and Aiding the Enemy," 80.

20. Prasad, *They Love It But Leave It*, 64. The convicted broadcasters in Europe were John Best (life imprisonment); Herbert Burgman (20 years); Douglas Chandler (life); Mildred Gillars (12 years): and Martin Monti (25 years): see Hurst, *Law of Treason in the United States*, 236–63 and appendix, 260–77; Steinhaus, "Treason, A Brief History with Some Modern Applications"; and Edwards, *Berlin Calling*. Ezra Pound, identified as a renegade because of his pro-fascist broadcasts from Rome, was arrested in May 1945 and sent back to the United States where he was declared insane and committed to a mental institution, from which he was released in 1958; see Redman, *Ezra Pound and Italian Fascism*.

21. *New York Times*, December 13, 1963; Loane discusses the complexities of Kawakita's case and the legal Catch-22 of dual citizenship whereby the individual is subject to two incompatible obligations, in "Treason and Aiding the Enemy," 66–7. The large Tomoya Kawakita file in the J. F. Kennedy Memorial Library contains no indication of why President Kennedy acceded to this request when he had previously denied all similar requests. Kawakita quit the US to live in Japan.

22. Loane discusses voluntary expatriation and the United States Nationality Act in "Treason and Aiding the Enemy," 64–5.

Chapter 1

1. For the detail of British executions see Viscount Templewood, *Shadow of the Gallows* and Pierrepoint's memoirs, *Executioner Pierrepoint*. Arrangements for John Amery's execution are minuted in HM Prison, Wandsworth, Register no 3992, John Amery December 18, 1945, 52–3; and the autopsy report, Governor HM Prison Wandsworth, December 19, 1945, Register No 3992 John Amery, 20–1, PCOM 9/1117, PRO.

2. *The Star*, December 19, 1945; *Manchester Guardian*, December 22, 1945.

3. Here, as in certain places in the text, I refer to members of the Amery family by their first names. This is not to imply disrespect or familiarity, but to un-encumber the text when discussing family members who appear together.

4. See for example *Sunday Pictorial*, May 13, 1945; *Daily Herald*, November 29, 1945.

5. Hugh Quigley, "To the Editor," *Manchester Guardian*, December 1, 1945.

6. *Manchester Guardian*, quoted in *Spectator*, January 4, 1946.

7. The talks cobbled together the same material in different sequence. For the first to Britain, see "Calais (English Group) In English for UK 30 minutes" *European Magazine*, November 19, 1942. News Summary, Talk by John Amery; PRO KV2/78 85012 PRO.

8. Leo Amery, Typescript Diary Notes, November 19, 1942, Box 291, TSD LAP CAC. I have used Leo Amery's Typescript Diary Notes where they provide more information about family matters. The published diaries provide scholarly comment on politics and context, *Empire At Bay: The Leo Amery Diaries 1929–1945*.

9. Interview on Norwegian Radio Home Service, John Amery's Views on the British Situation, February 24, 1944, KV 2/78 85012 PRO.

10. See LSA TDN, November 19, 1942, Box 291, LSATD LAP CAC. See references to the King in speech at Ghent, May 11, 1945; and at Lyons, November 1, 1944, KV2/81 PRO.

11. Amery, *Sons of the Eagle*.

12. *Commander Burt of Scotland Yard*, Joyce, 1–17 and Amery, 18–28.

13. British Renegades Wanted List. WO 204/2556/18232 PRO.

14. Other commentators see Edward VIII in a less-positive light. For example Allen, *Crown and the Swastika*, and Picknett, *War of the Windsors*.

15. West, *Meaning of Treason*. There are references to Joyce on most pages in the first 11 chapters.

16. Rollyson, "Rebecca West and the FBI."

17. *Life Sentence: Memoirs of Lord Shawcross*, 78–84.

18. It is interesting to note that West had little time for Slade and his meticulous insistence in the many cases he defended, that British citizens charged as traitors still had civil rights, *Meaning of Treason*, 152–4.

19. *New York Times*, September 20, 1945.

20. Ibid.

21. Slade later observed that "treason was the one area of English justice in which it is practically impossible to get and give a fair trial," quoted in Simon, "The Evolution of Treason," 669.

22. See the daily medical reports in, Hospital Case Paper Reg no 3992, John Amery, November 28 to December 19, 1945, 23–7; 204–24 PCOM 9/1117 PRO.

23. Senior Medical Officer HM Prison Brixton, December 1, 1945, 359, HO 144/22823, 85153, Minutes to Head Office, HM Prison Wandsworth, November 29, 1945, 63, Subject 3992 John Amery, 63; Copy of Dr Methuen's Minute on HO pp888547/7 John Methuen, December 3, 1945, 61; Secretary, John Amery, December 8, 1945, Methuen, 58, PCOM 9/1117 PRO.

24. Brixton Prison, December 1, 1945, p 359, Hugh Emerson to Dr Methuen, 3755 John Amery, age 33, 359. HO 144/22823 85153 PRO.

25. See reference to Dr Grierson, 339; HM Prison Brixton, December 1, 1945, 3755 John Amery age 33 from Hugh Emerson, Senior medical Officer, PCOM 9/117 PRO.

26. Weale, *Patriot Traitors*; and, *Renegades*.

27. Murphy, *Letting the Side Down*.

28. Faber, *Speaking For England*.

29. 5 December 1945, Box 293, TSD LAP CAC.

30. For the process by which they were collected see, "John Amery. Messrs J E Lickfold & Sons Solicitors. Reports by Lord Horder and Dr E. Glover, 7-12-45", 178–212, HO 144/22823 85153 PRO.

31. They were Bernard Hart of Harley Street, J. R. Rees, a former Brigadier in the Royal Army Medical Corps and Director of the Tavistock Clinic, A. MacNiven, Superintendent of Glasgow Royal Mental Hospital and D. K. Henderson, Professor of Psychiatry at the University of Glasgow and co-author of a textbook of psychiatry, J. E. Lickfold to Home Secretary, December 14, 1945, 202, HO 144/ 22823 85153 PRO.

32. Psychiatric Report by Dr Edward Glover, 18 Wimpole Street on the case of John Amery, 224–33, HO 144/22823 85153 PRO.

33. See Home Office report which begins: Lord Horder sent by telephone, December 18, 1945, 292–3, HO 144/ 22823 85153 PRO.

34. Gathorne-Hardy, *Old School Tie,* 303.

35. Westfields, XI. Dear Madam, from Caroline Mead, 269–72, HO 144/ 22823 85153 PRO.

36. Statement by Miss I. M. Ironside. Headmistress of the Private School, Elveston Place, SW7 made on a psychiatric interview with Dr Glover, 242, HO 144/22823 85153 PRO.

37. Mr Kenneth L. S. Tindall, Headmaster West Down, Winchester, December 1, 1945, 264–266 HO 144/22823 85153 PRO.

38. A. J. Boissier, John Amery, 160, HO 144/ 28832 PRO.

39. Sir Cyril Norwood, The Case of John Amery, December 4, 1945, 424–7; and Sir Cyril Norwood, to L.S. Amery, The President's Lodgings, St John's College, Oxford, 2.12.1945, 267–8, HO 144/22823 85153 PRO.

40. During the previous summer Jack had learned to drive a car while on vacation in Brittany.

41. Leander Jameson, December 4, 1945, 243–51, HO 144/ 22923 85153 PRO.

42. See the report which begins: "When in 1928 I undertook to tutor," 161–3; and Julian Amery Esq., from Kingsley Walton, December 9, 1945, 156–9, HO 144/ 28832 85153 PRO.

43. Statement made by G. C. Nock formerly private tutor to John Amery in a psychiatric interview with Dr Glover, 239–40, HO 144/22832 85153 PRO.

44. Psychiatric Report by Dr Edward Glover, 18 Wimpole Street, on the case of John Amery, 231, HO 144/ 22823 85153 PRO.

45. *Sunday Pictorial,* May 13, 1945.

46. Psychiatric Report by Dr Edward Glover, 224–33.

47. Points noted in conversation with Mrs John Amery, 253–4; Additional Points elicited in a psychiatric interview with John Amery's wife by Dr Glover, 255–6, HO 144/22823 85153 PRO.

48. Ibid.

49. For a discussion of the process of the law and legal reprieve see Christoph, *Capital Punishment and British Politics,* 13–34.

50. See report which begins: "Lord Horder sent by telephone," December 18, 1945, 292–3, HO 144/ 22823 85153 PRO.

51. There is detailed discussion of this legal question in the Home Office files, 10.11.45: John Amery. Messrs J. E. Lickfold & Sons, Appeal for a reprieve . . . .Response. Minutes and Reports, 343–51, HO 144/ 22823 85153 PRO.

52. See the regular discussions minuted between November 30 to December 10, John Amery. Messers J. E. Lickfold and Sons Solicitors appeal for a reprieve . . . Response, Minutes and Reports 343–51; 353–4, HO 144/22823 85153 PRO.

53. Letter to W. N. East Esq., MD, FRCP, December 10, 1945, 328; and Letter to J. S. Hopwood Esq., MB, BS, MRCS, LRCP, December 10, 1945, 329, HO 144/ 22823, 85153 Home Office Whitehall, To the Secretary Prison Commission Horseferry House, PCOM 9/1117 PRO.

54. Report by W. N. East & J. Hopwood, HM Prison, Wandsworth, December 14, 1945, John Amery, to the Under Secretary of State, 24–32, HO 144/ 22823 85153 PRO.

55. Report: Case of John Amery, initialed by Chuter Ede, December 10, 1945, 332–9, HO 144/ 22823 85153 PRO.

56. Home Officer Whitehall, December 17, 1945, to Secretary Prison Commission, 54 PCOM 9/117, PRO.

57. Report which begins "It is recognized that Amery is not insane within the meaning of McNaghten Rules," initialed "CE 15/12", 319–21; and comment that begins "The effect of the report submitted by the doctors is that Amery is a moral defective," initialed "OAN, 15/12/45," 322–23, HO 144/ 22823 85153 PRO.

58. J. E. Lickfold & Sons to Home Secretary, Enclosed statement December 14, 1945, 213–9 HP 144/22823 PRO; Private, John Amery, An Explanation, LSA 1946, 11ps, 93a–f, Canon Douglas Papers, Lambeth Palace Library. It is reproduced as an appendix to *Empire At Bay*, 1071–5.

59. Report which begins "Lord Horder sent by telephone," December 18, 1945, 293, HO 144/ 22823 85153 PRO.

Chapter 2

1. West, *Meaning of Treason*, 113.
2. Cannadine, *Decline and Fall of the British Aristocracy*.
3. McKibbin discusses the formation of the cultures of the old upper and the middle classes in, *Classes and Cultures*, 1–90, 235–59.
4. "Leo Amery" by A. P. Ryan, *Dictionary of National Biography, 1951–1960*, 16–9.
5. Amery, *Approach March*, 44.
6. Louis, *In the Name of God, Go!*; and "Leo Amery and the Post-War World, 1945–55."
7. Rubinstein, "Secret of Leopold Amery."
8. Leo Amery pays tribute to his mother's determination in, *My Political Life*. Vol. One *England Before the Storm*, 28–31.
9. Rubinstein, "Secret of Leopold Amery."
10. *Dictionary of National Biography*, 16–9; and *England Before the Storm, 1869–1914*, 28–31.
11. See 22 November 1933, Box 5 PC LAP CAC.
12. Louis, *In the Name of God, Go!*
13. Julian Amery provides an insider's analysis of the inter-war politicking around Imperial Preference in, *Joseph Chamberlain and the Tariff Reform Campaign*, 1010–30. McKenzie highlights the impossibility of the policy in the long run in, *Redefining the Bonds of Commonwealth, 1939–1948*, 17–30.
14. Constantine, "Bringing the Empire Alive."
15. Leo Amery's diaries contain regular references to his exercise regimen.

16. Martin Seedorf, "Hamar Greenwood," *Oxford Dictionary of National Biography*, Oxford University Press, Sept 2004; online edn. [http://www.oxforddnb.com/vie/article/ 33545, accessed January 15, 2008].

17. *Daily Express*, July 3, 1934, Box 8 PC. Typical was the gathering to farewell English headmistresses traveling to Canada to study the education of girls in the Dominions, *Morning Post*, February 14, 1931, Box 17, PC LAP CAC.

18. *Graphic* 20 November 1930, Box 8, PC LAP CAC; and Keene "At Home and Away with the Amery Family on Empire Day 1932."

19. Constantine, "Bringing the Empire Alive," 206. He notes that an edition of *The Book of Empire Dinners* sold out in the first week of its issue, 205.

20. "Bringing the Empire Alive," 207, 217.

21. *Sun*, December 19, 1927, Box 17, PC LAP CAC.

22. *Daily Sketch*, January 28, 1932; *Scotsman*, January 28, 1932; *Daily Telegraph*, January 27, 1932, Box 17, PC LAP CAC.

23. *Daily Sketch*, May 6, 1932, Box 17, PC LAP CAC.

24. *Scotsman*, May 16, 1932, Box 17, PC LAP CAC. During the campaign Leo offered one of his own favorites: Palestinian sauce made by whisking two English national mark eggs, three ounces of Canadian maple syrup, one-quarter pint of English cream and a liqueur glass of Cyprus brandy.

25. *My Political Life*, 399–474 and reception at Whitby, 461.

26. For example: "A tiresome letter from Inland Revenue clamouring for arrears in surtax," January 20, 1932, Box 285, TSD LAP CAC; or "I seem with all this to get no nearer the reduction of my overdraft," May 1, 1938, Box 290, TSD LAP CAC.

27. In 1938 Leo Amery's annual income was ten thousand pounds. See May 2, 1938, Box 290, TSD LAP, CAC. According to McKibbin, five hundred pounds provided the demarcation between a comfortable life with servants and the hard struggle that was needed in order to keep up appearances without household help. An income of two hundred and fifty pounds was the divide between the working and the middle classes. In this schema, the Amerys were in the very upper reaches of the high bourgeoisie. McKibbin also points out that members of the middle class in stable employment during the early thirties made real gains in income and that the tax burden on the rich was not onerous, in *Classes and Cultures*, 60–1, 44–5.

28. September 7, 1940, Box 290, TSD LAP CAC.

29. According to Julian, Pipette was unlike an English governess in that she believed in keeping the bedrooms hermetically sealed. And, from her, the children learned that there were two sides to every question as Pipette would disagree strongly with the interpretations of European history and France's place in it that were taught to English school children, *Approach March*, 29.

30. *Approach March*, 32. In August 1923, time taken out for a "month's holiday climbing in Chamonix with "'B' and our small boy Jack," *My Political Life*, 267.

31. Amery, *Approach March*, 32.

32. December 31, 1939, Box 289, TSD LAP CAC.

33. In 1923, Mrs Amery, Jack and Pipette accompanied Leo to Malta by sloop, *My Political Life*, 268. Leo's diary records time "horsing around" and "playing roughhouse" with Jack or enjoyable expeditions to the zoo. Leo taught both boys at an early age to play billiards and bridge; the family greatly enjoyed a rubber together after dinner. See January 1, 1932; January 2, 1932; January 10, 1932, Box 288, TSD LAP CAC. While Julian was at a crammer preparing for Eton, he and his father spent a long day together punting and

swimming on the Char; Leo having brought strawberries and cream, a tray of ham, salad and cakes for a picnic; July 10, 1932, Box 288, TSD LAP CAC.

34. Julian catalogues some of the incidents that became family lore such as his likening a distinguished admiral to the gorilla he had seen in the zoo; or his sticking drawing pins in the bottoms of grownups attending the unveiling of a portrait of his father, *Approach March*, 31.

35. *Approach March*, 27.

36. As a small boy, Julian met the Jaffir Pasha Al Askiri of Iraq and King Feisal who presented him with a golden dagger and scimitar, *Approach March*, 33–4.

37. *Approach March*, 26–7.

38. *Adelaide Register*, October 20, 1927; *Brisbane Courier Mail*, November 9, 1927.

39. *Approach March*, 45.

40. Leo's typescript diaries are filled with plans for his sons' future careers and his own efforts to foster them.

41. The information in this section comes from Henderson, *Old Friends and Modern Instances*, 29–35.

42. *Approach March*, 73: "Summerfields," 36–43; and "Eton", 36–3, 49–60, 73.

43. Heavy rain caused Leo for the first time ever to miss an electoral meeting in Birmingham. He used the unexpected free time to take Mrs Amery to the movies though their guilty feelings rather spoilt the outing. May 2, 1938, Box 290, TSD LAP CAC.

44. May 2, 1938, Box 290, TSD LAP CAC.

45. *Sunday Times*, June 19, 1932. At Randolph's twenty-first birthday party Churchill described his son as "a fine machine-gun and it was hoped he would accumulate a big dump of ammunition and learn to hit his target," *Evening Standard*, June 17, 1932. And Randolph's own observations in, *Twenty-One Years*, 109.

46. "Cassandra," January 1947, clipping CHUR 1/41/ 42 Winston Churchill Papers, CAC.

47. October 13; November 11, 1940, TSD LAP CAC. At the time that Julian was anxious to enter the Special Operations Executive, Hugh Dalton who oversaw the organization noted in his diary that he would "win the heart of Mrs Amery for ever" if he could make a place for her son" and that she was "all over" [Dalton] "by reason of her son," in his *Second World War Diaries of Hugh Dalton 1940–45*, 97, 185.

48. "The cheek of the young brute was almost more than I could bear," *War Diaries 1939–1945 of Field Marshal Lord Alanbrooke*, 276.

49. J. E. Lickfold 7 Sons to Home Secretary, Enclosed statement December 14, 1945, 213–19 HP 144/22823 PRO.

50. Between the wars the great public boarding schools faced falling enrolments and the costs of staff salaries rose, McKibbin, *Classes and Cultures in England*, 235–48. Sir Cyril Norwood's education committee favored the differentiation between children's abilities, the consequences of which was to solidify class differences within British education, *Classes and Cultures in England*, 223–7.

51. Gathorne-Hardy, *Old School Tie*, 297–304.

52. February 21, 1926, Box 285; and January 19, 1927, Box 286, TSD LAP CAC.

53. John Amery won a prize for French which delighted his parents, on November 24, 1926, Box 285, TSD LAP CAC.

54. See his comments in the interview with the Medical Superintendent, Brixton Prison, 1945. Randolph Churchill, also, recalled unhappy school days: at Sandroyal Preparatory School a master had encouraged the boy to masturbate him; at Eton he

had been "lazy and unsuccessful"; and made few friends, in *Twenty One Years*, 23, 31, 108.

55. February 21, 1926, Box 285, TSD LAP CAC.

56. February 21, 1926, Box 285, TSD LAP CAC.

57. February 21, 1926, 3 July 1927, Box 286, TSD LAP CAC.

58. September 1, 1926, Box 286, TSD LAP CAC.

59. September 1, 1926, Box 286, TSD LAP CAC.

60. February 21, 1926, Box 286, TSD LAP CAC.

61. February 21, 1926, 3 July 1927, Box 286TSD LAP CAC.

62. January 17, 1927, Box 286, TSD LAP CAC.

63. See Leo's report "John Amery born March 14, 1912," 235.

64. January 25, 1926, Box 285 TSD LAP CAC.

65. Ibid.

66. Ibid.

67. Ibid.

68. January 25, 1926, Box 285, TSD LAP CAC.

69. February 16, 1927, Box 286, TSD LAP CAC.

70. Mr Ferenc of Bishopsbridge Court to the Home Office recalled that prewar John Amery was "eccentric and crazy" and "completely film-mad"; "wore collars of a positively enormous size" and had some "outlandish schemes" to raise money for making movies via London stockbrokers, December 18, 1945, 373–4, HO 144/ 22823 PRO.

71. Statement by Mr W. H. Barrett Assistant Master at Harrow School, formerly Housemaster to John Amery in a Psychiatric Interview with Dr Glover, 235–6, HO 144/ 22823 85153 PRO. Worsley, a student and a master, emphasizes the central place of beatings in public school life, in *Flannelled Fool*.

72. When contacted by Leo Amery in December 1945, the retired Dr Maurice Wright could recall the consultation, but not the year. The date of July 1945 on the affidavit is curious suggesting that Lickfold had begun to prepare a defense of insanity as soon as John Amery had been brought back to England. Presumably, this defense had been abandoned and then later taken up again. See Maurice Wright for Lickfold and Sons, June 10, 1945, 257–8, HO 144/ 22823 85153 PRO.

73. Nock's affidavit is short on detail but long on self-righteous condemnation of Amery, which may be Nock's way of covering up his own failures as a guardian. Statement made by G. C. Nock formerly Private Tutor to John Amery in a Psychiatric Interview with Dr Glover, 239–240, HO 144/22832 85153 PRO.

74. Leo considered the master's comment on Jack's Latin an "exaggeration" because he could translate from Latin to English, but was without the grammatical structures to translate in the other direction.

75. Mrs Amery explained in an interview in Australia that "film direction was not exactly the career we had mapped out for John but his heart was so set upon it that we had no course other than to agree to it." She also noted that "he has done wonderfully well in this work so far," *Melbourne Herald*, May 21, 1932.

Chapter 3

1. Constantine, "Bringing the Empire Alive," 209; and Hollins, "The Conservative Party and Film Propaganda Between the Wars."

2. The film reconstructed the dangerous climbs on Mount Kanchenuga and the losses of life with avalanches, *Evening Standard,* July 20, 1932.

3. *Daily Herald,* October 7, 1930, Box 17, PC LAP CAC.

4. Keene, "At Home and Away With the Amery Family."

5. Amery's diary entries from February to September 1932 catalogue constant and intense activities relating to the Ottawa meeting, in *Empire At Bay,* 232–59.

6. August 11 to September 12, 1932, *Empire At Bay,* 250–59.

7. *Joseph Chamberlain and the Tariff Reform Campaign,*1026. McKenzie, *Redefining the Bonds of Commonwealth,* 20–1.

8. *Empire At Bay,* 237.

9. *Melbourne Herald,* May 21, 1932.

10. *Daily Herald,* October 7, 1930, Box 8, PC LAP CAC.

11. *Daily Herald,* October 7, 1930, Box 8, PC LAP CAC.

12. *Birmingham Evening Despatch*, January 23, 1932, Box 26 PC LAP CAC.

13. *Daily Film Renter,* September 22, 1930, Box 8; *Irish Independent*, October 6, 1930, Box 8; *Daily Express,* January 23, 1932, Box 26, PC LAP CAC. The correspondent in the *Daily Film Renter* expressed some reservations: "although it is the day of youth" he would "feel more confident if [Amery] were a few years older to be embarking on a production of this magnitude," January 27, 1932, Box 26, PC LAP CAC.

14. *The Star,* January 23, 1932; *Northampshire Evening Telegraph,* January 28, 1932, PC Box 26, LAP CAC.

15. See for example *Birmingham Evening Despatch*, January 23, 1932, Box 25, PC LAP CAC.

16. *The Star,* January 23, 1932, Box 26, PC LAP CAC.

17. Richards, "Boy's Own Empire"; "Patriotism with Profit," 245–56; and "Cinema of Empire." For a list of the films see Roberts, "Africa on Film to 1940."

18. *The Star,* January 23, 1932, Box 26, PC LAP CAC.

19. *Daily Sketch,* January 27, 1932; *Birmingham Evening Despatch*, January 23, 1932, Box 26, PC LAP CAC.

20. Paris, *Wright Brothers to Top Gun,* 105; and Omissi, "The Hendon Air Pageant," 189–220.

21. *Cinema,* April 8, 1932; *Sunday Times,* April 10, 1932, Box 26, PC LAP CAC.

22. *Birmingham Daily Mail,* January 23, 1932; *Birmingham Evening Despatch*, January 23,1932, Box 26, PC LAP CAC.

23. *Daily Film Renter,* January 27, 1932, Box 26, PC LAP CAC.

24. *Birmingham Daily Mail,* January 23, 1832, Box 26, PC LAP CAC.

25. *Sunday Times,* April 10, 1932, Box 26, PC LAP CAC.

26. *The Star,* April 25, 1932, Box 26, PC LAP CAC.

27. There had been criticism of bombing as a method in imperial air policing and several protests opposed the indelicacy of the displays at Hendon in which native villages with air force men disguised as natives were blown up from the air. See Omissi, "The Hendon Air Pageant," 211–5.

28. *Birmingham Post,* March 26, 1932, PC Box 26, LAP CAC.

29. *Birmingham Post,* March 17, 1932, PC Box 26, LAP CAC.

30. Metropolitan Police Special Branch, December 11, 1942, John Amery, KV 2/78 85012 PRO.

31. September 7, 1932; December 12, 1932, Box 26 TSD LAP CAC.

32. The details in this paragraph are from Rotha, *Documentary Diary*, 66–7.

33. December 25, 1932, Box 26 TSD LAP CAC.

34. *Times* (London), September 14, 1932.

35. September 8, 1932, Box 26, TSD LAP CAC.

36. The report from Special Branch of the Metropolitan Police, December 11, 1942 was solicited for the Amery file in the Renegades List. It cites Una Wing's arrest in the West End and conviction at Marlborough Street Police Court on June 13, 1931 and fine 40/–for soliciting. The description may be exaggerated as it was collected when Leo was attempting to stop John and Una's marriage, Metropolitan Police, Special Branch, Subject John Amery, KV 2/78, 85012, PRO.

37. August 23, 1932, Box 26, TSD LAP CAC.

38. September 30, 1932, Box 2, TSD LAP CAC.

39. September 30, 1932, Box 2, TSD LAP CAC.

40. Read, "Three Political Dissenters." I am grateful for the help from Professor Donald Read, the historian of Reuters and John Entwisle, the Reuters Archivist.

41. The ceremony caused a rift within the Anglican Church especially among those working for interfaith ecumenicalism. Canon Douglas, the Amery's local vicar and family confidant, sought assurances from the Archbishop of Athens that John and Una had not been required to re-baptize, Canon Douglas to Bishop of Westminster, Douglas Papers, Lambeth Palace Library.

42. The Editorial Department issued instructions that "nothing was to be printed on Amery Junior without reference to the Editor-in-Chief," Editorial Department, May 18, 1933; an editorial note instructs that Leo Amery is to be informed of all developments, The Editor-in-Chief, May 30, 1933, "To MD", JAF RA.

43. *Times* (London), May 31, 1933.

44. *World Press News,* June 1, 1933.

45. In the John Amery file, the errors in his notes to the editor and the night manager have been circled with a thick red pencil or marked with an exclamation mark. A note to the chief editor refers to him as the "problem child of the Mail and Features Department." October 1, 1936, signed "ADSC," JAF RA.

46. Dear Sir Roderick, Mail & Features Dept., July 1, 1936; Dear Mr Amery, October 15, 1936 from Bernard Rickatson-Hatt, JAF RA.

47. Private and Confidential, John Amery. September 30, 1936, JAF RA.

48. To Mr Rickatson-Hatt, May 26, 1936, 3pps, JAF RA. In Franco's Spain there was an expanding enterprise in propaganda, including filmmaking, dominated by Nazi institutions, see Bowen, *Spaniards and Nazi Germany*, 34–54; and Waddington, "Anti-Komintern and Nazi Anti-Bolshevik Propaganda in the 1930s," 582–7.

49. *Daily Mail*, July 7, 1936. On the Reuters file cutting, someone has written "I thought JA was now gun running in Spain"; and on another "Amazing Youth"; *Daily Telegraph* 25 November 1936; Press Association, John Amery "Window Dressing in the Film Industry," December 18, 1936, JAF RA.

50. "Amery. Heavy Business and Lavish Living," Reuters Copy, August 17, 1937, JAF RA.

51. Information from Patrizia Dogliani, University of Bologna. For the Spanish Foreign Ministry material see Chapter 6 FN 31.

52. Burns, *Use of Memory*, 81.

53. John Amery and Spain, G.E.Wakefield, July 15, 1945, KV 2/81 85012; Darling Toto, January 25, 1940, Estoril Portugal, KVV2/78 85012 PRO.

54. *Approach March*, Chapters 8 and 9.

55. *Approach March*, 112. It is worth noting that despite his antipathy to the International Brigades as communist dupes, when Julian was recruiting individuals to serve in the underground behind the German lines in Yugoslavia, he actively sought out British ex-International Brigaders because they were acceptable to Tito and had proven their anti-fascist commitment in battle, Dalton, *Second World War Diaries*, 545.

56. Roberts, "The Spanish Precedent"; and "Freedom, Faction, Fame and Blood."

57. March 22–25; June 14, 1940; July 5, 1940; July 8, 1940; August 1, 1940, TSD LAP CAC.

Chapter 4

1. Quoted in Thévenot, *L'Age de la télévision...*, 78–9, 146. See also, Taylor, "Propaganda in International Politics, 1919–1939."

2. Smith, *International Telecommunications Control*, 101.

3. Louis L. Snyder provides the extraordinary figure of fifteen hundred Germans in the first year of the war arrested for listening to foreign broadcasts, in *Encyclopedia of the Third Reich*, 279. Most of the arrests were as a result of talking to friends who reported them to the Gestapo, Smith, *Last Train from Berlin*, 87.

4. Bergmeier and Lotz, *Hitler's Airwaves*, 23; Buchbender and Hauschild, *Radio Humanité*.

5. See Bergmeier and Lotz, *Hitler's Airwaves*; Sorlin, "Struggle for the Control of French Minds," 245–69; and among an enormous number of earlier writings, Whitton, "War by Radio."

6. Bergmeier and Lotz, *Hitler's Airwaves*, 24.

7. See files, Dietze, Roderick Anton Eduard, including his statement, broadcasts and the recommendation by M15 not to charge him as a traitor, in KV2/428 118 252 PRO.

8. Dr Fritz Hesse, The England Committee, describes the ramshackle nature of the authority lines within the broadcasting sphere, KV2/81 85012 PRO.

9. Hesse, The England Committee.

10. *Hitler's Airwaves*, 29.

11. Otto Dietze, a regular participant in Goebbels' conferences, noted that "this game" was a frequent ploy to out-maneuver a competitor, quoted in *Hitler's Airwaves*, 30.

12. Doherty, *Nazi Wireless Propaganda*; Bergmeier & Lotz, *Hitler's Airwaves*; Murphy, *Letting the Side Down*, 49–99; and Edwards, *Berlin Calling*.

13. Statement of My Political Activities in Europe in Condensed Form 1936–1945. John Amery at "R" Internee Camp, Terni, Italy, 23/5/1945, 8pps, HO 45/25773 PRO.

14. *Ibid*, 8.

15. See Hoare, *Ambassador on Special Mission*.

16. See British Embassy, Personal, October 29, 1940, Part XIII, 17(69); December 4, 1941, XIII, File 18; Personal 1942, XIII, 19 (61) TP CUL. Another friend, in Lisbon, also sent parcels to Jack and passed letters to his mother, CEL Postal and Telegraphy Censorship, Mrs Amery to Mme Oulman, Lisbon, KV2/ 78 85012 PRO.

17. LA to SH, Personal, December 11, 1942, XIII 19 (60), TP CUL.

18. See the receipts, Relief Payments of Distressed, Nice, September 6, 1940, and Talarru Isère, June 30, 1942, HO 144/22822 PRO.

19. War Office, Statement by Wilfred Brinkman, May 26, 1945, 90, HO 4525773 PRO.

20. Statement by Wilfred Brinkman.

21. MI5 Liaison Section, C. P. Hope, Paris, September 7, and Statement by Alexander Ogilvie, September 2, 1945, KV 2/81 PRO. An intercepted message from the *Daily Herald* correspondent in Lisbon reported a rumor that Amery had acquired a diplomatic passport and was smuggling checks into Spain in the English diplomatic pouch. It is likely that the rumor was based on the communications from the British Ambassador through the intermediary in Occupied France. And as far as the Ogilvie case goes, it could be said that in hoarding dollars Ogilvie had been breaking a Vichy law.

22. See Spitzy, *How We Squandered the Reich*, 53.

23. The statement was made as part of an Allied interrogation, but has the ring of authenticity: British Legion against Bolshevism, Statement by Dr Hesse on September 17, 1945 by J. M. Davies, 242a, 3–4, 85012, KV2/81 PRO. The details of Hesse's statement tally with those in, Extract of Statement from Dr Haferkorn . . . July 13, 1945, 85012 KV2/81 PRO.

24. Lambauer, *Otto Abetz et les français; Ou l'envers de la collaboration*, 399–422; and Davey, "The Origins of the Légion des Volontaires Français contre le Bolchevisme," 29–45.

25. The German military were equally unenthusiastic about Doriot's Legion, in, Lambauer, *Otto Abetz et les Français*, 409.

26. Lamb, *Churchill as War Leader*, 15–20; and Reynolds, "Churchill and the British 'decision' to fight in 1940."

27. The British press read the early broadcasts as peace feelers. See for example, John Amery's Peace Feeler on Hun Radio, *Daily Mirror*, November 20, 1942.

28. Smith, *Last Train from Berlin*, 44, 96. There are frequent references to the two clubs in the memoirs of American broadcasters. See for example Flannery, *Assignment to Berlin*, 73, 110, 156; and Shirer, *Berlin Diary*, 522.

29. Smith, *Last Train from Berlin*, 44.

30. Flannery, *Assignment to Berlin*, 156.

31. Spitzy, *How We Squandered the Reich*, 355.

32. Flannery, *Assignment to Berlin*, 166.

33. Pressmen from democratic countries, "nauseated with fighting their way through the feathers of propaganda," often suffered the "Berlin blues," Smith, *Last Train from Berlin*, 43–51.

34. William Joyce earned four thousand marks a month while the others received between four and six hundred a month; the salary of the young German women at the station was one hundred and ninety-eight marks a month, even though many of them, as Doherty points out, worked long hours and spoke several foreign languages, in *Nazi Wireless Propaganda*, 27. According to the exchange rates applied in Jersey, 9.6 Reichmarks were the equivalent of 1 BP, http://eh.net/htmit/exchangerates/exchange.answer.php (14/5/06).

35. Statement by Dr Hesse taken on September 17, 1945, 242a , 3, KV2/81 85012 PRO.

36. He cultivated the friendship of P. G. and Ethel Wodehouse in Beverley Hills in 1927 and when Wodehouse made a series of shortwave broadcasts in Berlin, Plack was the chaperone and interpreter. Later in Paris in 1943, Plack moved the Wodehouses to the Hotel Bristol, in McCrum, *Wodehouse*, 242.

37. Flannery, *Assignment in Berlin*, 35; and *Hitler's Airwaves*, 154.

38. See J. A.'s statement, Complete Accounts, attached to Memorandum for The Foreign Office concerning my activities since my departure to Belgrade on November 14, KV/2/81 85012 PRO. In May 1941, the British Foreign Office used an exchange rate of

175 FF to 1 BP, and in 1944 it was set at 200FF to 1 BP, see "British official Relief, Acknowledgement of Loan" form completed by J. A., September 6, 1940, HO 144/22822 PRO.

39. Inspector of Police, May 7, 1944, Gaumont Palace Cinema, deposition in *The King v John Amery*, September 21, 1945, 33, CRIM1/1717 PRO.

40. See Lambauer, *Otto Abetz et les français*, 238–61, 350–78; and Burrin, *France under the Germans*, especially 291–305 and 411–36.

41. Document received by Major Burt from the military authorities in Italy and admitted by Amery to be his property, Memorandum for the Foreign Office Concerning My activities since my departure to Belgrade on November 14, 306–15, HO144/22822 85012 PRO.

42. Spitzy, *How We Squandered the Reich*, 354. A more unsympathetic view came from a pro-British source who, observing her at the Hotel Adlon in late 1942, observed that she was "very dark, outrageously made up, garish, flamboyant and behaving in a vulgar fashion in front of half a dozen other people." See, Extract from the Statement by Hewitt [SHAEFF MI5 Liaison] KV2/79 85012 PRO.

43. *How We Squandered the Reich*, 353–6.

44. Rumors abounded about the cause of death but an autopsy carried out by two German university professors concluded that she had died as a result of asphyxiation brought on by vomiting and inebriation, *Rapport du procurer general, le tribunal de 1er instance de Berlin en date du 21 avril 1943, Hesse Deutsche Botschaft*, Paris, KV2/84 85012 PRO.

45. The observor for British intelligence added primly, "her table manners are not good," Appendix Secret SIR, August 23, 1944, KV2/72 85012 PRO.

46. According to Bourdrel, a French journalist who has written extensively on the movement in *La Cagoule: Histoire d'une société sécrète du Front Populaire à la Ve République,*165–79. Soucy emphasizes the importance of Franco's Spain to the Cagoule, in *French Fascism*, 47, and Pugliese, "Death in Exile: The Assassination of Carlo Rosselli." The Cagoule assassinated the Italian Rosselli brothers: Carlo, an International Brigade veteran in the Spanish civil war, was an organizer with his brother of the *Justice and Liberty* anti-fascist exiles in France. In recompense, the Cagoule received a load of weapons.

47. Quoted in Leo Amery TSD, October 17, 1945, LAP CAC. Julian and Leo were highly amused at the references that praised John for his military demeanor and bravery.

48. Louis Malle's film *Lacombe Lucien* (1974) evokes the corruption and self-interest of French fascists in Toulouse in 1944. Under the protection of the French milice they ply the black market across the French border into Spain where San Sebastian provides a safe and luxurious haven for fleeing French fascists.

49. See Hérold-Paquis, *Des illusions... disillusions!*, 161; and Amery's "chats" scheduled for December 29 and 30, 1942 and January 9 and 10, 1943, in Rapport sur les emissions de Radio Paris, KV 2/79 85012, PRO.

50. Lambauer, *Otto Abetz et les Français*, 408–19; and Barthélemy, *Du communisme au fascisme*, 235–46.

51. Lambauer, *Otto Abetz et les Français*, 419.

52. See Millet, *Doriot et Ses Compagnons*, especially 82; and Keene, *Fighting For Franco*, 135–87. It was reported that Amery promoted the idea that the British legion in the east would use loud hailers to exhort enemy troops to cross the lines. This was a practise that was common in the Spanish civil war where the tactic was used by both Republican and Nationalist troops. In Spain both sides spoke the same language and the front was settled

into a stable configuration, neither of which pertained on the European fronts in the East. See the reference to Amery and loud hailers in "Extract from statement of BQMS John Henry Owen Brown, War Office, May 14, 1945," KV 2/80 85012.

53. Randa, *Dictionnaire commenté de la collaboration française*, 137.

54. Hesse statement, September 17, 1945, KV2/81 PRO.

55. The series of posters that advertised Amery's talk depicted a British soldier with blood pouring out of his eyes above the caption "Don't Wait Until Truth Stabs Your Eyes Out." Another showed a Russian soldier shooting a child and in a third, a group of British Tommies wore the German uniform but with a flash of the Union Jack on their sleeves. Another image carried a battlefield in which the German, the British and the American flags flew together in a confrontation with the Russian flag.

56. See the notice of the Camp Committee protesting Amery's visit, April 20, 1943, 107B KV2/79 85012 PRO. Kenneth Berry, an uneducated eighteen-year-old who joined up and later became part of the SS was under the impression that John Amery was the English Foreign Minister. Taken to Paris and Berlin, Berry met Amery and Barde, later sending them good wishes along with their dog Sammy and their friends Mr and Mrs Plack, Statement of Kenneth Edward Jordan Berry, July 3, 1945, CRIM 1/485 85012 PRO. West refers to him as Kenneth Edward, *Meaning of Treason*, 155–62.

57. See the depositions from Saint Denis internees, including Walter Brinkman, in *King v John Amery*, September 21, 1945, CRIM1/ 1717 PRO.

58. Seth, *Jackals of the Reich*; and Murphy, *Letting the Side Down*, 115–42.

59. Barthélemy, *Du communisme au fascisme: L'histoire d'un engagement politique*, 483; and Myriam Petacci's memoir of her sister and Mussolini's circle and of their exile, *Chi Ama è Perduto: Mia Sorella Claretta*.

60. *Ma Vie*, December 2, 1945; *Ma Vie*, December 3, 1945, Prison Commission, Outgoing Letters to Mrs Michelle Amery, PCOM 9/1117 PRO; and Petacci's memoir of her sister and Mussolini's circle, *Chi Ama è Perduto*.

61. For example a female colleague from German radio described Amery as a "dreadful type who was always accompanied by a French woman who was even worse," Statement by Dr Schorberth, Director of the Political Division German Radio Luxembourg, May 28, 1945 85012 KV2/ 81 PRO; Despite being Amery's mentor, Hesse noted with chagrin that wherever he was the Englishman's "drunken habits caused constant trouble" in his Statement, September 17, 1945, KV2/81 85012 PRO.

62. Spitzy, *How We Squandered the Reich*, 353.

63. Deakin traces the labyrinthine workings of these groups around Mussolini, in *Last Days of Mussolini*; and Breitman, "A Deal with the Nazi Dictatorship," 411–30.

Chapter 5

1. John Amery's voice can be heard on CD track 19 in Doherty, *Nazi Wireless Propaganda*.

2. *England Faces Europe; L'Angleterre et L'Europe, (traduit de l'Anglais) Documents et Témoignages Collection d'Essais Politiques no 1; Engeland en Europa door John Amery, Dokumenten en Getuigenissen Reeks Van Politieke Verhandelingen No 1*, 64; *John Amery Speaks; Charles Dickens et les Workhouses.*

3. Copsey, "John Amery: The Anti-Semitism of the 'Perfect English Gentleman'," 14–27. See also Seth's dismissal of Amery's writings as a "farrago of lies," in *Jackals of the*

Reich, 32; Weale, *Patriot Traitors*, that "detailed analysis is unnecessary," 190; and Faber, in *Speaking For England*, 462.

4. *England Faces Europe*, 20. See the editors' comments on Amery and Ethiopia, *Empire at Bay*, 326–40 and entries for December 1935, 404–5.

5. Kaplan, *Reproductions of Banality*, 51.

6. There are a great many references to "heroic little Finland" and her valiant efforts to stand up to the "wicked Jewish Bolsheviks." For example in *England Faces Europe*, 9, 10, 16, 27.

7. See for example Camerati . . . Camaraden . . . 267–86; Talk in Oslo; Talk Radio Paris, March 10, 1944; and Talk Gaumont Palace, Clichy, May 7, 1944, Speech in Antwerp, May 9, 1945, 144–47, Speech in Ghent, 148, HO 144/22822; Lecture in Belgrade, November 21, 1943, KV2/78 85012 PRO.

8. In parliamentary performance Leo Amery was often criticized for long-windedness and an inability to cut to the point, see Louis, *In the Name of God Go!*, 102–3. The tendency is belied in the newspaper reports of his performance on the hustings and the scripts that remain of his radio work. Perhaps the time constraints posed by these mediums were conducive to a pithy style.

9. February 13, 1939; June 11, 1940 and March 17, 1941, TSD LAP CAC; and Mr Amery's Appeal to Yugoslavia, *Times* (London), March 27, 1941. On Italian broadcasts, March 17, 1939 early June 1940, TSD LAP CAC ; and, Mr Amery's Warning, *Times* (London), June 12, 1940.

10. Original French version of a speech delivered by Amery in Belgrade, November 27, 1943, 117a KV2/79 85012 PRO.

11. See The German New Service, *Transocean*, in English attached to, Secret War Office Whitehall, D. C. Orr to E. B. Stamp, November 26, 1942, KV2/78 85012 PRO. Some of the interview smacks of the fabulist, whether from Amery himself or the journalist who describes Amery accompanying Mussolini's Blackshirts into Ethiopia and, seated behind the wheel of his Hispano Suiza, driving ahead of the German Panzas as they entered Vienna and Prague.

12. Leo Amery's diary carries frequent notations of press responses and his scrapbooks of reports and articles were carefully maintained. For John's self-assessments, see Memorandum for the Foreign Office Concerning My Activities Since My Departure . . . 306–12, HO 144/22822 PRO.

13. November 19, 1942, TSD LAP CAC.

14. LA to SH, December 11, 1942, Part XIII 19 (60) TP CUL.

15. Private and personal, My dear Winston, November 20, 1942, CHURCH 20/55/38 Churchill Papers CAC.

16. Postal & Telegraphic Censorship, addressee a wealthy French Jewess in Lisbon who is known to have sent parcels to John Amery . . . 28/12/42, KV2/78 85012 PRO.

17. LA to SH, December 11, 1942.

18. My dear Leo, December 29, 1942, BBK/c/7, BP HOL.

19. *Daily Mirror*, November 18, 1942. Mrs Amery had told Dalton in November 1941 that her son was in a TB Sanatorium in France, in *Second World War Diary of Hugh Dalton*, 305.

20. India Office, LA to Lord Beaverbrook, December 24, 1942, BP HOL. The Prime Minister received a telegram asking how the Secretary of State for India could retain his cabinet rank, with full knowledge of the Empire's fighting program, when his son broadcast over Berlin, Telegram, Glasgow South, CHUR 20/55/36, CP CAC.

21. LA to SH, November 19, 1942, TSD LAP CAC.

22. Rubinstein argues that Leo Amery's Jewishness was his "greatest secret" and that for John, anti-Semitism constituted Oedipal rebellion, "Secret of Leopold Amery." It was well-known, however, that the Amerys were partly Jewish: William Joyce was bitter that the Germans gave Amery's favored treatment when he was "one quarter Yid," in Martland, *Lord Haw Haw: The English Voice of Nazi Germany*, 64–5. According to a New Zealand defector it was common knowledge that John Amery was Jewish, Roy Nicholas Courlander, Statement September 16, 1944, KV/79 85012 PRO.

23. December 31, 1942, TSD LAP CAC.

24. LATSD, January 13, 1943, AP, CAC.

25. Amery, *Sons of the Eagle*.

26. May 2, 1945, TSD LAP CAC.

27. July 8, 1945, TSD LAP CAC. The Labour candidate for Sparkbrook said he would "never hit below the belt by attacking Amery on matters regarding his private family affairs" and the Communist candidate also distanced himself from such politicking, in *Birmingham Evening Despatch*, June 30, 1945.

28. There is a curious letter from Lickford, written after the verdict, asking the home secretary for a reprieve on the grounds that the defense had made the wrong plea, in "1 Brick Court Temple, December 7, 1945," 394–5, HO 144 22823 85153 PRO.

29. The Duke of Alba's correspondence is included in the substantial file in the Spanish Foreign Ministry Archives relating to Amery's citizenship, *Asunto: Nacionalidad de John Amery...*, AG MAE. I am grateful for Marta Ruiz Jiménez's expertise in the MAE AG.

30. While in Madrid, Julian also met the sister of Mussolini's mistress, Clara Petacci, who told him what also appears to be a far-fetched story that when in Italy John had criticized German foreign policy and been in danger of arrest by the Gestapo, Mussolini had told the German Ambassador that the *Duce* willingly would go to jail in John's place, October 17, 1945, TSD LAP CAC.

31. In late 1945 after an extensive search of the records of Spanish Military and the Foreign Legion, the Spanish Foreign Ministry reported that John Amery had never enlisted with any of Franco's military forces. A file note, revealing the paranoia of the Franco government after the civil war, warns that the British government will prefer to find John Amery is a Spaniard to avoid the public disgrace of executing a British person as a traitor. *Asunto: Nacionalidad de John Amery*, AG MAE. For MI5 tracking Julian Amery in Spain and the Nice records, see John Amery, 7p, FO369/3175 85197; E. J. P. Cussen to Director of Public Prosecutions, October 9, 1945, 2p, KV2/81 85012 PRO.

32. July 9, 1945, TSD LAP CAC.

33. *Daily Mirror*, November 23, 1945 and August 20, 1945, TSD LAP CAC.

34. November 22, 1945, TSD LAP CAC.

35. July 9, 1945, TSD LAP CAC.

36. Leo noted in his diary, though not himself present, Jack appeared in court "harmless and happily Lickfold had persuaded him to wear ordinary clothes instead of a fascist Blackshirt," July 9, 1945, LATSD. John's later request to the Prison Service, via Lickford, for permission to be executed in his European fascist garb was initially granted because the prison official had "not realized that this dress was to all intents and purposes the uniform of the Fascists." Permission was subsequently withdrawn, File Note to Home Office, December 17, 1945, 301, HO144/22823 PRO.

37. FA to Lord Fitzalan of Derwent, November 30, 1945; FA to JCE, November 28, 1945; JCE to FA, November 29, 1945; FA to JCE, December 1, 1945, HO 144/22823 PRO.

38. FA to Dear Max, December 9, 1945; FA to Dear Max, December 21, 1945; Beaverbrook assured her that he had asked the Editor of the *Daily Express* to carry out her request, Beaverbrook to My dear Florence, December 28, 1945, BBK/c/7 BP HOL.

39. Proposed cable to Mme Michelle Thomas, September 16, 1945, KV 2/ 81; John Amery. Madame Michele Thomas, Messrs J. E. Lickford. 445–51 HO 144/22823 85153 PRO.

40. December 5, 1945, TSD LAP CAC.

41. December 7, 1945, TSD LAP CAC.

42. Florence Amery to Dear Canon Douglas, May 21, 1946, Canon Douglas Papers, Lambeth Palace Library; and December 18, 1945, TSD LAP CAC.

43. *Ceci est mon testament*, KV2/184 85012; and Prison Commission, Outgoing Letters to Mrs Michelle Amery (with enclosures addressed to Marie Térèse Horalimian), PCOM 9/1117 PRO.

44. December 19, 1945, TSD LAP CAC.

Chapter 6

1. Mendelssohn, *Japan's Political Warfare*, 12–3; and Robbins, *Tokyo Calling: Japanese Overseas Radio Broadcasting 1937–1945*, 175.

2. Whitton and Herz, "Radio in International Politics," 19.

3. There was a Russian station also transmitting from Shanghai in Russian, English and Chinese, in Mendelssohn *Japan's Political Warfare*, 53.

4. Daniels, "Japanese Domestic Radio and Cinema Propaganda, 1937–1945," and Ryo, "Japanese Overseas Broadcasting; A Personal View"; and Robbins, *Tokyo Calling*.

5. Mendelssohn, *Japan's Political Warfare*, 40.

6. Mendelssohn, *Japan's Political Warfare*; Meo, *Japan's Radio War*; and Robbins, *Tokyo Calling*.

7. Meo, *Japan's Radio War*, 33–7.

8. *Japan's Radio War*, 26.

9. Robbins, *Tokyo Calling*, 67.

10. At about the same time the *New York Times* criticized the "stuffiness" of Japanese musical selections that were always based on classical Japanese scores, in Robbins, *Tokyo Calling*, 68.

11. Morris, *Traveller from Tokyo*, 92–3. The Listening Post in Melbourne noted frequent technical hitches in Radio Tokyo broadcasts, Meo, *Japan's Radio War*, 35.

12. Ibid.

13. *Traveller from Tokyo*, 151–2.

14. Tolischus later discovered the name of his interrogator and that he had graduated from the University of California, been a court interpreter in the federal court in Oakland and a secretary in the YMCA, *Tokyo Record*, 234–4.

15. The incident is referred to in the deposition by Kira Namikawa, Tokyo, March 22, 1949, no 31712 R 5–6 Box 264 and the cross-examination of Tsigetsugu Tsuneishi by Wayne Collins CC 31712-R Vol VII, p 455, RG 118 NARA SB].

16. *Tokyo Record*, 266–9.

17. *Japan's Radio War*, 52–3.

18. Returning to Tokyo after serving as Japan's military attaché in Rome from 1936 to 1939, Lieutenant Seizo Arisue advocated the policy of using POWs to broadcast Japanese

propaganda, in "Affidavit by G Henshaw, 15/1/47 to the Military Board" A4393 72/c/66 NAA.

19. Tsigetsugu Tsuneishi cross examination Wayne Collins, July 11, 1949, 262–4 and July 14, 1949; 459, CC 31712 RG118 NARA SB.

20. NX69742 A/WO II John Harold Dooley, October 25, 1945; SP 185/1 42044 Part 24 B626, NAA.

21. *Secret Prison Diary of Frank "Foo" Fujita*, 49.

22. N Schenk, Statement Yokahoma, August 24, 1946 [attached to Cousens' submission to the Military Board 15/1/47] A 4393 72/c/66 NAA.

Chapter 7

1. According to Tim Cousens' assessment of his brother's situation, Melbourne, December 2004. I am glad to acknowledge Mr Cousens' generous help during the research for this book.

2. *Sunday Telegraph*, August 16, 1942.

3. Commonwealth of Australia, Attorney General's Dept., Charles Hughes Cousens, 1–2, in Major C. H. Cousens-Alleged Collaboration, A472 W30733 NAA.

4. Letters in the possession of Tim Cousens, Melbourne.

5. *Wireless Weekly,* September 2, 1938; *Radio Pictorial of Australia,* April 1, 1937; July 1, 1939; August 1, 1939. I am grateful to Bridget Griffen-Foley for these references.

6. Japanese Consul General to New Zealand Director General of Agriculture, June 26, 1935; Japanese Consul General to Messrs Grotjam, September 12, 1935, Consul General to Charles H. Cousens Esq., September 21, 1935, AW472 W30733 Part 2, NAA.

7. Bayly and Harper powerfully evoke the times in *Forgotten Armies: The Fall of British Asia, 1941–1945.* Hastings punctures the myth of the fearless Australian soldier in *Nemesis: The Battle for Japan, 1944–45.*

8. These descriptions come from the Australian doctor Rowley Richards in Malaya in his *A Doctor's War,* 70–1; and from Mydans, an American war correspondent caught in the fall of the Philippines, in *More Than Meets the Eye,* chapters 11 to 15.

9. Mant excoriated the fecklessness of the British way of life in Malaya, the clubs, from which Australian soldiers were excluded, the women with children in boarding school in England and the general contempt shown towards the "native races," in his *Grim Glory,* 33. McCarthy has enumerated the historical inaccuracies that underpin the Australian myth of English perfidy towards Australia's defense in the Pacific war, in "The 'Great Betrayal' Reconsidered."

10. Several people present made statements at the end of the war and in large part they are in agreement. See, Colonel James Henry Thyer HSO 1 8 Aust Div Nov 45; Colonel Wilfred Selwyn Kent Hughes, A.Q. HQ 8 Div, Malaya, 31 10 45, SP 185/ 1 42044 Part 2 B626; and Statement made by Major Cousens at Yokohama, October 25, 1945, A472/ W36733 Part 1 Attachment, NAA.

11. There is no evidence that the broadcast was ever transmitted to Australia.

12. A New Zealander at demobilization noted on his, Collaboration with The Enemy Form, that Changi prisoners frequently listened to Cousens and gave him the nickname of "His Master's Voice," Confidential New Zealand, Singapore A4393 72/c/66, NAA.

13. Several weeks later in an internment camp in Hong Kong Hishikari offered a young journalist, later to become the Sydney radio identity André, the inducement of a luxurious

life if she would became a broadcaster on Japanese shortwave in Shanghai. When she de-murred, Hishikari suggested a job at Domei in Tokyo, telling her that Charles Cousens was already ensconced in Japan. MSS 5184 Dorothy Gordon Jenner Papers, Mitchell Library, Sydney. I am grateful to Bridget Griffen-Foley for this information.

14. Cousens provides a slightly different versions of the event in Statement made by Major Cousens at Yokohama on 25-10-1945, witnessed by G. S. Guysi, SP 185/1/42044 part 2 B 622, NAA.

15. Samuel Wilfred Thompson, ex 2/19, Aust In Bn, November 8, 1945, 175/ 1/170, NAA.

16. G. E. Ramsay to H. G. Horner, September 29, 1945; Bill Cousens to My dear H.G., June 2, 1942, A4393 72/ c/66 NAA.

17. Note handed to Col Ramsay by a Nipponese officer, Greetings, Bill Cousens, June 19, 1942, A 4393 72/ c/66 NAA.

18. Dobie discusses the United States Army efforts to keep up the "firing rate" of sol-diers in the infantry, that is those who fire their weapons in combat, versus those who avoid doing so or desert, in "AWOL in America: When Desertion is the Only Option."

19. There are a number of eyewitness and second hand accounts of the incident. See Statement by Major Cousens, Yokohama and Guysi interrogation of the same date. See also Cousens' description and cross examination in San Francisco in *USA v. Iva Ikuko Toguri D'Aquino*, August 15, 1949, San Francisco Court of Northern California NARA SB.

20. The sources for this paragraph are contained in, Cross-examination of Foumy Saisho, Sydney, SC 185/1 42044 Part 9 B622 NAA; Yuman Ishihara deposition taken in Tokyo Japan, March 22, 1949, no. 41712R and Akira Namikawa Deposition Tokyo, March 22, 1949, Box 264 RG 118; Tsigetsugu Tsuneishi cross-examined by Wayne Collins CC31713 RG 118 NARA SB.

21. Tsigetsugu Tsuneishi cross-examined by Wayne Collins, July 14, 1949, CC 31713 RG 118 NARA SB.

22. See cross-examination of Foumiko Saisho, *Rex v. Charles Cousens*, Sydney, Septem-ber 24, 1946, SC185/1 42044 Pt 11 B622 NAA.

Chapter 8

1. There are a great many descriptions of Bunka Camp and Broadcast House in Tokyo. They include: Statement made by Major Charles Cousens at Yokohama, October 25, 1945, 42; Interrogation of Major Charles H. Cousens by Col B J Dunn and George S. Guysi CIC Met. unit, October 13, 1945 and October 25, 1945, 25, part 1 Attachment, A472 W36733; NX69742 A/WO II statement by John Harold Dooley, October 25, 1945, 22, SP 185/1 42044 Part 24 B626; statement by L.A.C. Kenneth George Parkyns, October 23, 1945, 33, SP 1851/ 1 Part 4 B626, NAA. Federal Bureau of Investigation Reports of Darwin H. Dodds, File no. 61–236; Newtown Light, File no. 61–180; Frank Fugita, File no. 61–121; George H Henshaw, File no. 61–614; Edwin Kalbfleisch, File no. 61–263; Edwin Kalbfleish, File no. 61–162; James Martinez, File no. 65–1363; Ramon Martinez, File no. 65–1363; Stephen Herman Shattles, File no. 61–614; Norman Reyes File no. 61–38, RG 118 no. 5 6/6 NARA SB. Statements by J. T. Hirakawa, Hideo Mitusio, Hisao Yoshii, Hiroshi Niino, Foumy Saisho, Margaret Kato, Roy Osaki, Kaji Domoto, George Kazamuro Uno, and Shisetsugu Tsuneishi, SP 185/1 42044 Part 3 B 622 NAA. Diary of Lt, George H. Henshaw while interned at Bunka Camp Kanda Ward, Tokyo, Japan, is a daily record

of camp life between November 1943 and August 1945, 198, NAA. See also Henshaw's Affidavit, Tokyo Japan, November 1946, 5 attached as Appendix G to Charles Cousens' application to the Australian Military Board, A4393 72/c/66 NAA; and Fujita, *Secret Prison Diary of Frank "Foo" Fujita*.

2. Fujita, *Secret Prison Diary of Frank "Foo" Fujita*, 123.

3. Much of the writing about Australian prisoners of war has emphasized the mateship among the men, especially those laboring in teams on the Burma-Thai Railway. My careful reading of all the material on Bunka is that prisoners were careful not to rely too closely on one another. See Garton on the narrative forms in the telling of POW stories and the difficulty of integrating them into a national narrative that relies on the Anzac legend, in *Cost of War: Australians Return*, 208–18. Daws as well as Hank Nelson and Tim Bowden emphasize the role of national origin in determining the behavior of Allied POWs: Australians followed a collective mode, whereas Americans replicated the individualist ethos, in Daws, *Prisoners of the Japanese*, 23–24; Nelson and Bowden, *POW Prisoners of War*, 63–8. In Bunka Americans tended to side with Cox and the rest with Cousens.

4. On the cookhouse see FBI LA, File no. 65–1363, San Antonio, Texas, 4/17/48 William H. Buckler, Treason, Interview with James G. Martinez, 3, RG 118 Item no. 5 4/6 NARA SB.

5. *Secret Prison Diary of Frank "Foo" Fujita*, 204.

6. See Cousens, Yokohama Statement, October 25, 1945, 23.

7. Henshaw Diary, December 2–10, 1943, 3–10.

8. Norisane Ikeda recalled the same incident and that Tsuneishi told the camp interpreters that it was better for prison morale that the prisoners believed that Williams had been killed for disobedience, International Military Tribunal for the Far East, Tokyo, Japan, Affidavit, Norisane Ikeda, November 1946, Appendix H to CHC application to the Military Board, 3, A4393 72/c/66 NAA.

9. Morris, *Traveler from Tokyo*, 145.

10. Richards, *A Doctor's War*, 109. On the practice of *binta*, see Townsend, "Culture, Race and Power in Japan's Wartime Empire," she quotes Lee Kwan Yew's recollection that having his face slapped by Japanese soldiers turned him into an anti-imperialist, against all empires, 113.

11. For example on learning that Parkyns was born in Sydney Ikeda asked him what he thought of people from Melbourne, indicating that he understood the historic rivalry that is supposed to exist between people living in Australia's two largest cities. Statement by Kenneth Parkyns, 23/10/45, SP 185/1 42044 part 24 B.626 NAA; and Diary of George N. Henshaw while interned at Bunka Camp Kanda Ward, Tokyo, Japan, 2–3, SP 185/1; and Ikeda's Affidavit, November 1946, A4393 72/c/66 NAA.

12. See Henshaw Affidavit, 4 and Diary Feb to March 1944; and Confidential Statement Joe T. Hirakawa, October 6, 1945.

13. Mydans, *More Than Meets the Eye*, 105–7. Ichikoka, "The Meaning of Loyalty: The Case of Kazumaro Buddy Uno." See also Uno's testimony, Confidential Statement to Headquarters Counter Intelligence Corps area no. 1 U.S. Armed Forces, Pacific APO 75 1945, A 4393 72/c/66 NAA.

14. The term comes from Ichioka in the powerful analysis of Uno's experiences that asks what disloyalty means in a racist society and why Japanese-Americans who favored Japan have been written out of the American story, in "The Meaning of Loyalty."

15. Confidential statement to Headquarters Counter Intelligence Corps area no. 1 U.S. Armed Forces, Pacific APO 75 1945 NARA SB.

16. "Factions" is Dooley's term, Statement October 25, 1954, 13.

17. Confidential statement Mark Lewis Streeter, November 6, 1945, 2, Exhibit VIII A4393 72/c/66 NAA.

18. Several witnesses described Provoo as "having homosexual tendencies." For example, FBI File no. 61–57, Dallas, Texas, April 9, 1948, Efton A. Stanfield, Treason, Interview Jack K. Wisner, 6, RG 118/Item no. 5, 4/6 NARA SB; and Headquarters Fourth Army, Fort Sam, Houston, Texas, File no. 4A-150375, November 17, 1947, Provoo, John David, RG 118/2/7no. 2, 1/7 [1943–1949] Treason, NARA SB. Henshaw's diary contains detailed entries throughout about Provoo and Streeter.

19. Henshaw Diary.

20. See his Yokohama statement, 15.

21. Hearder found the professional involvement of medical POWs kept morale and self-esteem high and ensured survival rates higher than for the average POW, in "Careers in Captivity."

22. This testimony is rather contradictory, as Cousens had advocated both of these approaches in his earlier pronouncements on how to be a successful announcer.

Chapter 9

1. The Princeton Listening project, that tracked American shortwave listeners from early 1940 to mid-1941, concluded that the broadcasts had little effect on listeners' attitudes. However, the survey excluded Italians and Afro Americans and preceded The United States' entry into the war, Childs, "America's Short-Wave Audience." Radio Zeesen was famous for the elaborate lengths the station went to contact listeners abroad, in order to back up the Nazi message, but also to check the range of transmissions, Whitton and Herz, "Radio in International Politics," 19.

2. The Nazi censor cut the story from Shirer's broadcast on the grounds that "American listeners would not understand the heroism of the German woman in denouncing her friends," in *Berlin Diary*, 288.

3. Bergmeier and Lotz, *Hitler's Airwaves*, 90; and on British POW families listening for POW information, Doherty, *Nazi Wireless Propaganda*, 147.

4. *Hitler's Airwaves*, 125–128.

5. Weekly Summaries of Radio Paris Propaganda, KV 2/79/85012 PRO.

6. McKernan, *This War Never Ends*, 25.

7. Mrs Adelaide Levy letter, July 21, 1946, ST 295/1 N46452 Vol 1 NAA. The Japanese government eschewed UN protocols on the treatment of enemy prisoners that included providing lists of names of those who had been taken into captivity.

8. Minutes of the Sub-Committee on Enemy Propaganda of the Prime Minister's Committee on Morale, November 3, 1942, quoted in Meo, *Japan's Radio War on Australia*, 168.

9. Kitayama, quoted in Robbins, *Tokyo Calling*, 94.

10. Daws, *Prisoners of the Japanese*, 129.

11. Meo, *Japan's Radio War on Australia*.

12. Testimony of Fred E. Hahn, New York, [April 1949] RG 118 Item no. 2 1/7, NARA SB.

13. For example see the lists in MP151/1 429/201/477.

14. The National Archives in Australia holds a poignant collection of these messages, written in pencil on wisps of paper, some include greetings and others simply give the prisoner's name and home address.

15. John Parkes' Personal Papers. I thank John and Vera Parkes for their support and for aiding this research through *Vic Eddy: The Official Journal of the Eighth Division Signals.* I also thank Mrs Dawn Edsall for correspondence on her husband as a POW.

16. Strong, "When 'Tokyo Rose' Came to Albuquerque."

17. Guysi, who interrogated Cousens in Yokohama about the authenticity of the information contained in this broadcast and the following example, was skeptical at Cousens' claim that he was sure it would have been written by one of the men who had arrived at Bunka from one of the camps, Interrogation by Guysi and Charles E Ernst CIC, October 25, 1945, 16, A472 W30733 Part 1 Attachments NAA.

18. Japanese Propaganda Broadcasts from Batavia, Defence Committee Agenda, Secret, A5799 81/ 1942 NAA; and Meo, *Japan's Radio War On Australia*, 282.

19. The author heard these stories in childhood and again researching this book.

20. Thanks to Norman Dillon for sharing this story and family letters in Woy Woy, NSW, March 2006.

21. Statement by J. H. Dooley, October 25, 1945; Statement Concerning Timothy Dooley by Major C. H. Cousens, Yokohama, A439 72/c/66 NAA.

22. Statement by 34163 L. A. C. Parkyns: Kenneth George, Sydney, October 23, 1945, 1–30, SP 185/1 402044 Part 7 B.622 NAA.

23. Statement by J. H. Dooley, October 25, 1945; Statement Concerning Timothy Dooley by Cousens, Yokohama, A439 72/c/66 NAA.

24. Henshaw refers to this individual frequently, shortening his name to "man on the whole floor."

25. Cousens in Colonel Ben J. Dunn, Australian Military Forces, October 13, 1945, 41, SP185/1 42044 Pt 14 NAA and *Daily Telegraph*, September 20, 1946; Streeter urged the Japanese, as gesture of goodwill, to repatriate all American prisoners over the age of 45, the badly disabled, and all the Mormon Elders, "Statement by M. C. Streeter," November 6, 1945, 1 NAA.

26. C. H. Cousens, Reports Re: Incoming Radio Broadcasts, SP 185/1 42044 Part ii B 622 NAA. The transcript is annotated by hand with, "Cousens Radio Tokyo 12 8 42." A number of listeners testified to the Australian Security Service that they had heard Cousens making treasonous broadcasts, attacking Churchill and Roosevelt and urging Australia to "cut herself off from the British Empire," Lieut. Col. J. M. Prentice, 24 10 45, SP 1048/6 C12/1/706 B 31; and Miss Goody Reeves, 2GB, who knew his voice well, only heard him "broadcasting general news from a Japanese point of view," ST 2951/1 N 46452 Vol. 1, NAA.

27. Rivett, *Behind Bamboo,* 77. For transcripts of some, including Rivett's own long letter that was recorded in *The Listening Post* in Melbourne, see, Japanese Broadcasts from Batavia, Commonwealth of Australia, Prisoners of War Information Bureau, June 15, 1942, MP 151/1 429/201/477 NAA.

28. Tokyo, Friday, February 4, Report on Incoming Shortwave, The War Without Purpose, ST 2951/ 1 N46452 Vol. 1 NAA. At the same time as the Cousens' broadcast, the Commander of the Eighth Division, Major General Gordon Bennett, who had escaped from Singapore and returned to Australia, was giving the same reassuring message to Australian families, McKernan, *The War Never Ends,* 19.

29. *Truth,* August 16, 1942. Mrs Cousens identified her husband's voice to the Department of Information and requested that he be released or included in an exchange as a prisoner on the grounds of hardship, in Minister NX34932 Captain C. H. Cousens by T. R.

McDermott, Major 31/5/46, A4393 72/c/66 NAA. Mrs Cousens received a number of messages from her husband. See the long transcript, June 16, 1945, urging her to acknowledge the message through Radio Melbourne, ST 2951/1 N46452 Vol 1 NAA.

Chapter 10

1. References to the policy are in: Testimony of George Mitsushio, 5, RG 118 Item no. 2 1/7, RG 118 ; Testimony of Kenchiki Oki, 2p RG 118 Item no. 2 1/7; and cross-examination of Shigetsugu Tsuneishi, CC 31712, RG 118 NARA SB.

2. Years later veterans from the Pacific war could recall the music, see Rosa Maria Fazion, "The Effects of the Broadcasts of 'Tokyo Rose' During World War II."

3. Cousens testified at Iva Toguri's trial that she would give him a small "v" sign to indicate that she had good news to impart; or would say "Praise the Lord and pass the ammunition" if the news for the Allied side was not so good, in cross-examination CC 31712 RG 118 NARA SB.

4. Cross-examination of Charles H. Cousens, August 17, 1949, 3350–3354, CC 31712 RG 118 NARA SB.

5. Robinson, *By Order of the President*, 8–44.

6. Masoaka, spokesman for the Japanese American League, recalled growing up in Utah in a family where he and his brothers spoke no Japanese and his mother no English, *They Call Me Moses Masaoka*.

7. Hayashi gives statistics for these occupational patterns, *Assimilation, Nationalism and Protestantism*, 40–45.

8. Hayashi points out that by 1940 only one percent of Nisei in Los Angeles County held professional or semi-professional jobs even though their educational profile was like that of the Anglo American community, *Assimilation, Nationalism and Protestantism*, 43.

9. Well-educated Nisei girls faced great difficulties, most worked as maids and nannies.

10. Yamamoto, "Cheers for Japanese Athletes: The 1932 Los Angeles Olympics and the Japanese American Community." He notes that the Japanese Olympians disdained their Japanese American hosts as "immigrants and their children" and therefore of low status, 428.

11. Ichioka, "Japanese-Immigrant Nationalism: The Issei and the Sino-Japanese War, 1937–1941." McWilliams, a contemporary, provides a reminder that some Japanese Americans opposed the export of scrap metal to Japan and were subjected to intimidation by both the Los Angeles Police and the Japanese Consul, *Prejudice: Japanese-Americans Symbol of Racial Intolerance*.

12. Ichioka, "*Kengakudan*: The Origin of Nisei Study Tours of Japan," 35.

13. McWilliams, *Prejudice*, 315.

14. McWilliams, *Prejudice*, 315.

15. *Nisei* Survey Committee of Keisen School, *The Nisei: A Study of Their Life in Japan*, Tokyo, 1939, quoted in McWilliams, *Prejudice*, 315.

16. Yamashita Soen, *Nichibei o Tsunagu Mono (Those Who Link Japan and America)*, (Tokyo, 1938), 173–4, quoted in Tomita, *Dear Miye*, 11. There were also the children of overseas Japanese from Latin America, Korea. Manchuria and Southeast Asia.

17. *Dear Miye*.

18. December 22, 1939, *Dear Mye*, 61.

19. Tolischus, *Tokyo Record*, 46.

20. As a child she was delighted by fireworks on her birthday for the national day. Biographical information is from, Dale Kramer Testimony, RG 118 Item no. 2, 1/7 Ted 4; FBI File 61–614, A. J. Roberts, 12/29/1945; and 11/23/45 NARA SB.

21. Scott Thompson, President of Compton College to Miss Mary L. Cottrill, Classification and Parole, Federal Reformatory for Women, Alderson, West Virginia, January 9, 1950. Iva Toguri's Prison Record NARA SB.

22. See for example FBI Report on UCLA interrogations, File no. 61–614, 44, RG 118 no. 4 4/4 NARA SB.

23. FBI Report 61–158, Iva Ikuko Toguri, RG 118 Item no. 44/4 NARA SB.

24. FBI Report 61–614

25. FBI LA 61–614, 11/23/45 Albert J. Roberts, ITT Tokyo Rose Rg. 118 #4, Criminal case 4/4 3172 1–44; G. A. Sawtelle, April 1, 1949, RG 118 #5 Criminal case 31712, 2/6.

26. FBI Report File no. 61–64, 13–15, RG 118 No 4 4/4 NARA SB.

27. FBI Report File no. 61–614, 44, RG 118, no. 4, 4/4 NARA SB; and, *New York Times*, July 8, 1949.

28. Transcript of notes of interview with Clark Lee of the International News Service, Tokyo, September 5, 1945, CC 31712 RG 118 no. 2, 7/7, NARA, SB.

29. The neighbors' interviews are contained in FBI Report 61–614, December 29, 1945, 37, RG 118 no. 4 , NARA SB.

30. FBI Report File no. 61–614 Mrs Viola Young, 11–12, RG 118 no. 4, 3/4 NARA SB.

31. Testimony of Dr Clair Steggall, Report of S. A. Satelle, 4–18–49, CC 31712 RG 118/ 1/7 #2 1/7 NARA SB.

32. Testimony of Chiyeko Ito, CC 31712 RG 118, IT no. 2 1/7 NARA SB.

33. Before November 1941, United States citizens did not need a passport, it being sufficient for departure and entry to the country to have proof of having been born there. Kutler, "Forging a Legend: The Treason of 'Tokyo Rose,'" 1347.

34. Seymour Korman, "Tokyo Rose's words quoted against her," *Chicago Daily Tribune*, July 8, 1949, 4.

35. Testimony of Dale Kramer, CCRG118 Item no. 2, 1/7 NARA SB.

36. The family was at least in intermittent and brief contact with Iva in 1943 when her father sent a Red Cross telegram with "some good news" that her brother had married, Tokyo Rose File, JANM.

37. Sworn testimony by Iva Toguri, 5098–5101, CC 31712 RG 118 NARA SB.

38. Testimony of Chiyeko Ito to the FBI. In May 1947, without any questions or consequences, Ito returned to her prewar life in the United States.

39. *Chicago Tribune* interview Filipe D'Aquino.

40. Filipe D'Aquino testimony, *New York Times*, September 7, 1949.

Chapter 11

1. Written transcriptions by Federal Communications Commission of Acetate Recordings August 14, 1944; Cross-examination Charles Cousens, August 17, 1949, 3341–63, CC 31712 RG 118 NARA SB.

2. Ronald Yates, *Chicago Tribune*, March 22–23, 1976.

3. Material on the Radio Tokyo women announcers is contained in, Deposition by Mary Higuchi, RG 118 Box 264 NARA SB; and Confidential Statement Margaret Yakeo Kato, 2, A4393 72/c/66 NAA.

4. Cross-examination C. H. Cousens, August 16, 1949, 3316–3324; Testimony by Sugiyama Harris, 2, CC 3172 RG 118 Item no. 2 1/7 NARA SB.

5. Deposition George Kazumaro Uno, Tokyo, March 22, 1949, RG 21 Box 264,10–14, 23–25. NARA SB. See also the interview in *Yank,* June 29, 1945. Myrtle Liston was an American national of biracial Filipino-American parents. Originally married to an American, she transferred her allegiance to Japan when she began to broadcast with Ken Moriyama. Her American accented voice was heard regularly across the Pacific. Theodore Tambo, "War and Propaganda," *Rafu Shimpo: Los Angeles Japanese Daily News,* May 14, 1973; May 18, 1973. There were female announcers in Batavia, Radio Saigon and a female announcer in China, referred to as the "Nanking Warbler."

6. A Japanese American woman with an American passport endured terrible years working in a wartime factory in Tokyo. Coworkers treated her as the enemy, always referring to her as "the American" even though she had never visited that country, Mydans, *More Than Meets the Eye,* 98–104.

7. A colleague described her as always giving an impression that "she had outside interests," in Supplemental Testimony of Seizo (Dave) Huga, May 2, 1949, 2, RG 118 Item no. 2 1/7 NARA SB.

8. Supplemental Testimony of Seizo (Dave) Huga, May 2, 1949, 4, RG 118 Item no. 2 1/7 NARA SB.

9. FBI Report File no. 61–158, NARA SB.

10. Mrs Thomas Burch, FBI Report File no. 1–614, 19, CC 3172 RG 118NARA, SB.

11. For this paragraph see FBI Report File no. 61–57 S. A. Chester Orton Item no. 5 4/6; FBI Report File no. 61–158; FBI Report File no. 61–132; FBI Report File no. 61–174; FBI Report File no. 61–378; Toguri Item no. 4 4/4, 7 CC 3172 RG 118 NARA SB.

12. FBI Report File no. 61–378, Item no. 4 1/4; Deposition of Koichi Jimbo, March 22, 1949, Tokyo, Box 264, CC 3172 RG 118 NARA SB.

13. *Dayton Journal Herald,* January 8, 1977, Tokyo Rose File, JANM.

14. FBI Report File no. 61–378 # 4 1/4 Frederick Donald Julius, CC 3172 RG 118 NARA SB.

15. FBI Report File no. 61–378; FBI Report no. 61–590, CC3172 RG 118 NARA SB.

16. *Dayton Journal Herald,* January 8, 1977, Tokyo Rose File, JANM.

17. For Oregonian informants FBI, LA, CA, report Portland, Oregon, January 26, 1948 by Howard B. Patterson, RG 118 Box 3 Item no. 5 5/6 NARA SB.

18. FBI Oklahoma City, May 9, 1949, Report by Charles W. Sizemore, FBI File no. 61–121 RG 118 Box 3 Item no. 5 6/6 NARA SB.

19. FBI File no. 61–120 on Ben F. Chatfield, RG 118 Box 3 Item no. 5 5/6 NARA SB.

20. FBI Phoenix, January 2, 1948, Report William B. O'Mahoney, File no. 61–40, RG 118 Item no. 5 5/6 Box 3 NARA SB.

21. FBI Report File no. 61–31, Mark B. Mabry, RG 118 7/7 NARA SB.

22. FBI Seattle Washington, February 5, 1946 report Ernest A. Johnson (A) File no. 61–202, RG 118 item no. 4 1/4 NARA SB; and Al Dopkin, FBI Kansas City Missouri, January 30, 1946, File no. 81–164, RG 118 Item no. 4 4/4 NARA SB.

23. FBI Atlanta, April 27, 1949, Report Thomas A. Erwin Jr, File no. 61–120, RG 118 Box 3 Item no. 5 6/6 NARA SB.

24. FBI San Francisco Interview Thomas McShane Special FBI agent, San Francisco, 5, RG 118 Item no. 5 6/6 Box 3 NARA SB.

25. Testimony of Marshall Hoot, RG 18 Item no. 2 1/7 NARA SB FBI Alhambra, CA, report S.A. Sawtelle, April 18, 1949; Testimony August 3, 1949, 2203–2205, Box 266, RG 118 Item no. 2 1/7 NARA SB.

26. Testimony Ted E. Sherdeman, RG 118 Item no. 2 7/7; FBI North Hollywood, CA, April 8, 1948, interview S. A. Sawtelle, file TED RG 118 Item no. 2 7/7 NARA SB.

27. Statement Gilbert Velasquez, FBI File no. 61–614, RG 118 Box 3 Item no. 5 5/6, February 8, 1948, NARA SB.

28. FBI, Los Angeles, CA, February 9, 1948, Chester C. Orton, Interview by Harold Eugene Lima, 5–6, RG 118 Item no. 5 5/6 Box 3 NARA SB.

29. Testimony of David I. Gilmore, CC 3172 RG 118 Item no. 2 1/7 NARA SB.

30. "Iva Ikuko Toguri, with aliases Mrs Philip Jairus D'Aquino; Orphan Annie; Ann; Tokyo Rose; Tokyo Japan, April 30, 1946"; and "Iva Ikuko Toguri, with aliases . . ." FBI Report File no. 61–614, January 23, 1948, 66, RG 118 Box 3 Item no. 5 5/6, NARA SB.

31. Lee, *One Last Look Around*, 85.

32. *Chicago Daily Tribune*, July 15, 1949; *Los Angeles Times*, July 19, 1949.

33. The Federal Justice Department in Washington concurred with the military Counter Intelligence Corps that there was no evidence of Toguri's wrongdoing. Tom de Wolfe, the Assistant Attorney General in the Ministry of Justice, surveyed the evidence and recommended that the department not go ahead with the trial. When directed by his superior, the U.S. Attorney General, he became the chief prosecutor of the government's case in San Francisco.

34. When it was pointed out to Winchell that many of the GIs enjoyed the Tokyo Rose broadcasts, he replied that "they were probably communists," quoted in Kutler, "Forging a Legend: The Treason of 'Tokyo Rose'," 1358.

35. *New York Times*. September 26, 1948.

Chapter 12

1. The previous case had been in the Supreme Court of Victoria in 1855, see Fricke, "The Eureka Trials."

2. For prisoner of war figures see *Oxford Companion to Australian History*, 531.

3. Correspondence and cuttings in DT 22/7/46, A 4393 72/c/66 NAA and letters to the editor in the *Daily Telegraph* and the *Sydney Morning Herald*, July to November 1946.

4. The term "quitters" was used by a number of ex-POWs interviewed by the author. The Department of Defense and the Returned Servicemen's League opposed compensation for prisoners that was not also paid to rank and file soldiers. See Garton, *The Cost of War*, 219–27.

5. *Melbourne Herald*, January 1–2 and February 22, 1946.

6. The files are in ST 2951/1 N46452 NAA.

7. Confidential Statement Kennoske Sato, Army 175/1/170 3445, November 27, 1945, Tokyo, SP185/1 42044 Part 2 B 622, NAA.

8. Statement by Baron M. Takasaki, October 26, 1945, A4393 72/c/66. NAA.

9. Townsend, "Culture, Race and Power in Japan's Wartime Empire."

10. I am grateful to Dr Judy White for this information.

11. Oliver, "Japanese Relationships in White Australia."

12. Torney-Parlicki, "Selling Goodwill: Peter Russo and the Promotion of Australia-Japan Relations, 1935–1941"; and *Behind the News: A Biography of Peter Russo*.

13. Federal Controller of School Broadcasts, December 18, 1939, B2111/1 Edu/3 NAA.

14. Australian Military Forces, Director of Legal Services, Minute paper, Major C. H. Cousens, Confidential, January 2, 1946, 4 A4393 72/c/66 NAA.

15. The case plugged into long-standing tensions between the Australian federal government and the Australian states. For a discussion of the legal ramifications of the case and its significance for Australian state and federal relations, see Keene, "Treason and the Trial of Traitors in Twentieth Century Australia." For voluminous pre-trial preparation with discussion of Casement and Joyce as precedents, see SP 185/1 42044 Part 14 NAA.

16. See copy of Information (General Purposes) sworn by Wilfred Blacket in SP 185/1 42044 Pt 4 Bundle 1 NAA. This was the procedure that had been used in the prosecution in England of Roger Casement for treason in 1917.

17. *State Reports (NSW)* 47, 145–50.

18. Between June 1946 to January 1947 the *Sydney Morning Herald*, the *Daily Telegraph* and the afternoon tabloid the *Sun* carried daily reports and letters to the editor.

19. Statement by Major Cousens at Yokohama, October 25, 1945, and interrogation by George S. Guysi CIC Met, unit, October 13, 1945; and October 25, 1945, A472 W36733 Part 1 Attachment NAA. And for Guysi in Sydney, Memos and Reports A472 W30733 Part 2 NAA; and *Daily Telegraph,* July 14–15, 1946.

20. *Daily Telegraph,* July 15, 17, 29, 20, 22, 1946.

21. Information on this paragraph is in F G Galleghan to Mrs Margaret Iwata, July 4, 1947; Miss Saisho and Mr Niino Japanese witnesses; Note Massey Stanley, 31/1946; ST 2951/1 N46452 Vol. 1 NAA.

22. Material on Fumiko Saisho, *Daily Telegraph*, June 29, 1946; July 9, 1946; February 27, 1947; July 30, 1947; Memo Crown Solicitor Canberra, witness, November 27, 1946; Statement re Hiroshi Niino, Japan, A 472/6 W 30733 Part 3; Dear Sir [request to move from "unpleasant atmosphere" in Japanese house], 3, ST 2951/1 N46452 Vol. 2 NAA.

23. "Foumy Saisho Meets Us Australians," *Daily Telegraph*, February 27, 1947.

24. *Daily Telegraph,* July 15, 1946. For material relating to Hiroishi Niino, see Memo Crown Solicitor Canberra, Memo Major Cousens Case: Report re: Hiroshi Niino Japanese witness, November 27, 1946; Statement re: Hiroshi Niino, Japanese, Witness in Cousens case, A 472/6 W 30733 Part 3; telegrams and letter covers to and from Tokyo family to Mr Niino, A5103 30/3/1 NAA.

25. Statement re: Hiroshi Niino.

26. The broadcasts are contained in the attachment to A472 W30733 Part 1; SP 185/1 42044 Part 19 B 624 Script of Commentaries, as well there are transcripts of broadcasts included in SP 185/ 1 42044 Part 14 NAA. The New South Wales Records Office in "Special Bundle—Charles Cousens" for transcripts of cross-examinations, trial preparation, minutes, memos and notes. Chapman closely follows the trial in *Tokyo Calling.*

27. Statement by Saisho, October 4, 1945, 5, SP 185/1 42044 Pt 4 Bundle 1 NAA; and cross-examination August 10, 21, 22, 1946, 1–89, SC185/1 42044 Pt 9 B622 NAA.

28. Testimony and cross-examination of Cousens by Dovey KC, September 24, 1946; September 26, 1946, SC185/1 42044 Pt 11 B622 NAA.

29. Summing up by Shand KC, October 3, 1946, SC185/1 42044 Pt 14 B622 NAA.

30. Kutler highlighted the role of middle-level legal officers in the Department of Justice, in *American Inquisition: Justice and Injustice in the Cold War.*

31. Draft Statement Regarding the Cousens Case [by Minister for the Army, Cyril Chambers read in House of Representatives, March 20, 1947], A4393 72/c/66 NAA.

32. Maj. C. H. Cousens. Australian Military Forces, Eastern Command Victoria Barracks, January 29, 1947, including Cousens' submission and sworn statements as to why he should retain his commission, A4393 92/c/66 NAA.

Chapter 13

1. The voluminous documents, depositions, transcripts and the full decision as well as those relating to the subsequent appeals are held in Records Related to the Criminal case 31712 *U.S. v. Iva Toguri D'Aquino*, Treason ("Tokyo Rose Case" 1943–1969) RG 118 NARA SB. Duus, provides detailed day-by-day proceedings in *Tokyo Rose: Orphan of the Pacific*; Kutler, "Forging a Legend: The Treason of 'Tokyo Rose,'" demonstrates in Toguri's treatment by the government, the pernicious interaction of personal hubris, bureaucratic self-interest and political will. Howe, *The Hunt for "Tokyo Rose,"* adds the ingredient of hindsight with later interviews of some of the protagonists.

2. Dower, *Embracing Defeat*, 443–484. See also Bloxham, "The Trial that Never Was," 285.

3. Dower, *Embracing Defeat*, 454.

4. Ronald Yates, "Tokyo Rose 'just a scapegoat': her husband," *Chicago Tribune*, March 23, 1976.

5. The moving spirit behind JACL, Mike Masaoka, in a long and detailed autobiographical history of himself and the organization, never mentions Iva Toguri, her trial or the pardon, *They Call Me Moses Masaoka*.

6. *Pacific Citizen*, September 18, 1948. Wayne Collins acted for this group, as he did for a great many similar cases.

7. *Pacific Citizen*, May 22, 1948.

8. See Tomoya Kamakita File Archives, J. F. Kennedy Memorial Library.

9. See the comments that the JACL's avoidance of the trial was prompted by a desire to prove that Japanese were "flag-waving Americans" with the point made "almost to the point of subservience," *San Francisco Examiner*, January 19, 1977.

10. *Pacific Citizen*, July 17, 1948.

11. "A Nisei in Manhattan" by Roku Sugahara, *Pacific Citizen*, September 4, 1948. When Iva Toguri was released it produced angry letters in *Newsweek*, echoing the 1948 sentiments and written in response to a single sympathetic letter, see *Newsweek*, February 20, 1956 and March 5, 1956.

12. W. C. Peterson, City Clerk, City of Los Angeles to U.S. Attorney General, December 8, 1947, and Resolution, National Iva Toguri Committee Papers, JANM.

13. Dr Clifford I. Uyeda was the moving force behind the group.

14. Hatamiya, *Righting a Wrong*.

15. Indeed this fraught question is still not resolved. See Dower's sensitive discussion of the matter in *War Without Mercy*, and the stridently anti-Japanese position of Lillian Baker and her Americans for Historical Truth, *The Japanning of America: Redress and Reparation Demands by Japanese Americans*.

16. Dower lays out the way in which a discourse of the victim was created in postwar Japan, in which Japanese people are victims of the excesses and maladministration of the American occupation and of the atom bomb, *Embracing Defeat*, 206.

17. There are many tributes to Wayne Collins (1899–1974) and his work is honored in the exhibition of Japanese Internees at the Japanese American National Museum in Los Angeles and the eulogies printed in *Pacific Citizen*, Tokyo Rose Files JANM.

18. *Pacific Citizen*, June 15, 1979.

19. Duus suggests that the pay rates were such that a number of witnesses were able to use them to set up businesses back in Japan afterwards, *Tokyo Rose: Orphan of the Pacific*, 148. Howe notes that the witness payments enabled Kenchiki Oki to launch a successful advertising business in Japan, in *The Hunt for Toky Rose*, 316.

20. *Sydney Morning Herald*, August 17, 1949 and September 1, 1949.

21. Letters J. Edgar Hoover and the Director General of the Australian Commonwealth Investigation Branch between February 1946 and February 1948, in SP 1714/1/0 N46460 NAA.

22. Wayne M. Collins to U.S. attorney general, June 23, 1949, RG 118 Item no. 4/7 NARA SB.

23. The prosecution legal team wrote long weekly reports to the attorney general in Washington evaluating the trial and the prosecution's progress. The prosecution's prior agreed strategy of discrediting witnesses including Allied POWs who could have proved that Japanese placed Toguri and the prisoners under duress is set out in Frank J. Hennessy to A M Campbell, August 20, 1949; and described in cynical tones on July 15, 1949, RG 117 Item no. 3/7 NARA SB.

24. Cross-Examination of Charles Cousens, NARA SB.

25. *Sydney Morning Herald*, September 1, 1949.

26. Toguri cross-examination, 4909–6011; denial of broadcast on the Battle of Leyte, 5512–16. Redhead jokes were as common in 1940s as blond jokes were in 1990s; as given in court: What are the twenty-one reasons why you could not sleep with a redhead? Because no one ever went to sleep when in bed with a redhead, Cross-examination Charles Cousens, August 16, 1949, CC 3317 RG 118 NARA SB.

27. Tony Montemari, "2200 Documents Recently Released by Government on Tokyo Rose Case," *Chinese American Daily*, July 14, 1976.

28. *San Francisco Chronicle*, September 30, 1949; October 1, 1949.

29. John Mann, quoted in *San Francisco Chronicle*, September, 1976.

30. Ronald Yates, *Chicago Tribune*, March 22, 1976.

31. *New York Times*, January 29, 1956; *Chicago Times*, January 28, 1956; February 12, 1956.

32. *New York Times*, January 28, 1956; January 31, 1956.

33. *Washington Post*, March 22, 1957; *Hokubei Mainichi*, January 31, 1956; May 14, 1956.

34. *Hokubei Mainichi*, March 17, 1957.

35. *New York Times*, July 11, 1958.

Epilogue

1. Prison Commission file, John Amery, May 4, 1948, with regard to Prison Chaplain meeting Mrs Amery, HO 144/22823.

2. Correspondence 1946–1947, HO 144/22823; and PCOM 9/1117 PRO. Colonel E. J. P. Cussen, a member of British military intelligence, who had overseen John's capture and transport to Britain, left instructions to prevent the release to Julian Amery of

documents and court evidence to prevent his being able to publish a justification of his brother's behavior, "Secret, British Renegades. Documents and Articles found in possession of Renegades charged with treason..." February 21, 1946, HO144/22823 85153 PRO.

3. Faber, *Speaking for England,* 531–4.
4. *New York Times,* August 18, 1978.
5. *New York Times,* August 18, 1978.
6. *Chicago Daily News,* November 17, 1972.

Bibliography

Manuscripts and Sources

Amery Papers, Churchill Archives Centre, Churchill College, Cambridge.
Beaverbrook Papers, House of Lords, London.
British Public Record Office, Kew.
Canon Douglas Papers, Lambeth Palace, London.
Churchill Papers, Churchill Archives Centre, Churchill College, Cambridge.
Japanese American National Museum, Hirasaki National Resource Center, Los Angeles.
J. F. Kennedy Memorial Library.
National Archives and Records Administration, Washington & San Bruno, California.
National Archives of Australia, Sydney & Canberra.
New South Wales Records Office, Sydney.
Reuters Archive, London
Spanish Foreign Ministry Archives, Madrid, Ministerio de Asuntos Exteriores, Archivo General, Madrid.

Published Sources

Alanbrooke, Field Marshal Lord. *War Diaries 1939–1945 of Field Marshal Lord Alanbrooke.* London: Weidenfeld & Nicolson, 2001.
Allen, Peter. *Crown and the Swastika: Hitler, Hess and the Duke of Windsor.* London: Robert Hale, 1983.
Amery, John. *Charles Dickens et les Workhouses: Sur les conditions d'existence du people anglais suivi les declarations de M. John Amery, fils de l'actual Ministre d'Etat pour l'Empire des Indes, Ancien Premier Lord de l'Amirauté.* Paris: Col, Mai 1944.
———. *England Faces Europe.* Paris: April 1943.
———. *Engeland en Europa door John Amery, Dokumenten en Getuigenissen Reeks Van Politieke Verhandelingen No 1.* Brussels: 1943.
———. *John Amery Speaks* ND [Paris: 1943].
———. *L'Angleterre et L'Europe,* (traduit de l'Anglais) *Documents et Témoignages Collection d'Essais Politiques no 1.* Paris: 1943.
Amery, Julian. *Approach March: A Venture in Autobiography.* London: Hutchinson, 1973.

————. *Joseph Chamberlain and the Tariff Reform Campaign: The Life of Joseph Chamberlain Volume Six 1903–1968*. London: Macmillan, 1969.

————. *Sons of the Eagle: A Study in Guerilla War*. London: Macmillan, 1948.

Amery, Leo. *The Empire at Bay: The Leo Amery Diaries 1929–1945*. Edited by John Barnes and David Nicholson. London: Hutchinson, 1988.

————. *My Political Life. Volume One. England Before the Storm, 1869–1914*. London: Hutchinson, 1953.

Australian Law Commission. *Review of Sedition Laws*. Issues Paper 30, 2006.

Baillie-Stuart, Norman. *The Officer in the Tower*. London: Leslie Frewin, 1967.

Baker, Lilian. *The Japanning of America: Redress and Reparation Demands by Japanese-Americans*. Medford Oregon: Webb Research Group, 1991.

Barthélemy, Victor. *Du communisme au fascisme. L'histoire d'un engagement politique*. Paris: Albin Michel, 1978.

Bayly, Christopher and Tim Harper. *Forgotten Armies: The Fall of British Asia, 1941–1945*. London: Allen Lane, 2004.

Bergmeier, Horst J. P. and Rainer E. Lotz. *Hitler's Airwaves: The Inside Story of Nazi Radio Broadcasting and Propaganda Swing*. London: Yale University Press, 1997.

Bloxham, Donald. "The Trial that Never Was: Why There was No Second International Trial of Major War Criminals at Nuremberg." *History: The Journal of the Historical Association* 87 (January 2002): 41–60.

Bourdel, Philippe. *La Cagoule: Historie d'une société secrete du Front Populaire à la Ve République*. Paris: Albin Michel, 1992.

Bowen, Wayne. *Spaniards and Nazi Germany: Collaboration in the New Order*. London: University of Missouri Press, 2000.

Breitman, Richard. "A Deal with the Nazi Dictatorship: Himmler's Alleged Peace Emissaries in the Fall of 1943." *Journal of Contemporary History* 30 (1995): 411–30.

Buchbender, Otto and Reinhard Hauschild. *Radio Humanité: Les Émetteurs Allemands Clandestins,1940*. Traduit de l'allemand par Wanda Vulliez. Paris: Éditions France-Empire, 1984.

Burns, Tom. *Use of Memory*. London: Sheed and Ward, 1993.

Burrin, Philippe. *France under the Germans: Collaboration and Compromise*. New York: New Press, 1995.

Burt, Leo. *Commander Burt of Scotland Yard by Himself*. London: Heinemann, 1958.

Cannadine, David. *Decline and Fall of the British Aristocracy*. New York: Vintage Books, 1992.

Céline, Louis-Ferdinand. *Bagatelle pour un massacre*. Paris: 1937 (reprinted 1941).

————. *L'Ecole des cadavres*. Paris: 1938 (reprinted 1941).

Chapman, Ivan. *Tokyo Calling: The Charles Cousens Case*. Sydney: Hale and Iremonger, 1990.

Childs, Harwood L. "America's Short-Wave Audience." In *Propaganda by Short Wave*, edited by Harwood L. Childs and John B. Whitton. New York: Arno Press, 1972.

Christoph, James B. *Capital Punishment and British Politics: The British Movement to Abolish the Death Penalty 1945–57*. London: George Allen & Unwin, 1962.

Churchill, Randolph. *Twenty-One Years*. London: Weidenfeld & Nicolson, 1964.

Constantine, Stephen. "Bringing the Empire Alive: The Empire Marketing Board and Imperial Propaganda, 1926–33." In *Imperialism and Popular Culture*, edited by John M. Mackenzie. Manchester: Manchester University Press, 1986.

Copsey, Nigel. "John Amery: The Antisemitism of the 'Perfect English Gentleman'." *Patterns of Prejudice* 36 (2002): 14–27.

Cottle, Drew. *The Brisbane Line: A Reappraisal*. Leicestershire: Upfront Publishing, 2002.

Dalton, Hugh. *Second World War Diaries of Hugh Dalton, 1940–45*. Edited by Ben Plimlott. London: Jonathon Cape in association with The London School of Economics and Political Science, 1986.

Daniels, Gordon. "Japanese Domestic Radio and Cinema Propaganda, 1937–1945: An Overview." In *Film and Radio Propaganda in World War II*, edited by K.R.M. Short. London: Croom Helm, 1983.

Davey, Owen Anthony. "The Origins of the Légion des Volontaires Français contre le Bolchevisme." *Journal of Contemporary History* 6 (1971): 29–45.

Daws, Gavan. *Prisoners of the Japanese: POWs of World War II in the Pacific*. Melbourne: Scribe Publications, 1994.

Deák, István. *Essays on Hitler's Europe*. Nebraska: University of Nebraska Press, 2001.

Deák, István, Jan T. Gross and Tony Judt. *Politics of Retribution in Europe: World War II and its Aftermath*. Princeton: Princeton University Press, 2000.

Deakin, F.W. *Last Days of Mussolini*. Middlesex: Penguin, 1962.

Dictionary of National Biography, 1951–1960. Edited by E. T. Williams and Helen Palmer. Oxford: Oxford University Press, 1971.

Dobie, Kathy. "AWOL in America: When Desertion is the Only Option." *Harper's Magazine* (March 2005): 33–44.

Doherty, M.D. *Nazi Wireless Propaganda: Lord Haw-Haw and British Pubic Opinion in the Second World War*. Edinburgh: Edinburgh University Press, 2000.

Dower, John. *Embracing Defeat: Japan in the Aftermath of World War II*. Middlesex: Penguin, 1999.

———. *War Without Mercy: Race and Power in the Pacific War*. New York: Pantheon Books, 1986.

Duus, Masayo. *Tokyo Rose: Orphan of the Pacific*. New York: Kodansha International, 1979.

Edwards, John Carver. *Berlin Calling: American Broadcasters in Service to the Third Reich*. New York: Praeger, 1991.

Encyclopedia of the Third Reich. New York: Paragon House, 1989.

Faber, David. *Speaking For England: Leo, Julian and John Amery; The Tragedy of a Political Family*. London: Free Press, 2005.

Fazion, Rosa Maria. "Effects of the Broadcasts of 'Tokyo Rose' During World War II." M A diss., Department of Speech, Pennsylvania State University, 1968.

Flannery, Harry W. *Assignment to Berlin*. New York: Alfred A. Knopf, 1942.

Fricke, Graham. "The Eureka Trials." *Australian Law Journal* 71 (1977): 59–69.

Fujita, Frank. *A Japanese-American Prisoner of the Rising Sun: The Secret Prison Diary of Frank "Foo" Fujita*. Denton: University of North Texas Press, 1993.

Garton, Stephen. *Cost of War: Australians Return*. Melbourne: Oxford University Press, 1996.

Gathorne-Hardy, Jonathon. *The Old School Tie: The Phenomenon of the English Public School*. New York: Viking Press, 1977.

Hastings, Max. *Nemesis: The Battle for Japan, 1944–45*. New York: Harper Collins, 2007.

Hatamiya, Leslie T. *Righting a Wrong: Japanese Americans and the Passage of the Civil Liberties Act of 1988*. Stanford: Stanford University Press, 1993.

Hayashi, Brian Masaru. 'For The Sake of Our Brethren:' Assimilation, Nationalism and Protestantism Among the Japanese of Los Angeles, 1895–1942. Stanford: Stanford University Press, 1995.

Hearder, R. S. "Careers in Captivity: Australian Prisoner-of-War Medical Officers in Japanese Captivity during World War II." PhD diss., Department of History, University of Melbourne, 2003.

Henderson, Nicholas. Old Friends and Modern Instances. London: Profile Books, 2000.

Hérold-Paquis, Jean. Des illusions... disillusions!. Paris: Bourgoin Editeur, 1948.

Herz, F. "Radio in International Politics." In Propaganda By Short Wave, edited by Harwood L. Childs and John B. Whitton. New York: Arno Press, 1972.

Hoare, Rt. Hon. Sir Samuel. Ambassador on Special Mission. London: Collins, 1946.

———. The Shadow of the Gallows. London: Gollancz, 1951.

Hollins, T. J. "The Conservative Party and Film Propaganda Between the Wars." English Historical Review 96 (1981): 359–69.

Howe, Russell Warren. The Hunt for "Tokyo Rose." New York: Madison Books, 1990.

Hurst, James Willard. The Law of Treason in the United States: Collected Essays. Westport, Conn: Greenwood Publishing, 1971.

Ichioka, Yuji. "Japanese Immigrant Nationalism: The Issei and the Sino-Japanese War 1937–1941." California History 69 (1990): 260–74.

———. "The Meaning of Loyalty: The Case of Kazumaro Buddy Uno." Amerasia Journal 23 (1997): 45–71.

———. "The Origin of Nisei Study Tours of Japan." California History 73 (1994): 31–42.

Kaplan, Alice Yaeger. Reproductions of Banality: Fascism, Literature and French Intellectual Life, Theory and History of Literature. Minneapolis: University of Minnesota Press, 1986.

Keene, Judith. "At Home and Away with the Amery Family on Empire Day 1932." History Australia 1 (2004): 179–95.

———. Fighting For Franco: International Volunteers in Nationalist Spain during the Spanish Civil War. London: Leicester University Press, 2001.

———. "Treason and the Trial of Traitors in Twentieth Century Australia." When the Troops Come Home, Conference, University of Queensland, November 2007.

Kutler, Stanley. The American Inquisition: Justice and Injustice in the Cold War. New York: Hill and Wang, 1982.

———. "Forging a Legend: The Treason of 'Tokyo Rose'." Wisconsin Law Review (1980): 1341–82.

Lamb, R. Churchill as War Leader: Right or Wrong. London: Bloomsbury, 1993.

Lambauer, Barbara. Otto Abetz et les français; ou l'envers de la collaboration. Paris: Fayard, 2001.

Lee, Clark. One Last Look Around. New York: Duell, Sloan and Pearce, 1947.

Loane, Captain Jabetz W, IV. "Treason and Aiding the Enemy." Military Law Review 43 (1965): 43–81.

Louis, Wm. Roger. In the Name of God Go!: Leo Amery and the British Empire in the Age of Churchill. New York: Norton and Company, 1992.

———. "Leo Amery and the Post-War World, 1945–55." Journal of Imperial and Commonwealth History 30 (September 2002): 71–90.

McCarthy, John. "The 'Great Betrayal' Reconsidered: An Australian Perspective." Australian Journal of International Affairs 48 (May 1994): 53–60.

McCrum, Robert. Wodehouse: A Life. Harmondsworth: Penguin Books, 2004.

McKenzie, Francine. *Redefining the Bonds of Commonwealth, 1939–1948: The Politics of Preference*. London: Palgrave, 2002.

McKernan, Michael. *This War Never Ends: The Pain of Separation and Return*. Brisbane: University of Queensland Press, 2001.

McKibbin, Ross. *Classes and Cultures: England 1918–1951*. Oxford: Oxford University Press, 1998.

McWilliams, Carey. *Prejudice: Japanese-Americans Symbol of Racial Intolerance*. New York: Archon Books, 1971 [1944].

Mant, Gilbert. *Grim Glory*. Sydney: Currawong, 1955.

Martland, Peter. *Lord Haw Haw: The English Voice of Nazi Germany*. Lanham: Maryland, Scarecrow Press, 2003.

Masoaka, Mike with Bill Hosokawa. *They Call Me Moses Masaoka: An American Saga*. New York: William Morrow, 1987.

Mendelssohn, Peter De. *Japan's Political Warfare*. London: George Allen & Unwin, 1944.

Meo, L. D. *Japan's Radio War on Australia*. Melbourne: Melbourne University Press, 1968.

Millet, Raymond. *Doriot et ses compagnons*. Paris: Plon, 1937.

Morris, John. *Traveller from Tokyo*. London: Cresset Press, 1943.

Murphy, Sean. *Letting the Side Down: British Traitors of the Second World War*. Phoenix Mill, Gloucestershire: Sutton Publishing, 2003.

Mydans, Carl. *More Than Meets the Eye*. New York: Harper & Bothers, 1959.

Nelson, Hank and Tim Bowden. *POW Prisoners of War: Australians Under Nippon*. Sydney: Australian Broadcasting Corporation, 1985.

Oliver, Pam. "Japanese Relationships in White Australia: The Sydney Experience to 1941." *History Australia* 4 (2007): 1–20.

Omissi, David Enrico. "The Hendon Air Pageant, 1920–1937." In *Popular Imperialism and the Military, 1850–1950*, edited by John M. Mackenzie. Manchester: Manchester University Press, 1992.

Paris, Michael. *Wright Brothers to Top Gun: Aviation, Nationalism and Popular Cinema*. Manchester: Manchester University Press, 1995.

Petacci, Myriam. *Chi Ama è Perduto: Mia Sorella Claretta*. Rome: Puigi Reverdito Editore, 1988.

Picknett, Lynn, et al. *War of the Windsors: A Century of Unconstitutional Monarchy*. London: Hardie Grant Books, 2003.

Pierrepoint, Albert. *Executioner Pierrepoint*. London: Harrap, 1974.

Prasad, Devi. *They Love It But Leave It: American Deserters*. London: War Resisters International, 1971.

Pugliese, Stanislao G. "Death in Exile: The Assassination of Carlo Rosselli." *Journal of Contemporary History* 32 (1997): 305–19.

Randa, Philippe. *Dictionnaire Commenté de la Collaboration Française*. Paris: Jean Picollec, 1997.

Read, Donald. "Three Political Dissenters; John Amery: J. S. Barnes: John Peet." Unpublished Paper, 1994–5.

Rebatet, Lucien. *Les Mémoires d'un Fasciste: Les Décombres*. Paris: Pauvert, 1976 [1942]

Redman, Tim. *Ezra Pound and Italian Fascism*. Cambridge: Cambridge University Press, 1991.

Reynolds, Adam. "Treason: Defunct or Dormant." *Monash University Law Review* 26 (2000): 195–202.

Reynolds, D. "Churchill and the British 'decision' to fight in 1940: Right Policy, Wrong Reason." In *Diplomacy and Intelligence During the Second World War*, edited by R. Langhorne. Cambridge: Cambridge University Press, 1985.

Richards, Jeffrey. "Boy's Own Empire: Feature Films and Imperialism in the 1930s." In *Imperialism and Popular Culture*, edited by John M. Mackenzie. Manchester: Manchester University Press, 1986.

———. "Patriotism with Profit: British Imperial Cinema in the 1930s." In his *Visions of Yesterday*. London: Routledge and K. Paul, 1973.

Richards, Rowley. *A Doctor's War*. Sydney: Harper Collins, 2005,

Rivett, Rohan. *Behind Bamboo: An Inside Story of the Japanese Prison Camp*. Sydney: Angus & Robertson, 1946.

Robbins, Jane. *Tokyo Calling: Japanese Overseas Radio Broadcasting 1937–1945*. Florence: European Press Academic Publishing, 2001.

Roberts, Andrew R. "Africa on Film to 1940." *History in Africa* XIV (1987): 189–227.

Roberts, Elizabeth. "The Spanish Precedent: British Volunteers in the Russo-Finnish War." *History Australia* 3 (June 2006): 1–14

———. "Freedom, Faction, Fame and Blood: Soldiers of Conscience in Three European Wars." PhD diss., Department of History, University of Sydney, 2007.

Robinson, Greg. *By Order of the President: FDR and the Internment of Japanese Americans*. Cambridge Mass: Harvard University Press, 2001.

Rollyson, Carl. "Rebecca West and the FBI." *New Criterion* 16 (February 1998): 12–22.

Rotha, Paul. *Documentary Diary: An Informal History of the British Documentary Film, 1928–1939*. New York: Hill and Wang, 1973.

Rubinstein, William D. "The Secret of Leopold Amery." *Historical Research* 73 (2000): 175–95.

Ruddy, Francis S. "Permissible Dissent or Treason? The American Law of Treason From Its English and Colonial origins to the Present." *Criminal Law Bulletin* 4 (1968): 145–59.

Ryo, Namikawa. "Japanese Overseas Broadcasting: A Personal View." In *Film and Radio Propaganda in World War II*, edited by K. R. M. Short. London: Croom Helm, 1983.

Seth, Ronald. *Jackals of the Reich: The Story of the British Free Corps*. London: English Library, 1972.

Shawcross, Hartley. *Life Sentence: The Memoirs of Lord Shawcross*. London: Constable, 1995.

Shirer, William L. *Berlin Diary: The Journal of a Foreign Correspondent 1934–1941*. Boston: Little Brown and Company, 1941.

Simon, Walter G. "The Evolution of Treason." *Tulane Law Review* XXXV (1961):669–704.

Simpson, A. W. Brian. "Detention without Trial in the Second World War: Comparing the British and American Experiences." *Florida State University Law Review* 16 (Summer 1988): 225–67.

———. *In the Highest Degree Odious: Detention Without Trial in Wartime Britain*. Oxford: Clarendon, 1992.

Smith, D. *International Telecommunications Control*. Leyden: Sitjthoff, 1969.

Smith, Howard K. *Last Train from Berlin*. New York: Popular Library, 1942.

Sorlin, Pierre. "The Struggle for the Control of French Minds." In *Film and Radio Propaganda in World War Two*, edited by K.R.M. Short. Beckenham: Croom Helm, 1983.

Soucy, Robert. *French Fascism: The Second Wave 1933–1939*. New Haven: Yale University Press, 1995.

Spitzy, Reinhard. *How We Squandered the Reich*. London: Michael Russell, 1997.

Stammers, Neil. *Civil Liberties in Britain During the Second World War: A Political Study.* London: Croom Helm, 1983.

Steinhaus, Richard. "Treason: A Brief History with Some Modern Applications." *Brooklyn Law Review* 255 (1956): 254–77.

Strong, Lester. "When 'Tokyo Rose' Came to Albuquerque." *New Mexico Historical Review* (January 1991): 73–92.

Taylor, Philip M. "Propaganda in International Politics, 1919–1939." In *Film and Radio Propaganda in World War Two,* edited by K.R.M.Short. Beckenham: Croom Helm, 1983.

Thévenot, Jean. *L'Age de la télèvision...* Paris: Gallimard, 1946.

Tolischus, Otto D. *Tokyo Record.* Melbourne: George Jaboor, 1944.

Tomita, Mary Kimoto. *Dear Miye: Letters Home from Japan, 1939–1946.* Edited by Robert G. Lee. Stanford: Stanford University Press, 1995.

Torney-Parlicki, Prue. *Behind the News: A Biography of Peter Russo.* Perth: University of Western Australia Press, 2005.

———. "Selling Goodwill: Peter Russo and the Promotion of Australia-Japan Relations, 1935–1941." *Australian Journal of Politics and History* 47 (2001): 349–65.

Townsend, Susan C. "Culture, Race and Power in Japan's Wartime Empire." In *Japanese Prisoners of War,* edited by Philip Towle, Margaret Kosuge and Yoichi Kibata. London: Hambeldon and London, 2000.

United Kingdom, Law Commission of England and Wales. *Codification of the Criminal Law: Treason, Sedition and Allied Offences.* Working Paper 72, 1977.

Waddington, Lorna L. "Anti-Komintern and Nazi Anti-Bolshevik Propaganda in the 1930s." *Journal of Contemporary History* 24 (2007): 582–7. .

Weale, Adrian. *Patriot Traitors: Roger Casement, John Amery and the Real Meaning of Treason.* London: Viking, 2001.

———. *Renegades.* London: Weidenfeld and Nicolson, 1994.

West, Rebecca. *The Meaning of Treason,* with a new Introduction by the Author. London: Virago, 1982 [1949].

Whitton, John B. and John F. Herz. "Radio in International Politics." In *Propaganda By Short Wave,* edited by Harwood L. Childs and John B. Whitton. New York: Arno Press, 1972.

Whitton, John B. "War by Radio." *Foreign Affairs* 19 (1940–41): 584–96.

Worsley, T. C. *Flannelled Fool: A Slice of Life in the Thirties.* London: Ross, 1967.

Yamamoto, Eriko. "Cheers for Japanese Athletes: The 1932 Los Angeles Olympics and the Japanese American Community." *Pacific Historical Review* 69 (2000): 399–442.

Index